OUOLOF

SERÈRE

PEUL

DIOLA

BISSAGOS

MANDINQUE

BAMBARA

BOZO

DOGON

MOSSI

DAGOMBA

GONJA

BRONG
(BROM)

FANTI

ASHANTI

A

ATIE

DIDA

BAMBARA

FOULA

BOBO

LOBI

SENUFO
(SENOUFO)

BAULE
(BAOULE)

ABIDJAN

GR. BASSAM

BAMAKO

MALINKE

KOURO

ODIENNE

GURO
(GOURO)

BETE

SASSANDRA

FOULA

BOKE

BAGA

SOUSSOU

CONAKRY

KONO

LELE

KISSI

TOMA
or
BUZI

DAN
(YAKOBA)

MAN

QUOBE

GIO

GUERE

GEH

GREBO

KROU

MANON

GUERZE

KPELLE

BASA
(BASSA)

FREETOWN

TIMENE

MENDE

GOLA

WAI
(WEI)

DEY
(DE)

MONROVIA

GR. BASSA

SARACOLE

Atlantic Ocean

Region 1 (see main map)

AFRICAN SCULPTURE
SPEAKS

PABLO PICASSO: ". . . when the form is realized, it is there to live its own life."

HENRY MOORE: "The sculpture which moves me most is full-blooded and self-supporting, fully in the round; giving out something of an energy and power of great mountains, it has a life of its own independent of the object it represents."

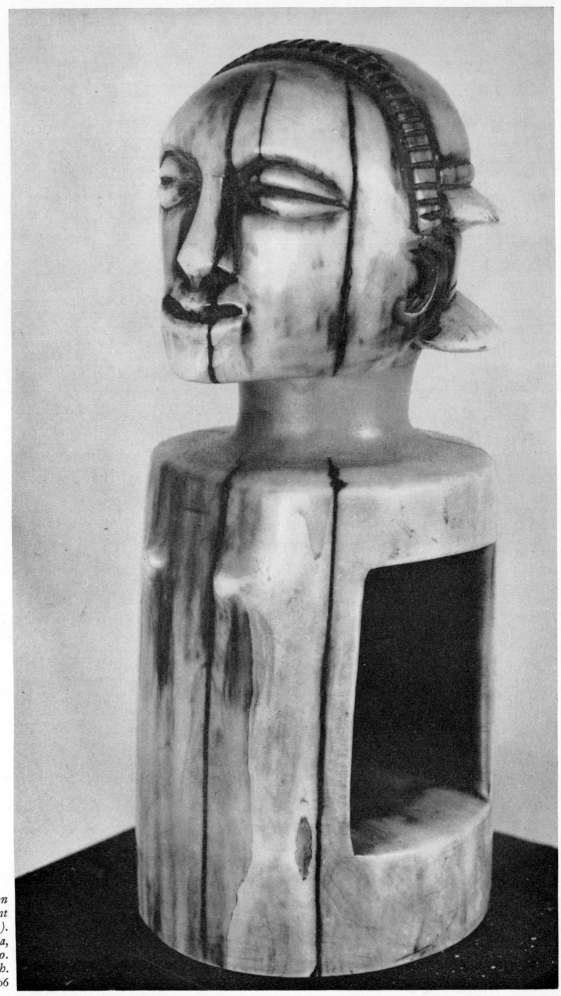

*Divination
instrument
(Katatora).
Ivory. Baluba,
Belgian Congo.
4½" high.*
SEE PAGE 206

AFRICAN SCULPTURE SPEAKS

LADISLAS SEGY

LAWRENCE HILL & CO., NEW YORK

CONTENTS

Part I. The Meaning and Sources of African Art

CONTENTS

Part II. The Content of African Art

CONTENTS

Part III. African Art and European Civilization

Appendix: Style Regions

CONTENTS

CONTENTS

CONTENTS

ACKNOWLEDGMENTS

THE books and articles consulted in the preparation of this book are listed in the bibliography, and I take this opportunity to express my gratitude to each author for his contribution to our available knowledge of African art.

In assembling the illustrations, these purposes were borne in mind: to present, for the first time in America, recently excavated African sculptures which shed a new light on historical-cultural backgrounds; to represent, wherever possible, each type of sculpture by an outstanding example; and to be as comprehensive as possible, including style regions not hitherto illustrated and thereby demonstrating the great variety and inventiveness of African sculpture.

To achieve this goal I revisited Europe. In the museums indicated below careful studies were made, not only of works on exhibit, but also of objects kept in the storerooms. A large number of these were photographed for reproduction here, their first appearance in any publication.

My first visit was to the magnificent London exhibition, "Traditional Sculpture from the Colonies," held at the *Imperial Institute* as part of "The Festival of Britain, 1951." With the help of one of its organizers, Mr. Webster Plass, reproductions of the most important objects were procured. I welcome this occasion to express my thanks to him and Mrs. Plass for their hospitality and their permission to reproduce objects from their very fine private collection. I wish also to thank the following for their assistance while I was in London: Mr. William Fagg of the British Museum and Dr. O. W. Samson of the Horniman Museum for their help, particularly in securing photographs for reproduction; Jacob Epstein, who permitted me to reproduce some objects from his collection, the finest in the world of their particular style; and Mrs. Eva L. R. Meyerowitz for her kind permission to reproduce her own photos of her findings in Nigeria. I recall with pleasure my discussion with Mr. Leon Underwood and my visit to the magnificent Gold Coast collection of Mr. Maurice Cockin. My thanks are also due to Mr. and Mrs. R. J. Sainsbury, for permission to use photos of objects in their fine collection.

I wish here to thank Prof. Dr. Frans M. Olbrechts, director of the Musée du Congo Belge, at Tervuren, not only for his valued help, but for his warm hospitality; and Dr. A. Maesen, his assistant, who made valuable suggestions regarding the Belgian Congo section of this book.

In Paris, at the Musée de l'Homme, Mme. Schaeffner permitted me to inspect the material in the storage spaces and to photograph many objects for this book. My thanks are also due to Mme. Helena Rubinstein for permitting me to photograph objects from her magnificent collection in Paris, and to Mlle. Madeleine Rousseau of Paris for helpful suggestions.

I wish also to express my gratitude to Mr. A. A. Gerbrands of the Rijksmuseum Voor Volkenkunde, Leyden, Holland, for his co-operation in securing photos of objects in the museum's collection and providing English translations of Dutch texts; also to offi-cials of the Institut Français d'Afrique Noire in Dakar for providing me with photos of objects in their collection, and to Pr. Leon Pales, chief of the Mission Anthropologique de l'A.O.F. in Dakar for the kind permission to use information contained in their ethnological maps of French West Africa.

In the United States numerous museums and private collectors were kind enough to grant me permission to use photographs of their collections, and their names appear on our list of illustrations with my very best thanks.

Last but not least, special thanks are due to Mr. A. A. Wyn, my publisher, who had the foresight to publish this volume, to Mr. L. E. Sissman for editorial assistance.

LADISLAS SEGY

AUTHOR'S NOTE. The subject of the present book is the so-called primitive Negro art of West Africa that flourished up to a generation ago, as distinguished from contemporary West African art, and from North, East, and South African art. When, for simplicity, we use the expressions "African," "native," or "African Negro," we always mean the West African Negro of past generations. The territories included in the term "West Africa" are shown in the end paper map.

To assure fluent reading, we have avoided footnotes, names of authors, and titles of books and quotations except where these were deemed essential.

L. S.

PART I

THE MEANING AND
SOURCES OF
AFRICAN ART

FIG. 1. *Divination statue. Bakuba, Belgian Congo. 2″ high.* SEE PAGE 203

FIG. 2. *Statue
of Shamba
Bolongongo,
93rd king of the
Bushongo. Bakuba,
Belgian Congo.
21½" high.* SEE
PAGE 199

1. THE APPROACH

I AM often asked how my interest in African art began.

It must have been some twenty-five years ago when, as a student in Germany, I visited an ethnological museum as part of a class assignment. In the African room I approached a showcase in which a wooden statue was displayed. As I looked at the statue, I felt a strange excitement mixed with anxiety.

This sensation, which combined pleasure and pain, I have never forgotten. Although I did not know then what had happened to me, I recognized it as a powerful, even an overwhelming thing. I felt impelled to see and know more of African art. I wanted to possess such a sculpture for my own.

From one of the museum publications on the subject, which I had bought, I selected an illustration as my model and tried to whittle a figure. But this did not satisfy my craving to live with and possess authentic African sculpture. Only after I had moved to Paris was I able to obtain a few pieces. In these I recaptured my first excitement.

What had moved me so deeply I did not know. It took me until now to find a tentative answer. The book reflects my quest for it.

What has been the fate of African sculpture in this quarter of a century? For the most part it remains a body of art stowed away in the dusty showcases of ethnological museums, though here and there its plastic qualities have been recognized.

As my research led me into the study of modern art, I discovered that others had anticipated me in the discovery of African art. In 1907 or thereabouts, African and South Sea sculpture created a flurry of interest in French salons. Artists in Paris discovered the power of these works of primitive man. Books and articles appeared. Some dealt with the subject from an ethnological standpoint; others confined themselves to the work's aesthetic merits; still others, by means of comparative illustrations, demonstrated its influence on modern art.

The emphasis in these pages will be different. We shall deal with African sculpture as a pure sculpture, speaking the language of plastic forms; but we shall deal also with its emotional content, through which it communicates with the beholder.

In approaching this field, the Westerner is often misled by what he brings from his own cultural background. Insofar as possible he should divest himself of the standards of his civilization and see African art in its own setting, keeping constantly aware of its ethnic sources and its specific socio-cultural functions.

Let him also hold on to his first emotional reaction to African sculpture. Through it a deeper rapport is established than by mere formal appreciation. Then, to the extent that he further succeeds in relating it to the cultural setting and in looking at it with an "African eye," his understanding and enjoyment will be deepened. He will feel its function and role in the life of the African, he will sense the activity and use that gave it its real existence.

It is the purpose of this book to show parallels between what the African projects freely in his art and what is buried in our own psychological roots. These parallels make possible our emotional identification with the content of African art. Such identification should then lead to a certain self-recognition, to personal rediscovery and renewed contact with our deeper instincts, now overlaid by "civilized" manners and conventions. By learning to understand the African sculptor's motivations and his relationship to his art, we can increase our understanding of ourselves and of our relationship to art.

Our age has been called by Auden "the age of anxiety," and by Camus "the age of fear." This anxiety and fear arise from the split or conflict between the intellect and the emotions in our lives.

In our emotional need we respond to African sculpture because it embodies an intense emotional life. To the extent that we feel its reality, that we sense the radiations of its emotional vigor, we gain the sensation of fulfillment, of nourishing something starved in ourselves.

This is a major value African art has for us. To realize it as fully as possible here, we will avoid the traditional highway of anthropology and follow instead the pathway of communication between the inner life-real-

ity of this art and our own emotional life.

THE BACKGROUND OF AFRICAN ART

In describing the life out of which African art arose, we work with uncertain data. Even the reports of ethnological field studies conflict. Their contradictions originate sometimes in differences of method, sometimes in differences of personality. Moreover, some studies were too hasty, or made by researchers whose command of the native tongues was insufficient, who were too unfamiliar with native customs to make correct interpretations or too unskillful to cope with the evasions of natives anxious to protect tribal secrets. It is even possible, according to one scientist, that divergences should be accepted as facts, since the phenomena observed were themselves variable. Finally, natives sometimes could not make intelligible reports where they were merely carrying on long-established traditions whose reasons or origins had been lost.

From the data which is available we can offer this generalized localization in time and space of the sculpture-producing African. His habitations lined the west and Guinea coasts, extended through the French Sudan and northern Angola, and reached eastward, across what is now the Belgian Congo, to the lake region—a territory about twelve hundred miles square, about half of equatorial Africa.

He was predominantly of Bantu stock and appears to have migrated to Africa from Asia. The date is unknown, but approximate indications would place the main influx around 3000 B.C. By the fourth century A.D., Negro states were well-established, and their history showed noteworthy political achievements.

We must bear in mind, however, that *Negro* is neither an African concept nor an African word. It is of Portuguese and Spanish derivation from words meaning "black," and was first used about 1550. In Africa each tribe has its own name and each individual identifies himself by membership in a tribe. The prefix *ba* (meaning people), in most African languages, signifies the tribe; the prefix *ma* signifies the individual tribesman. Thus, in a typical Belgian Congo group, the tribe is called *Baluba*, the tribesman *Maluba*.

Being mainly farmers, these African tribes under consideration were often bound to the region where they were settled; this factor promoted the cultural continuity so useful in the development of art. Their social structure was marked by a complex of authority—kings, secret societies, medicine men, etc. Virtually all social functions had the character of religio-magical ceremonies, in each of which sculptured images were employed.

Lacking writing, the Africans carried their mythologies—their literatures—in their heads, transmitting their legends orally from generation to generation. Sculpture was an additional language through which they expressed their inner lives and communicated with the invisible world, a language of emotional communication, used from birth to death. Virtually every act in the lives of the Africans had its ritual, and every rite had its appropriate image.

And the African came under the auspices of these statues even before birth. His mother, during her pregnancy, prayed to an image which functioned as the unborn child's protector. Another image assisted her through the delivery; and still another stood outside her hut, with an alms bowl before it, to secure help for her in the period when she could not work. Still another image watched over the child at birth and, if he was a twin, special sculptures guarded him against hazards to which this exposed him.

Every subsequent contingency of his life was provided for by images. In farming, hunting, fishing, in sickness, in litigation, he followed a specific rite employing a specific image. Such decisive periods as puberty, marriage, death called for a whole gallery of sculptures.

AFRICAN ART STYLES

Inevitably an astonishing wealth of sculptures was produced, the intensity of whose carving reflects the importance of the functions they served. If we now add that each tribe developed an art style of its own (classified in the Appendix), we begin to understand how extensive this material is. Since the creation of an art style is a major cultural achievement, the remarkable diversity of styles is in itself a testimony to the African's artistic inventiveness.

We shall trace here the primary ideas that provided the impetus for new styles. For those who are enthusiastic over this art, it is hoped a highroad to an aesthetic and emotional adventure will be opened. At first African sculpture may represent only an aesthetic pleasure. But another function will begin when we communicate with it, when what it touches in our inner selves is projected back into the sculpture itself.

THE AFRICAN CONCEPT

African sculpture springs from a specific concept of the world. It is the product of primitive mentality or primitive reason. This does not signify any basic differences, however, between the minds of primitive man and civilized man.

According to Franz Boas, the chief differences between primitive and civilized man lie in their types of association with the material. Tradition and institutions are more compelling for the primitive; his associations with the community are more emotional and less intellectual than ours.

In our society the goal is individual development, whereas in primitive society it is membership in the community. In both societies, however, the pressures for conformity are so great that in practice this difference proves to be less than it appears. When we examine our own behavior psychologically, we find that even the apparent intellectual differences are not so great. Our behavior is less rational than we think.

With the discoveries of depth psychology has come the realization of the extent and power of our unconscious life, of the emotional content of many of our actions and reactions. With this in mind, the mental and emotional attitudes of the African cannot long continue to be regarded as intellectual absurdities. We shall see here how many African beliefs and habits are analogous to residues deeply imbedded in our own life—how many, in fact, survive among us in deviated forms.

Primitive thinking is homogeneous because primitive life is conducted in small and relatively isolated groups held to rigid traditional patterns of behavior. The thought of the primitive therefore tends to be communal. The primitive man and his fellow tribesmen are inclined to think the same way that their forefathers did.

Primitive perception relates all objects emotionally. The primitive's attention was intuitively directed to inner reality; he achieved effortlessly the type of penetration Western man has to work to acquire when he faces a work of art. Western man must use outer reality to reach the inner reality, the real content of a work of art.

This emotional reaction is quite utilitarian. The African separated the world and its manifestations into what was good or bad, not in a moral sense but according to what was to his advantage or disadvantage, what was permitted and what was taboo. And he not only sought the good and avoided the evil; he sought to change the evil into good, or annihilate it. Toward this end he built up a magico-religious belief characterized by rituals which were, for the most part, centered on a magical use of sculpture.

We put such emphasis on the emotional tone of primitive man's reactions because this tone also characterizes his art creation. At the same time the primitive shows rudiments of the scientific mind in his observation of nature. His activities follow closely observed seasonal changes, etc. In his canoe-building, in his fishing and hunting, and above all in his farming, he uses his observations to secure the best results. He resorts to magic to influence nature only where his own labors seem to have no effect. Drought or flood can ruin the best-cultivated fields; storms can overwhelm the best fisherman. Here magic comes in—to influence the element of chance in the petitioner's favor.

Malinowski points out that, when fishing in the safe lagoons, the Trobriand Islander dispenses with magic. But for fishing on the dangerous open sea, an extensive magical ritual is performed to insure safety and a good catch.

The school of thought headed by the French scholar Lévy-Bruhl seeks to explain primitive mental processes as aversion to the rational, as follows: Not recognizing or comprehending any laws of nature, the primitive does not connect cause and effect, or distinguish between identity and contradiction. The primitive mind is prelogical, and its behavior patterns are largely inexplicable to Western man.

However, other schools hold that since the brains of primitive peoples have the same structure as ours and the same potential, and since all civilizations have developed out of the primitive, we must assume at least the groundwork of the rational among the primitives. This, indeed, is to be discerned in the African concept, which is a composite of many interlocking beliefs. The majority of these are magico-religious. As Delafosse expressed it, the Africans "are among the most religious people of the world."

FIG. 3. *Initiation ceremony mask. Bakuba, Belgian Congo. 13″ high.* SEE PAGE 205

FIG. 4. *Mask. Bekom, Cameroon. 18" high.* SEE PAGE 184

2. BASIC CONCEPTS

A STUDY of the art forms of any people must essentially take into consideration the cultural background from which the art springs. So for a better understanding and deeper appreciation of African art it would be well to examine the basic concepts underlying it. We must therefore concern ourselves with the manifestations of *animism*, *magic*, *fetishism* and *mythology* in the tribal civilization.

A. Animism

This is the belief that all objects—both "inanimate" and "animate," according to Western terminology—possesses vitality or are endowed with indwelling souls. Thus animals as well as men—and earth, water, vegetation, and minerals as well as animals—are invested with souls. The indwelling soul, moreover, is nonmaterial; it has its own thought and will.

Animism is carried over into the African's attitude toward sculpture. Both the creation of a piece of sculpture and its use in tribal rituals are based upon animism. The *power* of a statue or a mask is believed to be more real than that of a living being.

Those who possess the sculpture feel that they can depend on this power to protect them and promote their welfare.

The sculpture does not *represent* an idea, as a statue of Christ may be said to symbolize divine grace. The African sculpture *is* the spirit itself.

This concept, alien as it is to the rational mind, must be grasped if we are to understand and feel the force that African art radiates. An African sculptor's belief that he creates life is incomparably greater in its assurance than the "symbolic" or "representational" approach of the Western artist to his work.

African animism proved durable enough to resist the religious influence and other cultural-social pressures of invaders. Islam, for example, despite its intimate contact with the Sudanese states, left no impress on African art. The Christian missionaries, despite the effects of their medical work, have similarly made little impression on animism, though political and economic change, brought about by Western rule, have begun to break up the African social structure.

The vitality of animism is all the more striking in that, through centuries of external pressures, it did without the aid of or-

[19]

FIG. 5. *Magical statue. Bakongo, Belgian Congo. 24" high.*

ganized religious institutions and the teachings of great religious leaders, such as have sustained nearly all other religions. Moreover, the African's religion lacked writing and could therefore not preserve itself in records. Traditions were handed down orally with all the consequent risks of change and loss.

However, the Africans had certain things which helped to offset these lacks. One was their sculpture, which preserved their beliefs in powerful shapes. Through these they achieved a unification rare in the history of art.

The very strength of this integration and use of sculpture as a language may partially account for the fact that the art of writing never developed among the talented West Africans.

THE RANGE OF ANIMISM

Animism is not an exclusive African concept. It is found in varying degrees in nearly all religions. We find survivals in many highly developed religions despite the opposition of leaders. The occurrence of animism in the cultures of the Egyptians, Babylonians, and Greeks will be dealt with when we trace their possible influence on African art. We can easily detect animistic survivals in Hinduism, despite the Buddhist, Jain, and Sikh reformations, in the objects which fill Hindu temples and in the Hindu pilgrimages to sacred mountains and rivers.

Again, in the pre-Mosaic religion of the Hebrews, *telphim*, or "idols," apparently made of wood, were adored. The cumbersome wooden Ark of the Covenant which the Hebrews trundled over the desert is another example of the animistic belief in the inner life of inanimate objects.

Before Mahomet, the Arabs worshiped sacred trees, stones, and springs. The guardian spirit of each was later personified in a god or goddess. Despite Mahomet's opposition to animistic beliefs, he had to permit adoration of the black meteorite, the "Kaaba," and of the Zem Zem spring. Belief in them has persisted to this day.

Various Roman and Greek pantheons also showed a development from animism to animistic polytheism. The Teutonic-Scandinavian religions showed a similar development. A chief object of their worship was the "world tree" Yggdrasil.

In Mexico the culture of the Toltecs, Aztecs, and other tribes of the Nahuatlan stock was animistic and resembled that of the Africans. They, too, were noted for their sculpture, and their forms of human sacrifice and their cult of skulls showed similarities to ancient African practices.

An animistic survival may even be found among us in our nurseries.

DOLLS

When a little girl plays with a doll, she talks to it, handles it like a living being, takes it to bed with her. The doll is alive to the child. And experiment has shown that an expressionless doll is more stimulating to the child than a naturalistic one.

The word doll itself is a shortened form of the Greek word for image or idol—*eidolon*. The use of the doll as a toy is a comparatively late development in history.

The doll idea—that an inanimate figure has life—often occurs among neurotic adults. In the year of Catherine de' Medici's seclusion, dolls which she fed and cared for were her only companions. The Duchesse d'Enghien, niece of Cardinal Richelieu, treated dolls like her children, dressed them, fed them, and gave them medicine.

This behavior, a neurotic disorder called "doll fetishism," is a regression to an earlier, primitive state of mind.

A doll-like fetishism is connected with the mandrake or mandragora (also called "gallows man"), a plant in whose forked root men saw a resemblance to the human form. The plant was extensively used in magic rituals in Europe.

Thus we can see that all of us have been under the influence of a sort of animism in childhood. In some the influence retains sufficient power to be reactivated as neurotic behavior under some emotional stress.

Generally speaking, childhood patterns are only pushed down deep in the unconscious; they do not disappear completely. Knowingly or unknowingly, we carry remnants of them all through life. Such survivals in us help to explain our response to primitive arts.

Primitive arts were practiced in the services of animistic religion. These services, or rituals, were believed to have direct effects, to have the power called magic.

B. Magic

In magic, certain gestures, words, or acts, separately or together, are believed to invoke the direct assistance of supernatural beings in human affairs, or to give men control over the secret powers of Nature. In another sense, magic may be defined as the art of living in intimate union with Nature and sharing and using her secrets through ritual, or "doing." The Greek word for rite, as Jane Harrison has observed, is *dromenon*—a thing done. Thus a rite is a feeling or reaction expressed in an *act*. Moreover, since, in magic, spirits are influenced by appealing, cajoling, reconciling, conjuring, or subjugating them, magic may also be regarded as the *strategy* of animism. Freud remarked on the correspondence between the thing desired and the thing done in ritual; and magic may further be defined as wish fulfillment through ritual.

THE SCOPE OF MAGIC

Although in the broadest sense the field of magic might be said to include sorcery, or black magic, we shall make a distinction here. For the sake of simplicity we shall call magic that which is intended to have beneficial effects, and sorcery that which is in-

FIG. 6. *Crucifix statue (brass, XVI-XVII century). Lower Congo, Belgian Congo.
11" high.*

tended to do harm. The magician mainly serves the community; he performs rites to promote fertility and avert misfortune. The sorcerer, on the other hand, is employed privately, serving one man to harm an enemy. Sorcery is desperately feared by the African, despite the remedy of counterspells worked by another sorcerer.

The profession of magician is held in esteem. It is passed on from father to son. As priest the magician promotes the welfare of the community; as medicine man he heals the ailing.

The sorcerer's profession, on the other hand, is often an underground one. It is not only ill-regarded, but may suffer persecution by the magician. Its role is to procure somebody's injury or death by poison or by the prostrating fear the sorcerer instills. Among the Nyamsi of western Tanganyika the sorcerer is called *Lozi* (or poisoner), a name derived from a poison root.

By the user, however, sorcery is regarded as beneficial. Rightly or wrongly, he lays the blame for a misfortune he has suffered on another, an enemy. To retaliate gives him a feeling of justice and restored power.

A third type of practitioner is the diviner, whose "science" is exclusively focused on divination. Often, however, the magician is a diviner as well.

If we analyze our own behavior, we will find that we, too, often act on assumptions close to those of magic. Much of what we do is an acting out of what we desire. And we, too, may seek to evade responsibility for the misfortunes that befall us by transferring the blame to others.

MAGIC AND RELIGION

In the ancient Negro states, the ruler was the religious head. But since the white conquests the natives have had to dispense with religious leaders other than the local magicians, whose status and function vary from tribe to tribe.

The only African institution comparable to the hierarchy of organized religions is *patriarchy*. Thus it is the oldest man in the tribe who has authority in religious matters and in the division of land. His authority is backed by the secret societies, of which more later.

However, the African himself recognizes a distinction between his religious and his magical practices. The former are connected with events—such as birth, puberty, marriage, death—for which we too prescribe certain rituals. The province of magic, on the other hand, takes in unforeseen events of life—sickness, drought, accidents, battle risks.

Magic differs from what we hold to be religion in its lack of a hierarchical priesthood, of scriptures, of authoritarian heads such as a pope, and of revered founders such as Moses, Jesus, Mahomet, Buddha, etc. Nor are its practices carried out in large sacred edifices, such as churches, temples, synagogues, or mosques; nor does it have a principal center of worship and place of pilgrimage, such as Jerusalem, Rome, or Mecca.

Virtually all these characteristics of other religions are missing in African animistic cults, though the mythology is somewhat analogous to the scriptures of other cultures and unquestioning adherence to the precedents established by the mythology is obligatory, as in religious groups everywhere. In the African cults any infraction, even when accidental, is severely punished. Any lapse is believed to destroy the effectiveness of the rite.

The huts set aside for the storage of religious masks and ancestor sculptures cannot be compared with the edifices raised for worship in other religions. Nor does the same sanctity attach to them. Where the buildings consecrated to other religions are believed to contain emanations of the deity, no such sanctity is ascribed to the hut containing the magic statues. The African is not concerned with any universal God, but with the soul of the dead. Through the me-

FIG. 7. *Ancestor statue. Bena Lulua, Belgian Congo. 10″ high.* SEE PAGE 223

dium of the sculptor's art, this soul is re-installed among the living.

In other religions the believer trusts in prayer to a forgiving and protecting higher being. But the African believes that by magic he can directly control the forces of nature and make the spirits work for his advantage. He is so confident of his rights to this—given the proper magic—that a sculpture that fails to produce results may be destroyed and replaced by another. Thus the worshiper's attitude in the magic cults is active, not passive. Through his positive assertion against fear and despair, the African attempts to arrive at mental assurance and balance.

Another difference between religion and magic is that in the former abstract ethical principles are stressed; in the latter only results count. The magic rites have a clearly defined, practical aim: to satisfy physical or instinctual needs and desires.

Furthermore, religions are usually evangelistic. They hold themselves open to all comers, to everyone willing to believe. In the animistic cults the rites are restricted to the initiated.

In the African cults themselves, certain distinctions might be pointed out between what may be termed their religious and their magical practices. Where the ritual is collective it may be termed religious; where it is restricted and private it may be termed magic. Again, where the ritual is founded on family life it tends to have a religious character; magic is founded on the individual as a member of a secret society. Burials, which are connected with ancestor worship, involve the whole tribe and have a communal religious significance. Many other rites are secret and exclusive, at least of the opposite sex, as in the ceremonies held by the men's or women's secret societies.

THE MAGICAL ACT

The magical act protects one against mischances. When magic is used against the un-foreseen, the future loses its dread. Magic helps to transform the uncertain into certainty. It derives from the instinct for self-preservation, but it fulfills other instinctual needs besides.

Recent psychological discoveries throw a new light on the magical act. We now know that if deeply rooted impulses are unfulfilled, they create inner tensions. In the magical act, the African attempts to deal with his neurotic tensions.

The magical act assigns an important role to the expression of emotions. The magician or sorcerer acts out the emotion of his client. This emotional identification gives a conviction of the validity of the wish the magical act is to fulfill. The sorcerer works himself into a rage, which is actually supposed to terrify the object of his maledictions.

Malinowski offers an interesting speculation on the origin of such spells. When one is faced with an overwhelming difficulty, he may blurt out curse words remarkably similar to the words used in spells. This often tranquillizes the person by discharging his emotional tension, and gives him a curious feeling of confidence, as if he has done something to bring his desires a little nearer to fulfillment.

This may help to explain the importance of oral expression in the magical act. Though a ritual carving has had magical substances added to it, it assumes its magic power only when some qualified person—the chief, the magician, or the sculptor—pronounces that power to have entered into the carving. Among the Dogons a ritual rock painting incorporates the spirit it is assumed to represent only after the artist's pronouncement. Consecration rites include sacrifices, a dance, and an invocation setting forth the thought or wish the ritual is to embody. The Word, we see, is as important in primitive ritual as in organized religion.

Of course the user of magic does not thereby change the course of outer events.

FIG. 8. *Chief's stool. Baluba (Buli), Belgian Congo. 21" high.* SEE PAGE 208

FIG. 9. *Staff's head. Baluba, Belgian Congo. 2" high.* SEE PAGE 208

But the belief that he has produced emotional fulfillment furthers a later fulfillment in fact. When we have confidence in our actions, that confidence may help us to effect and fulfill our desires.

The magical act is of two basic kinds. One is an act with, the other without, a ritual object such as a statue or a carved mask. In the former case the ritual object is believed to have the power to bring about the desired end; in the latter, the spoken words and the imitative gestures are believed to suffice. But in most rituals both types of magical acts are performed.

WHY MAGIC SUCCEEDS

Whatever the forms may be, they rest on a common base, the user's faith in their potency. This faith in "the omnipotence of the thought," as Freud called it, is particularly powerful in African ritual because both the spirits and the statues they are believed to inhabit reflect the African's inner world. In this inner world he craves fatherly protection, and this is supplied in the ancestor spirit as concretized in the statues. In our search for security, we in the West build analogous image formations in our minds.

African ritual claims to be rigid and traditional. The oldest myths affirm that these rituals, in the forms in which they have been practiced ever since, began with the very genesis of the tribe. Unquestioning and undeviating observance is demanded of and willingly given by the natives, who are convinced that it is in their interest to do so. Observance gives them a comforting sense of belonging and relieves them of difficult personal decisions. The African knows no other way to assure success in his undertakings than magic; and he feels that without the ancestor cult there would be no safe haven for his soul after death.

We can see much the same process in the relation of the Catholic to his church. He is similarly relieved of anxiety and doubt, and many vital personal decisions are made for him.

SYMPATHETIC MAGIC

The anthropologist Frobenius describes a form of magic he witnessed in the Congo. A hunter traced a picture of an antelope in the dust with his finger and then shot an arrow into its neck. He returned from the hunt with an antelope killed in that manner. For Frobenius this was a living survival of the magic used by the Magdalenian cavemen who, some fifteen thousand years ago, drew pictures of the animals they hunted on the walls of their caves and shot arrows —as marks on the drawings indicate—at vulnerable places on the animal. There is no doubt but that the assurance gained in this symbolic killing gave the primitive hunter a surer eye and a steadier hand.

This is a variant of one of the most widespread of magical procedures—*sympathetic*, or *contagious*, magic. What is done to the image of an animal or a man is believed to be done, magically, to the original. It is the chief form of sorcery. Often the sorcerer does without an image or an effigy and makes use of a lock of hair, or a nail paring, or a piece of a garment worn by the victim. Where a statue is used, it is burned or broken up. Numbers of valuable works of art have been lost in this manner. A similar function is served by the "nail fetishes" into which nails are driven.

MAGIC WITHOUT RITUAL OBJECTS

The French anthropologist Feuilloley witnessed the following exorcism. A man said to be possessed by an evil spirit chewed a mixture of seeds and chicken blood given to him by the magician. He then spat the masticated matter into a dish which a condemned youth was forced to swallow. The youth immediately howled like an animal. This was taken to mean that the evil spirit had left the older man for the younger, and the exorcism had succeeded.

We can find versions of such beliefs in possession by evil spirits in fantasies and in private rituals of compulsion neurotics. The magician who effects a transfer of the possessing spirit performs an act similar to the transference which occurs when the psychoanalyst is accepted as a substitute for the patient's father, or any other person in regard to whom the patient is in emotional conflict.

In such exorcism cures an analogy of another sort may be seen. The cure here is the result of the patient's faith, just as are the cures at the miracle shrines of Lourdes or St. Anne de Beaupré, where the walls are lined with the crutches of hysterical paralytics who walked away "cured." This condition is realized at the ministrations of African medicine men, and we may assume a certain proportion of cures where illnesses are psychogenic. Unfortunately, Africans suffering from organic diseases have only the magicians to go to, and millions have died untimely for lack of a scientific medicine.

This does not mean, however, that the African medicine man works with nothing other than faith. Actually, he has command of a fairly extensive pharmacopoeia accumulated through centuries of observation of the effects of herbs and minerals and transmitted orally from generation to generation. The value of a number of these remedies has been confirmed by Western scientists. Indeed, the African healer's apprenticeship calls for many years of study, beginning at the age of twelve.

POSITIVE AND NEGATIVE ASPECTS

In their positive aspect, magical rites provide a man with the assurance necessary to carry out some undertaking with success. In their negative aspect such rites, when the victim knows about them, weaken his capacity to resist. Many instances are known of such victims apathetically resigning themselves to death by inanition. In psychiatric terms, paranoid fear of powerful persecutors or intense guilt feelings have thus been activated in the victim to induce self-destruction. Similar psychic mechanisms are observed in psychotics and neurotics in the West.

NEGATIVE MAGIC—TABOO

A manifestation of negative magic is the operation of restrictions or taboos. The psychologist Wundt called taboo (or tabu, derived from the Polynesian word *tapu*) "the oldest unwritten law of humanity." Freud defined it as the "objectified fear of demonic powers" and, in another connection, as "a command of the conscience, the violation of which causes terrible guilt feeling." Taboo is a series of socially and psychically sanctioned restrictions on behavior. He who violates a taboo faces not only the wrath of the community but his own horrified conscience.

How powerful this can be is shown in episodes reported by French missionaries. After eating a meal at the mission, one child learned that a banana, a food taboo of his tribe, was one of the ingredients. The resulting terror produced a paralysis of the respiratory muscles, and the child died before the missionary's eyes. Another child's taboo was being slapped, which was supposed to be fatal to him. Receiving a slap during a scuffle, the child fainted, and his life was saved only because a magician who could perform the necessary purification rites happened to be available.

THE MEANING OF SACRIFICE

Sacrifice is as old as taboo, as old as the feelings of guilt and fear, as old as humanity. Essentially, sacrifice is an appeasement of a higher power by one who fears hostility. It may be connected with taboos, violation of which involves guilt feelings and dread of punishment. In African terms, the superior life force (called *Nyama* among the Dogons of French Sudan) of a

FIG. 10. *Ceremonial cup. Bakuba, Belgian Congo. 9½″ high.* SEE PAGE 200

chief, a priest, or a spirit will destroy the taboo-breaker's life force unless appeased by a sacrifice. This higher power or stronger life force is connected with the image of the parent, from whom everybody experienced punishment as a child. Human sacrifice is rare. Usually animals, fruits, or cereals are offered. The vital force of the offering is believed to be absorbed by the person or image to whom the sacrifice is made.

Sacrifice is also thought of as expiation, and is thus a direct expression of the sense of guilt. Thus, in addition to the relief gained by appeasing a higher power, the worshiper gains inner peace through the absolution purchased by his sacrifice.

Analogies may be seen in the Catholic institutions of confession of sins, and the recovery of serenity through penance and absolution.

MODERN SURVIVALS OF MAGICAL BELIEFS

Though in a weakened state, much of our social behavior resembles the code of taboo. Our consciences are deep reservoirs of taboo. These may be so strong as to lead us to punish ourselves by neurotic symptoms for unconscious impulses that transgress the taboos. Actual survivals of magic in the West include superstitious beliefs in the evil eye, unlucky days and numbers (how many of our modern skyscrapers do without a thirteenth floor!), fears of black cats, the open penknife, the broken mirror, etc. Figures like Superman allow us, like the primitive in his ritual identifications with ancestor heroes, to identify ourselves with fantasy figures through whom we may fulfill infantile wishes for omnipotence.

DOGMA AND ART

Our concern here, of course, is with the effect of what we may call African dogmas on African art. The dogmas narrow the scope of the artist, but they also concentrate his emotions and thus intensify their power. The result may be likened to the concentration by a focusing lens, which imparts a burning heat to rays that, when diffused, are hardly felt.

The limitations of the dogmas are manifest in the rigidity of the African style traditions. The concentration is to be seen in the intense expressiveness of the sculptures. We may note here that early Christian art and the great Khmer Buddhist art showed a similar rigidity and intensity.

According to Gide, a work of art is the product of selection and discipline. In African sculpture the selection is imposed by a unified, religio-magical, animist idea, the discipline by a strong, though limiting, tribal art tradition.

AFRICAN SCULPTURE AND MAGIC

Most African sculptures are of a magico-religious character. Seldom have they been the product of a purely aesthetic intention. African sculptures have become works of art only to us. To Africans they were objects of use necessary to the successful performance of rituals and magic.

It is reported that on the Ivory coast today, the Baule and the Guro tribes experience aesthetic pleasure in sculpture and produce pieces with that purpose in mind. But even among these tribes, most of the sculpture is made upon recommendation of the magician and consecrated by the sacrifice of a cock. Thus the separation of the religious and the aesthetic in African sculpture is a late, incomplete, and still isolated phenomenon.

In addition to magical and religious sculpture, some figures serve as dolls; others as personal adornment, armor, or household utensils; and some carved masks are used in clowning. But even where the magic element is not predominant, it exisits. Thus a pot may have a carved lid in the form of a totem or a mythological animal which is believed to safeguard both the food and those who eat it. Sculptured figures on

weapons similarly protect the weapon itself and therefore the wielder.

Some writers hold that the famous statues
of the Bushongo kings should be classified
as secular monuments, products of a court
culture (Fig. 2). However, since the king
(or *nyimi*) was considered of divine origin,
his statue was also a religious representation.
A division into religious and non religious
African sculpture is hardly feasible. Its magical function is apparent even in the etymol-
ogy of the words. Perier points out that the
Bantu word *ngangu* means both talent and
magician.

African sculpture includes statues and
masks, used separately, but both believed to
have magic power. Some statues are used
for healing and some are commemorative
figures. In the West African term, statues
and masks are "spirit- or god-traps," embodying the spirits, providing homes for ancestors, containing their Vital Force and
that of mythical and totemistic animals.

FIG. 11. *Ivory whistle. Basonge, Belgian
Congo. 2½″ high.* SEE PAGE 215

c. Fetishism

The word *fetish*, which describes the
most widely used of magical objects, is not
of West African origin. It is an invention of
the Belgian, De Brosses, who used it in his
essay, "Du Culte des Dieux Fétishes," to
designate West African statues when compared with the ritual objects of the Egyptians. He derived the word from *phatah*, the
Egyptian term for their smaller idols. A
similar, earlier coinage by the Greeks was
pataic, for the figureheads on Phoenician
vessels.

Another derivation may be the Portuguese word *feitiço* or *fetiçao*, meaning "fab-
ricated" or "false," and derived in turn from
the Latin verb *facere*, from which come
such words as *factitious* and *fake*. The connotation for the Portuguese, who were the
first to see African carvings, was probably
that of false gods. It must be noted, how-

ever, that the Africans themselves never
thought of these images as gods.

As it has since come to be used, the word
fetish is applied mainly to statues, but it
categorizes *any* object credited with magical power. The African fears evil spirits
more than wild animals. Against the latter
he can defend himself, but against the spirits
his only defense is magic or spirit power,
mainly as incorporated in the fetish.

Any object over which the proper magical rites have been performed becomes a
fetish. It need not be a statue; it may be a
piece of wood, bone, feather, stone, animal
tooth, an animal skin, a bird's head, an herb,
or a string of beads. In Africa each fetish
serves a specialized function. A warrior, for
example, needs separate fetishes to protect
him against death by bullet, by club, by
drowning, by crocodiles encountered at
river crossings, etc. Consequently the African wears a number of fetishes, usually in a

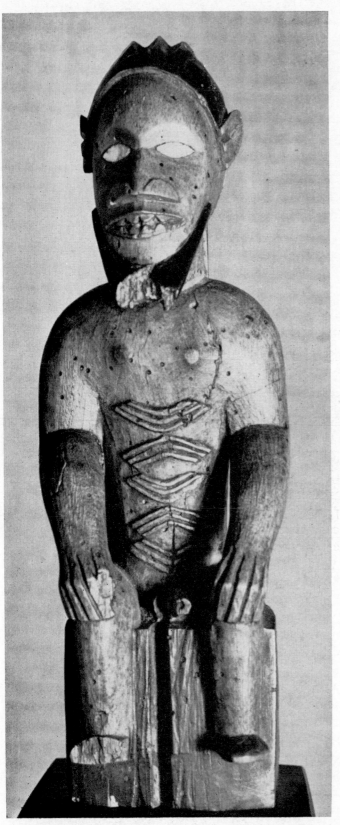

FIG. 13. *Head of a sceptre. Batshioko, Belgian Congo.* high. SEE PAGE

FIG. 12. *Ancestor statue. Babembe, Gabun (Moyen Congo). 7″ high.* SEE PAGE 186.

FIG. 14. *Head. Pangwe, Gabun. 15" high.* SEE PAGE 192

FIG. 15. *Statue. Pangwe, Gabun. 29" high.* SEE PAGE 192

small bag hung around his neck. Fetishes are also used in cures of the sick.

Attempts have been made to classify fetishes as defensive or offensive. It is true that the fetish worn on the body is supposed to be a protection against evil spirits and is thus defensive; and a fetish into which nails are driven is functionally offensive. Yet the nail fetish also has defensive functions, as indicated by the inset mirror, which is supposed to blind hostile spirits, and the dagger in the upraised hand (Fig. 5).

One may broadly differentiate the fetish from the ancestor statue by considering the first an article of everyday use with a specific function and the latter as reserved for the rituals of the ancestor cult.

There is, however, a diversity in the use of ancestor figures. Offerings to them (in the form of food) may vary in purpose. They may seek to appease the vengeful spirit; they may seek a cure for sickness (believed to be caused by the wrathful ancestor); they may solicit the ancestor's aid in an enterprise; or they may merely seek peace of mind through relief from guilt feelings.

The word *fetish* is interchangeable with *charm, talisman,* or *amulet.* These objects are as numerous as human desires or fears. They are used to conjure away evil and propitiate chance. The idea of hope is attached to such objects—not a passive hope, but an active influence upon destiny. Because a definite result is expected, the belief in the fetish becomes *faith.*

MODERN SURVIVAL OF CHARMS

It is interesting to note the magical concept in our word *charm* even when used, not to denote a fetish or a spell, but to describe the characteristics of a person who fascinates *as if he had cast a spell.* Surviving magical beliefs, intermingled with animism, are manifested by us in the use of such objects as lucky coins, rabbits' feet, elks' teeth, rings, lockets, and necklaces; they induce

us to hang horseshoes over our doors, to touch wood in order to avert harm, and so on. The Catholic Church uses magical rituals when it pronounces blessings over ordinary water, making it holy, or sells protective medallions and amulets with sacred images or inscriptions.

The cross itself, as used and worn, is endowed with magical power. Incidentally, the cross was readily accepted by the African natives when Portuguese missionaries, in the fifteenth century, brought it to the Lower Congo (then called San Salvador). The natives reproduced crucifixes and images of St. Anthony in the native manner, called them *Kangi,* vested magical power in them, and incorporated them into their own store of fetishes. These beautiful pieces are comparable to Byzantine works (Fig. 6).

DIVINATION

Another magical procedure, widely practiced in Africa, is "throwing the bones." As reported from Gabun, the practitioner uses a basket of small "bones"—*ngombo,* as the apparatus is called. The "bones," numbering about ninety, are small objects, each with its own meaning. A small carving of a crouching dog represents the soul of the dead; a human figurine represents a child; a long sliver of bone represents a traveler, etc. From their position in the basket, the diviner interprets a person's fate.

This resembles the methods of our fortune-tellers, who derive from the fall of cards, the lines on a palm, the shapes taken by tea leaves, etc. Indeed, another African form of divination directly resembles the last, the dropping of small sticks into a bowl of water and the reading of the "fortune" from the positions they assume. The earliest reports of divination in the Western world describe prognostication from the entrails of sacrificed animals, practiced by the ancient Babylonians, Egyptians, and Romans. Special small animal sculptures, used by

FIG. 16. *Maternity statue, steatite. Bakongo, Belgian Congo. 9″ high.* SEE PAGE 198

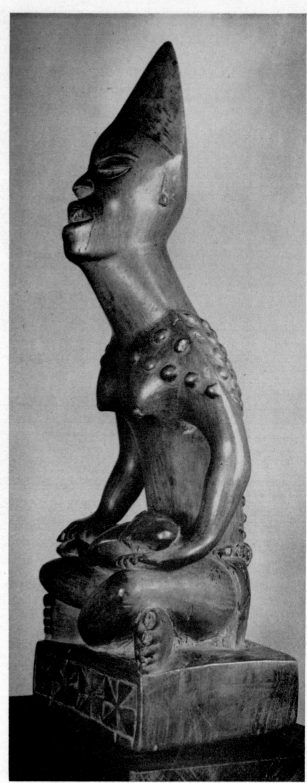

FIG. 17. *Maternity statue. Bakongo, Belgian Congo. 12" high.* SEE PAGE 198

the Bakubas, and called *itombwa*, mainly crocodiles, pigs, and dogs, some with human and some with animal heads, were used in divination (Fig. 1). The back of each was flattened, and during the divination this flat surface was moistened and a wooden disk rubbed on it. If the disk stuck, it was supposed to be an affirmative answer to a question asked at that moment. Torday reported the adhesion as so strong that the disk did not fall off when the statue was turned upside down. It seems probable that water was not used, but instead some mixture that became viscid on rubbing; and that the diviner let the disk stick when he thought he had a clue. For example, in using this magic to catch a thief, the diviner would call out the names of suspects. Nervous behavior on the part of a person on hearing his name might decide the diviner to let the disk stick at that point. Similarly a medicine man, using this method to hit on a remedy, might call out, "Do not smoke," "Do not eat meat," etc., and let the disk stick at what he considered the right prescription.

Itombwe images are of fine, abstract construction. The requirement of a flat surface was met with great ingenuity.

Magical objects did achieve results for the Africans. And in each case sound psychological reasons as to why they worked may be found.

D. Mythology

The historical past of the natives has dissolved in their myths which, while of little documentary value, served a major cultural purpose in providing subjects for symbolic sculptures.

The number of African tribal myths cannot be estimated. Each of the more than a thousand tribes had its own vast store, which took the place of written literature and survived for centuries in oral tradition. The French writer Blaise Cendrars, in his *Anthologie Nègre,* has offered a sampling of these myths, about a hundred legends selected from material in 591 African languages and dialects. He subdivides them into myths concerned with cosmology, fetishism, totemism, fantasy, tales, and poetry.

ORIGIN OF MYTHS

It is possible that some myths began with the recital of a chieftain's dreams. Since primitive people consider dreams a part of their everyday life (seeking guidance for future action in their dreams), the recital might have been accepted both by the narrator and his audience as real, and repeated in future recitals as actual occurrences. Succeeding narrators quite possibly selected and emphasized those features which corresponded with their own desires. Thus the original dream might have grown into a communal fantasy or myth. It is also likely that the chief, as the responsible moral authority of the community, edited his dreams here and there to carry a moral lesson, thus incorporating an ideological statement into the myth.

Most important, perhaps, are the creation myths and the myths of the origin of the tribes and of their institutions. Myths are always "stories," whose characters include human beings (either similar to those presently alive, or ancestor and cultural heroes) and the spirits of natural forces and animals. They are not symbolic figures; they act out events from tribal history; and their speech and behavior are those of contemporaries. To the African it is perfectly natural for animals or spirits to behave and talk like living people.

MYTHS IN EVERYDAY LIFE

Myths play an active part in the African's everyday life. They are a vital social force. They not only supply accounts of the tribe's origin but, as Malinowski pointed out, relate *precedents* to present-day beliefs, actions, and codes of behavior. It is taken for granted that beliefs and practices have existed unchanged since their adoption. Thus the reference to a precedent codifies and sanctifies the beliefs and places them beyond question or change. According to the myth, magical or religious ceremonies or actions produced results for the forefather; therefore the efficiency of the ritual is assured. The faith in myths is comparable to the faith in scriptures. Because myths also lay down laws of ownership, of behavior, etc., they are comparable to our legal codes, which also accord a high place to precedent.

The sacred myths are preserved by the secret societies and recited in a special language understood only by the members. The impressiveness of these myths is enhanced by the fact that they are revealed to the member for the first time at his initiation, the turning point in his life, when his fears have been excited, when he has been subjected to ordeals of pain and endurance, and when his tribal identification has been dramatized to the utmost.

Thus every subsequent repetition of the myth is bound to evoke strong emotional resonances.

MYTHS AS ART SOURCES

Myths are peculiarily accessible to the psychoanalytical approach, their symbols showing strong similarities to dream symbols and expressing similar repressed desires, fears, and compulsions. But the mythological symbols, although originating from the unconscious, carry ideological and spiritual concepts as well.

Like dreams, myths are inexhaustible sources of creative impulses. This is exemplified in African art works. Entire masks, and sometimes ornamental details on art work, have their origin in a mythological belief.

For an interesting parallel, dreams have also been used as inspirations in contemporary surrealist painting and sculpture. Physical reality seemed so precarious that surrealist artists sought attachment to something more secure, something in their own inner world not dependent on the ever-changing outside world, and they turned to the images in their unconscious.

Mythological precedents, as we have seen, also helped to establish a strong *art-style tradition*. In African mythology, invisible forces, the spirits of nature, the genii, are pictured as the ancestors of the Africans, who believe that the territories they occupy were previously held by the local genii. When a tribe moved to a new territory, rituals were performed asking permission from the spirits of the former inhabitants to occupy the new grounds.

The Dogons, in French Sudan, have a creation myth eight hundred verses long. Local genii, animals, and mythical "redmen" are their joint ancestors. In the recital certain masks and ancestor figures are used.

The Baules of the Ivory Coast start their creation myth with an immaterial God (*Aluru*). No cult, however, is devoted to him; therefore no sculptural representation exists. But *Nyama*, their spirit, genius, or demon of the sky, who rules over the future life of people, is represented by a ram mask. A bull mask with two or three horns represents another spirit, *Kaka-Huie*, and his wife, *Ago*, who supervise burials. The Demon of Agriculture, *Kuamanbo*, is also represented by a ram mask. *Zambie* and *Frete*, second-grade genii, are represented by an antelope head with long horns. *Obekre*, another second-grade spirit, has a monkey mask with a doglike head. *Bgogro-Kofi* has a hyena mask.

One could continue an endless enumeration of spirits, demigods, second-grade genii, etc. Sometimes the same mask serves two different spirits. To determine whether a mask refers to a myth, a totem, or a supernatural being, whether it embodies the protective spirit of a tribe or a secret society, requires long and careful study.

FIG. 18. *Ceremonial pottery jar. Mangbetu, Belgian Congo. 13" high.* SEE PAGE 225

FIG. 19. *Statue, ivory. Warega(?), Belgian Congo. 6" high.*
SEE PAGE 227

FIG. 20. *Ivory statue. Warega, Belgian Congo. 5¼" high.*
SEE PAGE 22

3. AFRICAN CULTS EMPLOYING SCULPTURES

THE intense emotionalism of African art can be best explained in terms of the rich tradition in which it has its roots. Sculptured objects are utilized not only for magical purposes in everyday life but in the religious rituals engaged in by the tribal cults. These are: the cult of the dead, the cult of totemism, and the secret society.

A. Cult of the Dead and Ancestor Worship

The cult of the dead, of which ancestor worship is an outgrowth, is one of mankind's oldest religious observances. Remains of the Neolithic Period (New Stone Age, 10,000 to 3000 B.C.), such as the dolmens (table stones), cromlechs (stone circles), and passage graves found in France, England, and Scandinavia, indicate communal burial sites which were used over long periods. Nowhere was this cult so highly developed as in Egypt, where traces from as far back as 6000 B.C. have been found, and where the world's vastest tombs, the pyramids, arose.

According to Freud, ceremonial burial derives from a deeply rooted instinct in man to return to the womb, to be laid in "Mother Earth." Many primitive peoples still bury their dead crouched in the foetal position (Fig. 7).

When an African king or chief died in ancient times, his companions, wives, relatives, slaves, and others connected with him, were killed to keep him company in the other world. Only exceptional people were then believed to have immortal souls; therefore only those were sacrificed who were deemed worthy of sharing the dead ruler's immortality.

In some regions the custom survived into the last century. According to Torday, in 1884, when the Bushongo king Bope Mobinji died, two thousand people were killed, not counting wives and personal servants. Similar human hecatombs in the Benin Kingdom showed certain variations. The trunks were buried in a common grave while the severed heads were raised on poles around it. Photographs of this grisly palisade were brought back by explorers. Elsewhere it became customary to bury sculptured heads or figures of the royal companions instead of killing them and interring their bodies.

Heads were frequently dried and the skulls used for ceremonial drinking cups. Because the Vital Force (or soul) resided in the head, by drinking from the skull the user appropriated the strength of the dead man. Most treasured of all was the skull of a powerful enemy, for this meant not only the acquisition of his Vital Force, but thereby, his complete extinction. The Bakuba cups which were carved in the form of human heads appear to be survivals of this custom (Fig. 10).

Subsequently, a carving of the dead man became an ancestor figure. So, instead of providing company for the dead man by slaughtering his former companions, a sculptured body was provided in which he could rejoin the living. Thus in Africa there evolved from burial rituals a system of worship of the spirits of ancestors. These were believed to retain their vital power after death.

UNIVERSAL ENERGY

Although the concept of God exists among the Africans, their attention is directed elsewhere. God is believed to have created the world, but to be indifferent to human beings. He is cosmogonic rather than religious. No cults, statues, or symbols are consecrated to Him. Because this God, variously called *Zamba, Nzame, Gumpa, Ngala, Nisaua, Emitay, Mahu*, does not concern himself with human beings, they in turn show no interest in Him, confining their religious ceremonies to the gratification of the spirits who are very much interested in human beings. These are not thought of in the sense of deities, but as emanations or agents of a superior, all-embracing Universal Energy.

Part of Universal Energy is the Vital Force, sometimes called Vital Breath or *Nyama*. It is a component of the soul of animate beings. But even inanimate objects have a share of the Universal Energy, which, though invisible, is omnipresent. The Universal Energy can see and hear everything and has volition; therefore a man's everpresent guilt feelings cause it to be feared, and attempts are made to appease it with flattering offerings and prayers.

Universal Energy is thought of as being distributed through all matter. It is remarkable how close this concept comes to the most modern understanding of matter and energy as different aspects of the same entity.

VITAL FORCE

The Vital Force (or Nyama, as we shall call it from now on) exists only in animate beings—men, animals, and plants. It differs from the rest of Universal Energy in that it can pass from man to man, from animal to man, and from plant to man or animal, etc. This transfer can be effected, as desired, by the use of the proper magic. The Nyama is indestructible. After death it reincarnates itself in other human beings, generally those of the same family.

The Nyama comes closest to our concept of the soul. However, unlike our soul, which is indivisible, the Nyama is transmissible in whole or in part. Our soul is specifically human, and after death goes off to the afterworld to receive divine justice. But Nyama exists in all animate creations. A man's Nyama remains on earth after his death and exerts power over living beings, with whom it maintains intimate connection. It can be augmented with additions of the Nyama of others; it can be appropriated by others; and it is not subject to divine justice.

As part of Universal Energy, the Nyama can fuse with it. Since Nyama is attributed to sculptured masks, it must be considered in any discussion of African art. The mask is regarded as the support or container of the Nyama; by wearing it the masker augments his own Nyama. It is necessary to trap Nyama, which may work harm when on the loose. In the consecration of the mask the blood of a sacrificed animal is poured

FIG. 21. *Mask with horns. Baluba, Belgian Congo. 18" high.* SEE PAGE 208

FIG. 22. *Initiation ceremony mask. Balunda-Batshioko, Belgian Congo. 14″ high.* SEE PAGE 21

over it, thus adding to its Nyama the Nyama of the animal. A human being may lose part of his Nyama by bleeding and add to it by eating. When he consumes a vegetable he acquires not only its Nyama, but the Nyama of the earth, rain, and sun which the vegetable has absorbed. Animistic ritual is mainly a matter of transference of Nyama from one organism to another.

The Polynesian concept of *Mana* is so strikingly similar as to suggest the possibility, despite the great geographical distance between the two peoples, of a common cultural origin.

We find this concept throughout the African continent. The Gold Coast Ashantis' word for it is *Kra* (how similar to the Egyptian *Ka* for the same concept!). As reported by Eva L. R. Meyerowitz, they define it as the overriding vital force which maintains an independent existence in the body and is the source of uncontrollable human impulses, dreams, and fantasies (how close to our concept of the unconscious!). Further, we find the design ⊙ on Ashanti gold weights, on Warega and Basonge ivories (Fig.11), and on some Egyptian carvings, including several in the Louvre. According to Ashanti explanations, the circle enclosing a dot represented the sun, upon which *Nyama* (the Ashanti Supreme Being) deposited her *Kra* after giving birth to the universe. Subsequently this symbol was restricted to the *Kra* or to the Universal Energy.

THE ANCESTOR CULT

To the African, death means that the Nyama leaves the body at the command of the Universal Energy. Death, consequently, is not destruction but a transformation or transfiguration.

This belief in the Nyama may be seen as another primitive solution of a psychic problem. Death was terrifying and repugnant to the African, who had frequent occasion to see putrefying corpses. Had his horror and fear led to flight from the place defiled by

the putrefaction, it might have resulted in a disintegration of his social structure through the continuous disestablishment of its centers. In addition, fear of death would have become a crippling obsession.

Here faith in the survival of his Nyama, his Vital Force, came to his rescue. Instead of flight he chose to confront and overcome his fear. He minimized physical death and emphasized the continuity of life. He knew that the Nyama of his ancestors survived. It was worshiped and venerated. Believing in this procedure, a man need not fear death. His Nyama, too, would survive to occupy an honored place in the family.

He was assisted in the development of this concept by his dreams or visions, in which dead persons returned. Dreams being as actual to him as reality, this was concrete evidence to him of the survival of the dead. The belief was dramatized by making every death and burial a communal event, and faith was concretized in the ancestor statue.

Using psychoanalytic concepts, the cult of the ancestor may be seen as an aspect of the father (or mother) image. This image may be externalized in the statue or internalized as conscience. Thus one of the various functions of an ancestor statue is its role as counterpart of the conscience.

An African, when he has a dubious impulse, consults his ancestor statue, first offering it food to gain its good will. Having procured his ancestor's sanction, he then carries out his impulse with an easy mind. The guilt feeling, so restrictive to our actions, is removed.

ANCESTOR STATUES

Among the Pangwe and Bakota and other tribes, ancestor worship involves preserving the skull of the dead in a container mounted with a sculptured head or figure (Fig. 23). Other observances include visits to the grave, where food is offered. But the commonest form of ancestor worship is the use of an ancestor statue or mask. The figure

FIG. 23. *Funerary statue. Bakota, Gabun. 22″ high.* SEE PAGE 186

is kept in the house on an earthen altar, or in a small adjoining hut erected for this purpose. Thus it is immediately accessible any time the ancestor's help is needed.

As we have seen, the soul of the deceased is believed to consist of two components: its Nyama with which the worshiper seeks to reinforce his own Nyama; and the powerful Universal Energy, whose good will it is important to have. The concept of the Universal Energy and the Nyama is not always clear-cut. Versions vary from tribe to tribe. In some form, however, the concept has been found in every tribe.

The ancestor statue contains this composite force, but not until certain rites have been performed to induce the spirit to take up his residence in it. After the spirit has thus been ritually inducted into it, the statue becomes a very important object. Up to

then the spirit was believed to have led a homeless existence, which embittered it against the living and made it dangerous to them.

There are two types of ancestor figure— one serving a family, the other serving the whole tribe. The latter is a representation of a tribal chief. It is kept in the custody of the magician of the village. So real are the spirits to the African that he considers the spirit—and the image in which it is embodied—to be literally alive, to function as an active member of the family, and, indeed, to have more potent vitality than the living.

Residues of similar attitudes may be observed here and there in Europe. For example, in Germany there have been instances in modern times of the place of the dead at the table being left unoccupied and the food set there at family meals.

Most common among the variety of pleas made to the ancestor figure are appeals for the use of his Nyama to strengthen the petitioner's Nyama, intervention in his favor with the spirits of Nature, protection against harm to him, and aid in his enterprises. The pleas are expected to be granted if the proper sacrifices have been made. The sacrifices also appease the ancestor's jealousy and resentment toward the living, signs of which are the accidents, misfortunes, and illnesses which the ancestor is asked to avert.

WESTERN ANALOGIES OF ANCESTOR WORSHIP

When we go into a cemetery and invoke the memory of the deceased, we, too, perform an act of ancestor worship. But the African's ritual is based upon animistic concepts. His mortuary figure has life, while our representation is merely symbolic. For this reason, perhaps, his figure is a powerful work of art, while our tombstones are among the most inartistic carvings man has ever produced. Instead of our occasional trips to the cemetery, the African can turn at will or need immediately to the ancestor figure beside him. Probably for the same reason, that is, to have the savior symbol near at hand, crosses with finely carved Christ figures have been set up on highways in various parts of Europe.

PSYCHOANALYTIC INTERPRETATIONS

In our society, neurotics, shrinking from threatening demands of the world, may regress to an infantile stage. The father (or mother) image in the mind then serves as a protection. To overcome this regression and regain confidence to face the world, the neurotic must resort to prolonged and painful analysis. The primitive, however, has a father image that he can touch, to whom he can go for protection and make sure of getting it by offering the right sacrifices. Wish is thus promptly translated into action; a feeling of well-being is achieved, and he faces his world with security.

However, the attitude toward the father is ambivalent. His protection is sought, but his restrictive authority is resented. Awareness of this appears in the Old Testament, in Exodus, where veneration of father and mother (the ancestors of African ritual) was codified: "Honor thy father and thy mother that thy days may be long upon the land which the Lord, thy God, has given thee." In Deuteronomy the commandment is repeated with the added words ". . . as the Lord, thy God, has commanded" and "that it may go well with thee." Thus to the redoubled command rewards are added— the promise of long life and material prosperity.

According to Freud, the revolt against the father among primitive peoples is expressed in the totem feast, when the totem animal, an ancestor image, is killed and eaten.

Fears, including the fear of the vengeful ancestor, are widespread in Africa, as everywhere. To deal with them, the African may be said to have worked out a psychotherapy of his own, of which ancestor worship is only one aspect.

Fears arouse two types of reaction in human beings: *flight* (or evasion) and *fight* (or struggle). In the case of a neurotic who chooses flight (whether the threatening force is a reality or a fantasy does not matter), this choice may end in panic or the collapse of the will to live. The African chooses to fight. To master his fear he "objectivizes" or "concretizes" it in images and rituals. One result has been creation of a great sculpture.

In this sculpture the African has followed natural forms, but he has deformed them, imposing his will upon them. From this have come abstractions, which we shall later discuss in detail.

With his fear unloaded in his sculptures, the African is able to dominate his fear, having captured and thus vanquished the threatening spirit, and imprisoned it in the wooden figure. This enables him at the same time to put greater power into the creation —reflecting the intensity of his animistic belief. In this way, too, he masters himself, for, as Freud has shown us, spirits and demons are man's projections of his own emotional impulses.

The African's positive struggle against fear, and the will to create that it stimulated, constitute a magnificent, wholesome, and epochal achievement.

To the African the spirits supply *logical answers* to manifold threats in life and Nature. What he cannot understand seems to him obviously the work of spirits. Rain, fecundity, sickness—each has its spirit and may be caused by the malevolence of the ancestor spirits. And the better to face them, he has simplified or objectified them by creating magical objects and rituals.

B. Forms of Totemism

Totemism, in Frazer's definition, "is an intimate relation . . . which is supposed to exist between a group of kindred people on the one side and a species of natural or artificial objects on the other side, which objects are called the totems." The totem in most cases is an *animal*, but sometimes a plant, a natural phenomenon, or physical object of some kind.

It would be safe to define totemism as a formalized human association with objects and symbols which the natives have charged with emotion. Sometimes the clan takes its name from the totem and uses it as a heraldic symbol or develops a system of magical observance around it. Where the totem is an animal, killing it is tabooed. As Freud pointed out, totemism and exogamy often existed together. Exogamy (prohibition of intermarriage or sexual relations within the clan) is frequently one of the totem taboos. It defines incest, inbreeding, and adultery. African peoples do not consider the totem animal to be the tribal ancestor, as do totem-observing peoples in other parts of the world. According to many African myths, the totem animal helped the founding father of the clan or saved his life, and thus became the protector of the clan, which adopted its name. Animals are seldom objects, in any other way, of a religious cult, although the serpent, among the Ouidahs in Dahomey and the Dogons in Sudan, etc., is considered sacred primarily as incarnation, or a symbol of local genii or ancestor protectors. This belief, however, does not exclude the possibility of the Nyama being conducted into an animal.

SOURCES OF TOTEMISM

We will use the totem concept here in its relationship to the concept of spirits, of a force operating in the African's world that he can draw upon for his own use or protection.

The African believes in an intimate affinity and relationship between men and animals, to whom he accords equal status. Each clan has a different protecting totem animal. To some clans the totem animal is sacred and cannot be killed, because its ancestor is believed to have given service to the clan's ancestor.

The use of animals as symbols for spirits had its origin in the "worm-soul" concept. According to Otto Rank's interpretation, the worm issuing from the decomposing human corpse was its departing soul. From this first concept grew the idea that other animals—snakes, leopards, etc.—were also "soul animals." There is a strong possibility that the worm-soul idea is unconsciously behind the African veneration of animals and their intimate usage in magico-religious ceremonials. Identification with animals, of course, presupposes the belief that animals have souls.

Concern over food provides an additional explanation. To assure an abundance of food animals and plants, the African must take care of them. To accomplish this and also to overcome his fear of the animals and not to become too dependent upon them, he establishes control over them through magical rituals.

In Boas' view, the totem originated as the guardian spirit of an ancestor revealed to him in a dream. As we observed earlier, dreams are considered real by the Africans and are often the basis of myth creations. Handed down from generation to generation, the dreams formed the mythology; thus, the dreamed power of the animals was considered a real power established by tradition.

While the spirits of ancestors and of natural forces are seen to some extent as abstract manifestations of Universal Energy and are generally connected with the dead, the totem animal is thought of as a living being. Yet the totem animal serves the same primary purpose as the cult of spirits—as a release from fear. In the totem animal fear is objictified in a living figure.

Totemism served still another function. It helped primitive people to feel themselves possessed of some enviable quality of

FIG. 24. *Ivory mask. Bakuba, Belgian Congo. 5″ high.* SEE PAGE 206

FIG. 25. *Ivory mask. Bapende, Belgian Congo. 6" high.* SEE PAGE 212

an animal—combativeness, strength, speed, endurance, and so on. When an African wears a totem-animal mask, he becomes the animal itself. This process of identification will be further explained (Part II) when masks are discussed.

TOTEMISM AND TRIBAL CUSTOMS

Certain social institutions derive from totemism. Because people in the same clan are considered brothers, they acquire a closely knit unity, not fostered by the ancestor cult or magical rites. But while totemism fosters unity within the group, it fosters differentiation from other groups. The system provides dramatic ritual affirmation of the human need for mutual aid. The totem helps to overcome elemental but destructive human emotions, such as hate, dissension, and jealousy, with the aid of a magical social unity sealed by the common bond of the totem animal.

Where a taboo against killing the totem animal exists, a day is set aside when its slaughter is permitted—a day celebrated as a holiday. The animal is butchered but at the same time mourned, and Freud sees in this an analogue of the child's ambivalent emotion toward the father—love and admiration for his power and hatred for standing so threateningly in the way of his sexual demands and his desire for independence. In Freud's interpretation the totem animal is a substitute for the father, and the simultaneous rejoicing and grief when it is killed reflects the conflicting attitudes toward the father.

TOTEMISTIC USAGES IN CIVILIZED SOCIETIES

Residues of totemistic usage may be detected in our everyday language, when we refer, for example, to "foxy," or "pigheaded," or "eagle-eyed," or "lion-hearted" people. Similar vestiges are to be seen in the use of animal mascots, in the figures on college rings and pins, in heraldry, and in emblems of all kinds. Our national symbol, the eagle, is such a survival. Of our forty-eight states, forty-five have animal emblems.

SECRET SOCIETIES AND INITIATION RITES

Initiation ceremonies, enrolling the youth into the tribe, make use of masks. The ceremonies are conducted by the secret societies to which men and women belong—the men in one, the women in another. These secret societies have authority over religious matters.

After the boy reaches puberty at about eleven, he is entered into the male secret society at its next initiation ceremony. The long and complicated ritual is a form of intensified education. The proceedings are carried on in a hidden place. Generally the boy remains there in seclusion for a longer or shorter period, according to the custom of the tribe. Among the Bakongo of the Congo, this is two to four months. Among the Hyondo of the Uabangi-Shari regions, the ceremonies last two years, and continued flagellation is administered to develop the endurance of the initiate. The timing of the ceremonies also differs from tribe to tribe. Some tribal secret societies meet every four years; some, like the Poro secret society in Liberia, once every twenty-five years (that is, once in each generation).

The boy's instruction includes complicated ritual dances, secret language, secret music, the sacred myths, religion, and magic. Respect for the aged is drilled into him. Among the tests of endurance he undergoes are circumcision, scarring the skin in prescribed patterns, and prolonged silence. The boys are also trained to work collectively, giving a hand where urgently needed.

Girls go through a comparable course of initiation. This has been most closely studied in connection with the feminine secret societies called *Bundu* in Sierra Leone, of the tribes of Sherbro Island, and of the Bijago on the Bissagos Islands.

In rites analogous to circumcision ceremonies, the membrane covering the clitoris

FIG. 26. *Initiation ceremony mask (Bundu).*
Mendi, Sierra Leone. 17" high. SEE PAGES 166,
169

is cut or an incision is made into the vaginal
lips, facilitating hygiene.* A hoodlike mask
is used in these ceremonies (Fig. 26).

SIGNIFICANCE OF THE MASK

The secret societies have a hierarchy into
which members are admitted by stages. Each
rank has its own name and is represented by
its own mask. During the dances it is the
mask that is recognized, not the individual

---

* According to H. T. Laycock, "Surgical aspects of female circumcision in Somaliland," published in the *East African Medical Journal* (Nov.
1950), the following operations are performed:
Clitoridectomy or excision, imfibulation (sewing
up) to prevent premature and illicit intercourse,
and the reverse, defibulation (cutting open). Imfibulation consists in cutting away part of the
clitoris and in scarifying the labia minora; defibulation consists in a short incision made to separate the fused labia minora.

who wears it. The mask is the spirit, the
mask has the power. The person who wears
it is depersonalized.

The mask also becomes the *law*, since
judgments and rulings are pronounced by
the masker in the name of ancestors or ancestor spirits who reside in the mask. These
pronouncements, like Papal bulls, are considered infallible. For the individual this
means that he can confidently attach himself to the protective power of the mask
(the Ideal Father), in place of the human
figure who so often causes deep psychic re-
sentments. When the individual wearer of
the mask dies, the mask is immediately as-
signed to another high-ranking member of
the secret society, thus achieving a continuity of the law and its institutions.

The initiation ordeal ends with a ceremonial dance, with the boy entered into the
first grade of the secret society. Among the
Bapendes, in the Belgian Congo, the youth's
body is painted white with a clay called
Mpembe, and he wears a mask (Fig. 27).

This mask, which represents the ghost of
his old life, is finally cast aside, symbolizing
the death or extinction of childhood as the
youth assumes manhood and adult respon-
sibilities. Simultaneously the initiate assumes
a new name when he returns to his clan.
Changes of name mean more to the African
than to us, though we too feel certain psychic effects. For the African the name
change involves a change in personality, for
the name *is* the person, as his shadow is part
of his body.

(Among the Orthodox Jews, when a child
is gravely ill, the parents change his name in
the hope of giving him a new identity, turning him into a newborn child free of the
sickness.)

As a badge of initiation among the Bapendes (Belgian Congo) or as a symbolic
manifestation of his new personality, the
youth receives a small ivory mask (Fig. 28),
similar to the large one used in the initiation
ritual (Fig. 27), which serves him as a pro-

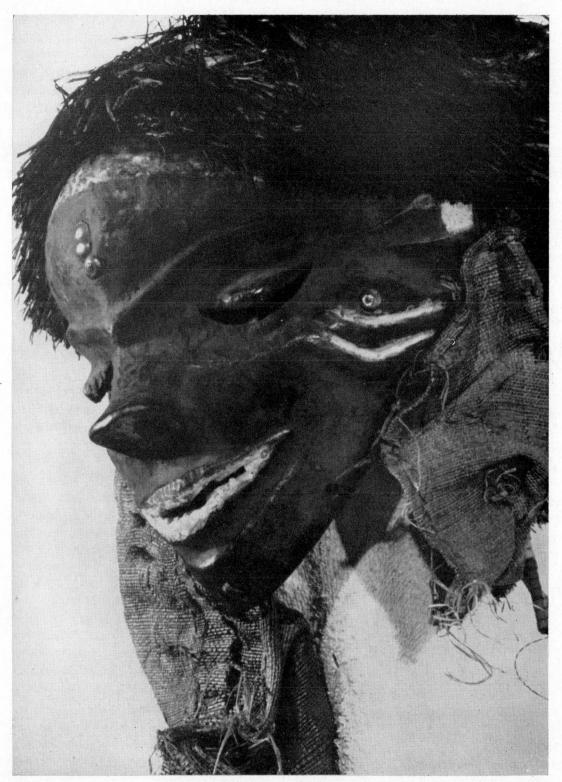

FIG. 27. *Initiation ceremony mask. Bapende, Belgian Congo. 11" high.* SEE PAGE 211

tective amulet in his new activities. Humans being a constant prey to insecurity, this enables the young native, whenever he feels uncertain in his new status, to reassure himself by touching his amulet.

PSYCHOLOGICAL IMPLICATIONS

Among the Mendis in Sierra Leone, the symbolic death and rebirth is thus dramatized. A "devil" represented by a mask "eats" the candidate, who is painted white, the spirit color, to symbolize his entrance into the world of spirits and the fact that he is not alive now but in communion with the spirits. (This symbolic death is also sought after by adults in trances that enable them to "travel to the country of the spirits.") The devil later "vomits" the candidate, who is thus resurrected from the dead as newly born. The candidate's head is shaven to simulate the hairless scalp of the newly born infant; then he is washed and given a new name.

In the Bakhimba secret society (Mayombe region, Belgian Congo) the final ceremony is a baptism of the initiated under water to wash away his past. He eats a morsel of sacred food to acquire part of its Nyama (which brings the Catholic institution of the Host to mind) and he acquires a new name.

We will realize what sound psychological reasons lie behind the initiation ceremony when we compare it with our own development. The transition from youth to manhood, with its sexual ripening, is accompanied, among us, with prolonged conflicts marked by varying degrees of frustration, guilt, and fears. In his initiation ceremonies, the African dramatizes this transition and its associated reactions against the emotional bonds of the child to his parents. The African father does not evade the issue of the coming manhood of his son, and it is made easier for him by having the responsibility for it assumed communally, by the assembly of "all fathers." At the same time, this may lessen the psychic resentment against the father, a resentment that sometimes inhibits a boy's sexual development.

Similarly, the problem of the boy's relationship to his mother is dealt with through ceremonies which help to cut the psychic "umbilical cord." In these rites he is born anew into his tribe. The African youth thus appears to be spared the agonies and fears that so often (and so tragically) overshadow adolescence in "civilized" countries. The rituals are the African's way of attempting to prevent mother fixations.

The circumcision ceremony, performed at the onset of virility in the youth, is made the occasion for his incarnating the Vital Force. The ceremonies have the effect of making him feel assured of potency and helping him to avoid the self-doubts that harass so many adolescents and adults in other cultures.

The initiation ceremonies also help to preserve the traditions handed down by sacred myths, which are the foundation of social unity in Africa. The youth undergoes fear, privation, physical pain; for the rest of his life he carries the scars of his ceremonial mutilation. The dramatic rituals impress deep into his consciousness the traditions of his tribe. The strength of African tradition, thus reinforced, also manifests itself in African art.

SOCIAL ROLE OF THE SECRET SOCIETY

A further word should be said here about the social role of the secret societies. The chiefs and magicians—who were the leaders of the societies—held the tribes together and assured continuity and order. With their influence discredited and their powers shorn after the white intrusion, with the magician largely displaced by the white doctor, with soldier and policeman hired by a remote foreign government as the new embodiments of power, the intimate contact with and participation in traditional religio-magical exercises have been disrupted. The result-

FIG. 28. *Ivory mask. Bapende, Belgian Congo. 2½" high.* SEE PAGE 212

ing confusion of the African is augmented by the preachments of missionaries. Their abstract divinity is alien to him. The idea that all men are equal before God can scarcely be a reality to him when in practice white men, including the missionary himself, treat him as a second-class human being.

For this reason the present-day art of the African has lost its root in tradition; with few exceptions it has become—at best—an empty copy of a once-vital art expression.

PART II

THE CONTENT OF
AFRICAN ART

FIG. 29. *Container. Baluba,*
Belgian Congo. 8" high.
SEE PAGE 208

FIG. 30. *Brass head of an Oni of Ife. Ife, British Nigeria. 14″ high.*
SEE PAGE 180

4. HISTORICAL BACKGROUND

THE body of information about the racial antecedents of the African tribes is somewhat sketchy. For example, stone implements of Paleolithic type and celts (primitive chisels) of Neolithic style have been discovered in Africa. This, however, does not prove, even assuming that the tools originated in Africa, that they belong to the same period of time as corresponding tools in Europe, or that they were produced by the ancestors of the present inhabitants of Africa. When the Bube tribes on the Island of Fernando Po off West Africa were discovered by Europeans in the late eighteenth century, they used Neolithic celts which they considered to be images of the thunderbolt.

The C. G. Seligman excavations in Egypt, however, indicate that Hamitic people, with characteristics similar to those of present-day Negroes, lived there in the last predynastic period, or about 3000 B.C. According to some theories, prehistoric invasions took place in Africa about 6000 B.C., probably from Asia through the Straits of Aden (Bab el Mendeb).

There is, as we have seen, a theory that the invasion route was from Asia through Somaliland or Madagascar. It is to be noted that Madagascar, in spite of its proximity to the African continent, differs in many aspects from Africa; thus it is possible that Madagascar was long ago connected with Asia.

The theory is advanced that this prehistoric invasion came in three waves: a "white invasion," which occupied, successively, Ethiopia, Egypt, and North Africa; a "black invasion" that mixed neither with the whites of the North nor with the Pygmies, and established itself around the equator to form the present Bantu people; and a second "black invasion," which reached the Sudanese plains and the Guinea coast, forming the Sudanese and Guinea Negro groups.

Probably the Pygmies now living in the Belgian Congo forests were the aborigines of Africa. They are mentioned as court clowns in Egyptian records dating from 3000 B.C. Even today Pygmies are noted for their mimicry. They are isolated from the surrounding Bantus and have no religious cult resembling West African concepts.

Besides the Pygmies, the Bushmen of the Kalahari Desert of South Africa and the Hamites of the northern part of the continent might have constituted the original inhabitants.

Of the many African stocks, it is the agricultural Negroes (the Bantu, Sudanese, and Guinea) bound to the land, who have developed an art of high quality. The nomadic Berber herdsmen and Pygmy hunters have produced no art worth mentioning. The Bushmen produced cave paintings.

New archeological excavations are beginning to enlarge our knowledge of ancient Africa. These excavations have brought amazing achievements to light, among them the bronze and terra-cotta heads of Ife, the stone figures of Esie, the stone heads from Nok, and the bronze figures of Tada and Jebba (all four in Nigeria), the terra cottas of the Chad region, and those found lately in the Belgian Congo.

HISTORICAL DOCUMENTS

Fortunately we have also some historical writings from which we can piece together the history of the tribal cultures.

The first historian to mention West Africa was Herodotus, in the sixth century B.C. He described the circumnavigation of Africa by the Phoenicians, who set out from the Red Sea and returned through the Straits of Gibraltar.

Later the Carthaginians, in a naval expedition commanded by Hanno, touched Senegal and Guinea. From the ninth to the nineteenth century A.D., powerful Negro states flourished on the Sudanese plains, along the coastal regions, and in the Congo.

References to these Sudanese states appear in Arabic literature—the reports of Ibn Khaldun, El Bekri, Yakut, and Edrisi. Other sources include the *Tarikh Es Sudan* and the *Tarikh El Fettach*, sixteenth-century chronicles compiled in Timbuctoo; the fourteenth-century references by the Arab traveler Ibn Batuta, who visited Mali; and the sixteenth-century accounts of Leo Africanus, who visited Gao and Mali.

The history of the indigenous native kingdoms interest us because it proves the existence of well-integrated political units.

The basis for the existence of these states was an agreement on fundamental cultural issues and, with the divine power invested in the kings, a great unification took place. Only under such conditions could such an expressive art emerge. A further contribution to the development of art was the great patronage of the kings, as the art products were necessary implements to maintain the different religious institutions which were the basic foundation of the political organizations in which every member of the community took part.

Prior to the nineteenth century, some reliable geographical information was available concerning the outer rim of the African continent. We now have a map dated 1351, in a museum in Florence, which already gives the coast line in fairly accurate detail. Early in the fifteenth century, cartographers of Majorca (one of the best-known of whom was Abraham Cresca) mapped the Senegal and the "Gold River." The information upon which these maps were based probably came from North African traders, who were in contact with the Sudanese Negro states.

More elaborate maps were made in 1700 by G. Delisle and in 1749 by B. D'Anville, but they indicate only coastal towns.

The interior remained unknown. Some mapmakers of the eighteenth century compensated for lack of knowledge by their imagination. They designated Lake Chad as the source of the Niger and sent rivers coursing across the Sahara.

Probably the first published document on the African West Coast was the Venetian Cadamosto's *Account of Voyages along the Western Coast of Africa*, in 1455–1457. A few years later, a narrative by Pigafetta appeared in Rome, based on the travels of a Portuguese monk, Fra Duarte Lopez. It was translated into French, English, Dutch, German, and Latin. This book made the first mention of African "idols." In 1599, J. V. van Linschoten's report on the Guinea coast,

FIG. 31. *Bronze figure (detail), Warrior, Jebba Island, British Nigeria. Whole figure 44″ high.*
SEE PAGE 180

FIG. 32. *Head of a ram. Yoruba (Owo region), British Nigeria. 20″ high.* SEE PAGE 179

the Congo, and Angola was published in The Hague. De Rochefort published his *Voyage to the Kingdom of Sénégal* in 1643; and Dr. Olfert Daper's *Description of Africa* appeared in Amsterdam in 1686. A year later, in 1687, an abundantly illustrated nine-hundred-page volume was published in Bologna by the Franciscan friar Giovanni Antonio Cavazzi, in which the Portuguese West African colonies were described. Here, too, mention was made of idols and magical rituals. From that time on the literature has become voluminous.

It is believed that the Normans were the first Europeans to reach Guinea, but they left no records. The Portuguese were the first to circumnavigate Africa after the Carthaginians. Under Prince Henry (called "The Navigator") this exploration was intensified, and to this fact we owe the abundance of reports on West Africa. The first shipment of Negro slaves appeared in Lisbon in 1469, brought in by a dealer named Fernand Gomez, who had received a monopoly for the slave trade from the king.

The Portuguese reached the Guinea coast in 1470 and the Benin Kingdom in 1472. In 1482, under Diego Cão, Portuguese ships reached the river Congo and sailed up ninety miles to Matadi. In 1490 they had established a small colony in the Congo. In 1508 the son of a Congo king studied theology in Lisbon, and in 1520 he was consecrated Bishop of Utica, the first Negro bishop, unless the earlier Coptic prelates may also be regarded as Negroes. In 1647 a Portuguese fleet from Rio de Janeiro sailed to conquer Angola.

NEGRO EMPIRES AND KINGDOMS

The northern or inland states (Ghana, Shonghay, Manding, and Hausa) came under Islamic influence around the year 1000. Many of their rulers embraced the Mussulman religion, but animism was not suppressed; the majority of the people retained the old cults. The court conversions had political motives rather than religious ones.

Flourishing Negro states were in existence even before the Islamic penetration. Their religious life was based on animism. And an abundance of sculpture was produced. Islamic influence waned; the tribes returned to animism, which lasted in a vigorous form until the recent influence of the Christian missionary. This suggests that the natives have been sculpturing as long as they have lived in Africa, probably some fifteen centuries.

Along the coast, independent empires and kingdoms—Ashanti, Dahomey, Fanti, Yoruba, Benin, and, further south, Loango and the empire of Congo—which were not infiltrated by Islam flourished. Here the art of carving also flourished without interruption and was encouraged by powerful rulers. A very strong conventional art tradition developed, such as that of the Yorubas (Ife) and of the Benin Kingdom. The richness of the Congo sculpture is probably due to this continuity, upon which early European contacts left no effect. Only during the last fifty years has coastal colonization led to organized exploration of the interior and attendant missionary activities, which threatened and in many cases destroyed the social and religious structures of the Negroes, thus causing the decline of African art.

Under Islamic influence or outright rule, the African art tradition often persisted. The lack of art objects from antiquity (except for the bronzes from the fourteenth to the eighteenth centuries) is due solely to the perishable materials used, which were mostly wood. From our knowledge of the rigid traditional style unity of each tribe and the fact that little perceptible change has occurred in the last century, we may assume that the existing objects are the product of an art developed over many centuries.

Why Islamic influence failed to reach Equatorial West Africa has been tentatively answered by Messrs. Haardt and Dubreuil, leaders of the Citroën expedition in 1926.

They observed that the limits of Islamic penetration stopped with the areas infested by the tsetse fly, carrier of the fatal bacteria of sleeping sickness.

THE AFRICAN STATES

The *history* of the African states is evidence of the Negro's ability to organize empires, to install systems of jurisprudence and produce powerful leaders.

Ghana (also called Kumbi), probably the first of the Negro empires, was founded possibly around 300 A.D., on the Sudanese plains. In the ninth century, Ghana had large cities and an army of 200,000. Many houses in the capital, Kumbi, were built of stone. The empire traded with caravans from beyond the Sahara in ivory and gold dust or gold worked into wire. But Ghana weakened, was defeated in war, and in 1203 became part of the Soso Empire.

The Empire of Manding developed on the left bank of the Niger (above the northern borders of present French Guinea) with its capital at Kangaba, and lasted thirteen centuries. The first time the outside world learned about the Mandingos was in 1050, when one of their kings, converted to Islam, made a pilgrimage to Mecca and startled the East by the wealth and splendor of his retinue. Under Gonga Musa, about 1320, the Mandingo Empire was at its height. It then comprised nearly the whole of what today is French West Africa. Gonga Musa also made a pilgrimage to Mecca in 1324, leading what was probably the greatest procession ever to leave Africa on such a mission. His caravan numbered sixty thousand and carried more than a ton of gold.

The Songhay Empire, with its capital at Gao, was probably founded in the seventh century along the bend of the Niger River. In 1325 it fell under the sway of the Mandingo Empire for a shorter time; but later turned the tables under the leadership of Sonni Ali. The latter, though a Moslem convert, was not a zealot. He allowed religious freedom to his people, most of whom remained animists. He was perhaps the first ruler to separate church and state. After his death in 1492, Askia, a devout Mussulman and a great organizer, consolidated the Songhay Empire, whose prosperity continued for about a century, when Moroccan troops, including three thousand Spanish renegades equipped with firearms, invaded the country.

The Mosi states, a cluster of principalities with two important capital cities, developed south of the Niger in the present Upper Volta regions. They resisted Mussulman influence and clung to animism. They developed a highly mature native judiciary system.

The Hausa city states developed west of Songhay, on the west bank of the Niger but further inland, in what is now northern British Nigeria. They flourished about the fifteenth century under Mussulman kings, and their cities, Zinder, Gober, Kano, and Zaria, became famous.

On both sides of Lake Chad, the Burnu Kingdom existed until the end of the twelfth century under an animistic state religion. Under native kings converted to Islam it lasted until the twentieth century.

Other kingdoms, such as the Fula of Massina, the Bambara (Banmana) of Segu, and those of Bagirmi, Wadi, and Kanem, existed in the eighteenth and nineteenth centuries but never reached the importance of the earlier Negro states.

Along the Guinea coast, independent kingdoms developed, such as Ashanti, Dahomey, Benin, and Yoruba, maintaining, for unknown periods, the institution of animism. This was reflected not only in the strength of their art tradition but also in the surprising tenacity of their resistance to the European occupation, which began in earnest about fifty years ago.

We do not know much about the Ashanti Kingdom, except that it successfully resisted the English invasion until 1894. About the year 1700, during the reign of King Osai Tutu, the institution of a wooden throne of heavenly origin began and the carving of such thrones and stools spread toward the Cameroons.

Dahomey (also called Danhome) was noted as early as 1507 by Leo Africanus and was charted on maps published in Amsterdam in 1627. This kingdom has a rich art tradition. It became known for its Amazon regiment, established by the fourth king of Dahomey, Agasa, who used one thousand of his superfluous wives first as bodyguard and later as soldiers. Their chastity was enforced by enormous penalties. Dahomey grew very rich on the slave trade. Its last king, Behanzin, resisted the French until 1904.

British Nigeria includes several old native states: on the north, the kingdoms of Hausa and Bornu; on the south, the kingdoms of Lagos, Nupe, Ife, Yoruba, and Benin.

Ife came into prominence in 1936 when highly sophisticated bronze heads were excavated there (Fig. 30). With regard to these and the bronze figures found at Tada (Fig. 33), Sir Richmond Palmer suggests that possibly between 600 and 950 A.D. an important casting industry had been established at Kaukau on the Niger which spread to Nupe (where Tada was located) and was carried by the Yorubas first to Ife and then to Benin. Another possibility is that Persians, Jews, or Greeks introduced the method in the Nile Valley, whence it made its way westward. In either case, the discovery of the Ife heads forced revisions of our estimates of Benin art. It may now be assumed that the art of bronze-casting traveled to Benin by way of Ife, where a highly developed state must have existed.

About the Benin Kingdom we have abundant information. The Portuguese reached it under Ruy de Sequeira in 1472, and thirteen years later sent to it their first missionary, Alfonso d'Aveiro, who persuaded the *oba* (king) Esignie to send an ambassador to the King of Portugal. The ambassador returned with missionaries and presents. The mission, founded in 1530, built three churches, but was abandoned in 1699. We know of a line of thirty-three obas, or Benin kings, among them Oba Oguola (*c.* 1280), who built the great city wall and imported the Ife technique of brass-casting. Benin's pioneer brass-smith, Egueigha, is still venerated as the patron saint of the craft.

Dutch visitors to Benin included Dapper and Nyendael, who published their accounts in 1686 and 1702 respectively. The British first reached Benin in 1533. In 1896 a British expedition numbering two hundred fifty men disregarded the Oba's warnings and entered the city of Benin during secret religious ceremonies. The entire troop was massacred. A year later, a British punitive expedition took out some three thousand objects, which were immediately purchased by English and German museums.

We have little information of the Negro states which might have existed between the Gulf of Guinea and the Congo River. We know of the kingdom of Loango and of the empire of Congo, the latter comprising several kingdoms, among them the Bushongo (Bakuba), Ansika (Batekas and Bayakas), Lunda (Baluba), and Bachimba. A Portugese ship first sailed up the Congo in 1482 (under Diego Cão) and established a colony christened San Salvador. But the Congo Empire and the other Negro states in this region kept expanding under native dynasties until the nineteenth century.

ANTIQUITY OF AFRICAN ART WORKS

For the majority of African sculptures (except Ife and Benin) we have no historic data. The older objects have disintegrated because of their perishable materials (wood, clay, straw, etc.). The only exceptions, to our knowledge, are certain objects collected before 1600, now in the museum at Ulm, Germany.

Here we must reiterate our belief that, although the majority of the objects are the products of the last century, they are representative of older periods as well, the forms remaining unchanged through the rigid adherence to tradition.

ORIGIN OF AFRICAN ART

The question now arises: Is African art indigenous or is it derivative? Leo Frobenius was the first to advance the theory that Negro art may have been influenced by Mediterranean cultures, and in addition by a civilization from beyond the Sahara Desert. The origins of West African art may lie in the Fezzan, Atlas, and Libyan Desert regions of North Africa. In Fezzan, Frobenius saw four rock pictures similar to the Egyptian images of their god, Bes. In the Sahara-Atlas Mountains were found pictures of rams with disks between their horns, resembling images of the Egyptian ram god, Jupiter Ammon. In the Libyan Desert, rock pictures similar in appearance to representations of the Egyptian god Set were found. The theory has been advanced that images in these rock pictures spread to Egypt.

Thus we see how early in human history art influences traveled from one country to another.

As we have seen, between the ninth and nineteenth centuries, contact was maintained between West Africa, the Western Sudanese Empires, and the Arabic world. This contact was commercial and intellectual as well as military. Islam, however, left no influence on West African art. One reason is undoubtedly the prohibition imposed by the Koran upon the use of human figures, which limited artistic expression among the Arabs to geometric decorations and calligraphy. This had no attraction to the vigorous African artists.

In the great epochs of the African empires, Egyptian caravans, traveling through the Sahara, established trade with the Negro states, exchanging goods for slaves. Egyptian navigators are reported to have steered their ships into the Bay of Benin.

Another direction of Egyptian infiltration and possible influence was across the equatorial region. Egyptian vessels could have sailed to Rejaf on the Nile near Lake Albert in northeastern Belgian Congo. From Rejaf the River Uele, a tributary of the Congo, is only a little more than a hundred miles away. Through the Congo tributaries the Egyptians could easily have reached into West Africa.

The practice of the Mangbetu people (living between the Nile and Uele) of pressing the craniums of their females into an elongated form shows startling resemblances to the head forms in Egyptian art. And according to an interesting study made by Jeanne Tercafs, certain dialects in the Uele region show words and pronunciations resembling those of ancient Egypt.

Thus in the north the Egyptians reached the Sudanese people through caravans, and in the south there is a possibility that they may have reached the Bantu people by boats. There is an astonishing unity in the plastic creations of the different African tribes, although we know of no direct contact between north and south. The Egyptians' infiltration might explain this unity.

When people of common cultural background meet, their artistic products are subject to mutual influence. Because Islam was alien to the Africans, it left no imprint on their works. Egypt or the Mediterranean countries, though further removed geographically than the territories ruled by Islam, appear to have exercised some influence on West African art.

COMPARISON BETWEEN EGYPTIAN AND AFRICAN RELIGIONS

Early Egyptian religion was animistic, with fetishes and magic. Its polytheism was a later development. Sculpture was used in

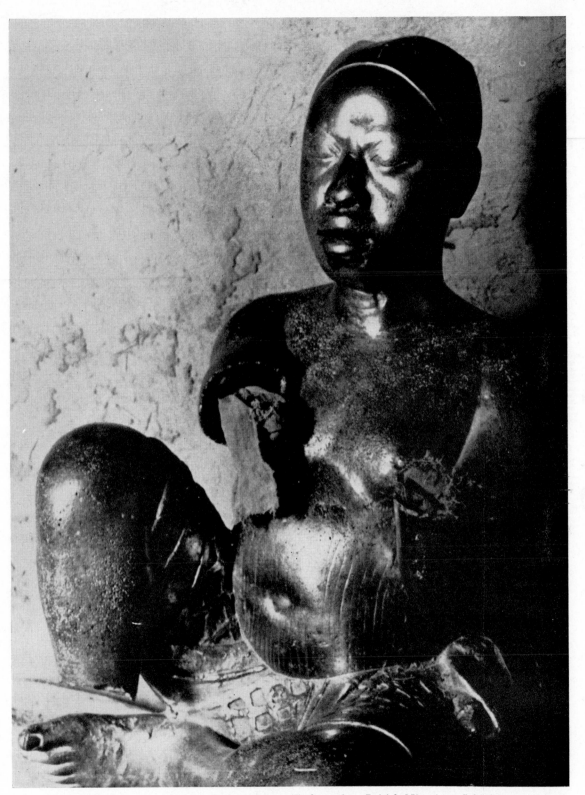

FIG. 33. *Bronze figure. Tada region, British Nigeria. 22″ high.* SEE PAGE 180

a religious or magical manner, as in West Africa. The Egyptian believed in the survival of the soul and incorporated it into statues. The Egyptian Soul Bird is comparable to the totem animal. The statues which the Egyptians placed in the tombs are analogous in meaning to the ancestor figures of the Africans which were kept on display and used in everyday rituals. For a parallel to the Egyptian custom of putting statues into the earth for eternity, we may note the West African practice of placing funerary figures in the baskets of ancestral bones in the "burial" huts to keep eternal guard over the ancestral spirits. The Egyptian idea of *Ka*, as the surviving substance of the personality, is similar to the West African *Nyama* (called *Kra* by the Ashantis). The shadow as a part of the personality is a concept common to both Egypt and West Africa. Sculpture in both Egypt and West Africa had a similar religious role.

In Babylon also, demons and animal gods were worshipped; prayers were incantations and divinations. That country's religion was also animistic; for it, too, polytheism was a later development.

In Greece, similarly, fetishism, animism, and even traces of totemism were found, as well as intimacies between gods and men such as the Africans knew between his totem animal and men. Potter remarks that "a very old statue of a goddess in the Parthenon itself was comparable to the crudest idols of African tribes."

COMPARISON OF ART FORMS

The most striking characteristics of African art are its architectonic quality, the sobriety and closeness of its forms, its feeling for the material, and the fact that its carving is done out of the mass. The same characteristics hold true for Egyptian art.

In their decorative schemes, some Egyptian vases and utensils resemble Congo pottery and utensils of Africa. Portraits of Egyptian kings, especially those of certain Pharaohs of the Fourth Dynasty, became cult objects, and the figures were portrayed in attitudes similar to the portraits of the Bakuba (or Bushongo) kings (Fig. 2). Statues of the First Dynasty resemble West African ancestor figures. A bronze statue found in Tada (Nigeria) (Fig. 33) is comparable to the famous early Egyptian "scribe" statue. The Egyptians also regarded the head as the abode of spirit power, and many of their sculptures exaggerate the head, as do West African sculptures. Negro headrests are similar to those of the Third to Eleventh dynasties; and some musical instruments found in West Africa are of the same design as the Egyptian.

There is also a possibility that the *cire-perdue* casting technique was imported from Egypt.

Cylindrical beads of the African natives (especially in the Benin Kingdom) resemble those found in Phoenician graves.

The astonishing Ife bronze heads (Fig. 30) may also indicate a Mediterranean influence. These heads have a classical Greco-Roman cast. The Yorubas, original inhabitants of this territory, never created any such works. The purity of the style could have been achieved only by artists already at the height of their development, artists for whom the style was an established tradition. We know that Greek sculptors wandered as far as Afghanistan to create the Gandhara style. Is it then not possible that some accompanied caravans to Ife? The nineteen heads found there might be the products of one master caster, or two or three, since certain signs indicate uniformity of handling. However, as soon as these heads were used as models by the Bini people, the Ife style was altered. Even the early Bini heads, although of portrait type, have the freedom typical of the Negro carving style. This would point to foreign influence in the Ife heads. As soon as the Negro influence became dominant, it imposed the West African style.

The artist was anonymous in Egypt, as he is in Africa. The objects which he fashioned were used exclusively in religio-magical rituals. There is uniformity in dimension and attitude and unchanging stylistic unity in both Egypt and Africa.

If, as this evidence suggests, African art is not indigenous, how is it that this art has such a dynamic liveliness, such a force of expression, and such a unity of style? The so-called "derivative" arts generally show signs of decadence: borrowed forms "perfected," then exaggerated, and finally drained of living content.

It appears that the African was able to absorb influences without succumbing to them. The strength and energy of his own outlook on the world, combined with the intensity of his religious feeling, proved stronger than any formal influence. He digested the imported forms and made something new out of them. African sculpture stood on its own, and continues to radiate life.

FIG. 34. *Group of stone figures. Esie region, British Nigeria.* SEE PAGE 180

5. CHARACTERISTIC FORMS

As we have seen in earlier chapters, the entire body of African art includes a wide range of material, from the object which is almost strictly utilitarian to that which possesses a highly religious or magical significance. These sculptures fall into three general classifications, however: statues, animal carvings, and masks.

A. Statues

African animism recognized two major groups of spirits—ancestor spirits for which the ancestor statues were created, and the spirits of nature (or genii). The latter are again divided into two groups: natural objects—earth, sky, mountains, trees, stones, etc.—to which sacrifices are made; and natural forces—rain, thunder, fecundity, etc. Included with these are sickness, but since this is often attributed to the wrath of the ancestor, it is also associated with the ancestor cult. Statues dedicated to the spirits of nature and those aiming at magical results will be referred to as magical statues to distinguish them from the ancestor figures.

The ancestor figures have a closed form.

The composition and frequently the facial expression manifest calm and dignity. They give an impression of other-worldly detachment. The magical statues, although also architectonic in their sculptural concept, are more aggressive in their facial expressions. Often their attitudes suggest latent movement.

MAGICAL SUBSTANCE

Usually magical statues did not acquire their power until after the addition of a magical substance whose ingredients might be anything—particles of earth, dead flies, a hair, a nail paring, or merely a grease rubbed into the statue. In many of the statues, cavities were hollowed out in the abdomen (Fig. 35), breast, back, or head, to be filled with magical substance and sometimes sealed with a mirror (Fig. 36).

For the significance of the mirror we have two interpretations. Bastian supposes that the purpose of the mirror was to reflect the image of, and thus identify, the person who caused a sickness; Peschuel-Loesche and Luoffer think that its purpose was to repel evil spirits, who were believed to be unable to withstand strong light. In a tropical country like Africa, mirrors re-

[70]

flect the sun with blinding brilliance, and this may have suggested the use of mirrors to the image makers. Possibly, too, the African might have felt that through the reflected rays he could use the power of the sun against evil spirits. Incrustations of glass, shell, or mirror in the eyes of many magical statues had a similar purpose.

Magical substance was not essential to endow a statue with magic power. With or without the substance, such power was believed to be invoked by the magical words spoken by the magician at the consecration of the statue.

In most of the statues in Western collections, the magical substance is missing. It has been removed to get rid of decaying organic matter or in the process of deconsecration by the native, to make the statue safe as a lay object.

It may be noted that deconsecration, as well as consecration, is also a practice of the Catholic ritual. And the power attributed to "relics" is analogous to magic power.

CLASSIFICATION OF MAGICAL STATUES

The variety, number, and uses of magical statues are great. The statues may have been family possessions, communal property in the custody of the tribal magician, or professional instruments of the medicine man. The last group is the most numerous. The African did not attribute sickness or death to natural causes but to spirits—the wrathful spirit of an ancestor or the hostile spirit summoned by a sorcerer. The remedy was appeasement through sacrifices, or the summoning of a more powerful spirit with the aid of the medicine man, who knows how to handle the magical statues.

In the following section we shall enumerate only the best-known types of magical statues to illustrate how African animism used sculpture.

FIG. 35. *Magical statue. Bateke, Belgian Congo. 18" high.*

FIG. 36. *Magical statue. Bakongo, Belgian Congo. 8" high.*

FIG. 37. *Animal with nails. Bakongo, Belgian Congo. 13" high.*

FIG. 38. *Nail fetish. Bakongo, Belgian Congo. 20" high.*

Although the use of magical statues is a common feature of animism everywhere, we shall begin with the Bakongo tribe (Belgian Congo), where such statues are especially abundant and have been most extensively studied by Maes and others. The statues in this region are used in a continuous warfare between the good spirit *Nkisi* and the evil spirit *Ndoki*.

1. Konde *or Nail Fetish*. One of the best-known types of statue in this region is the *Konde*, or nail fetish, the abode of the evil spirit Ndoki. The statues are large erect wooden figures, the legs and trunks roughly carved and without sex indications, and the feet flat on the base. In some figures one hand is on the hip while the other hand brandishes a dagger. Magical substance, here called *Bilongo*, is applied to both the abdomen and the head. In other statues both hands are on the hips, and the Bilongo is applied only to the abdomen. In both, the carving of the head is artistic. The expression is menacing, often with mouth half open as if the sickness is to be exorcised from it. Sometimes the tongue protrudes. The eyes are splinters of mirror. The cavity in the abdomen containing the Bilongo is square and is sealed with a mirror (Fig. 5). The nail fetish may also be in the form of an animal statue (Fig. 37).

Nails, pieces of metal, amulets, etc., stud the body. The head, emerging from the mass of metal, has an impressive effect. With the nails removed, the statue looks "naked" (Fig. 38).

The Konde housed extremely dangerous spirits, which could inflict diseases and "eat up" those whom they were set upon. Each Konde was kept in a special hut.

2. The Pezo *or* Panzu Mbongo. These were similar in function to the Konde but served only for minor ailments. The figures, painted red and white, are smaller; their expression is less terrifying; and they are more likely to be hung with bags and amulets than studded with nails (Fig. 39).

FIG. 39. *Magical statue. Bakongo, Belgian Congo. 8″ high.*

FIG. 40. *Statue of the twins (Ibeji). Yoruba, British Nigeria. 10″ high.* SEE PAGES 174, 177

FIG. 41. *Magical statue. Bakongo, Belgian Congo. 6" high.*

had stump-armed statues; and seated figures are also to be found among the Muserongo. Similar statues among the Bateke have filed teeth and scar patterns on the skin.

4. *The* Mbula *or Fire Fetish.* This belonged to the tribal chief to protect him against enemy medicine men. The fetish can be recognized by a tube protruding from the magical substance. Through this tube were inserted gunpowder and metal slugs, which exploded when enemy magicians tampered with the image. Many are known to have been killed by these homemade "magic" grenades.

5. *The* Makonda *and* Simbu. These minor magical statues of the Bakongos were designed for the protection of children. Pregnant women dedicated their unborn children to the first and invoked its protection for the child after birth. The second was placed in the hut after labor started, to facilitate childbirth.

3. *The* Na Moganga *or* Noganga. These are healing fetishes which belong to the *Noganga*, or village medicine man. They were the abode of the good spirit Nkisi. Their expressions are benevolent, and they helped the medicine man to recognize the plant whose potent spirit was the right one to cast out the evil spirit from the patient's body. In such cases, the medicine man actually relied upon a store of folk knowledge of the curative effects of herbs and minerals. The African, however, did not attribute these effects to the chemical properties of the plants, but to the spirits which resided in them.

The *Na Moganga* statues also contained magical substance, but they were carved with greater care than the nail fetishes. In some, however, the arms are mere stumps (Fig. 41). Others are in squatting attitudes with chin in one or both hands (Fig. 42).

The Basundi and Babuende tribes also

FIG. 42. *Magical statue. Bakongo, Belgian Congo. 5" high.*

6. Guardian of Home. A special type of fetish was placed at the doors to guard houses. It was supposed to contain spirits of the dead. The distinguishing marks of these images are oblong faces and protruding chins. The eyes are inset cowrie shells, and horns frequently crown the head. Similar figures were placed in the fields to protect crops against marauders.

7. Healing Fetish. These statues, which were placed beside the sick, occur in nearly all regions. Among the best-known are the Bateke (Lower Congo) statues (Fig. 35), which were also used for the child's protection until he attained adulthood.

8. Fertility Fetish. Figures with outstretched arms and disklike heads were made by the Ashanti of the Gold Coast. These were given to expectant mothers to facilitate childbirth and to young girls to render them fertile.

9. The Ibeji *or Twin Fetish.* This figure was produced by the Yorubas in Nigeria, Dahomey, etc. (Fig. 40). The statue was carved upon the death of one of a pair of twins. The mother cared for the statue and made offerings to it to assure the welfare of the surviving twin until the latter reached maturity, at which time he took over the care of the statue, continuing to make offerings to it for the rest of his life. This was done in the belief that twins shared one spirit, and therefore the survivor must be protected against the effort of the dead twin to seize the rest of his Nyama. Twins were also believed to be able to communicate more readily with ancestor spirits than other people.

A variant of the twin fetish is the *Ndugu* ivory (Fig. 43), a miniature statue which the surviving twin carried during his lifetime strung around his neck in a small bag with the head sticking out.

In this case, as in so many others, magical practice is founded on acute psychological insight. Twins brought up together are known to have a compulsive sense of be-

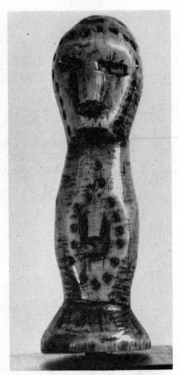

FIG. 43. *Ivory statue. Warega, Belgian Congo. 5" high.* SEE PAGE 227

longing to each other which may lead to neurotic behavior. For this reason it has been found advisable in our armed forces to separate twins.

10. The Bieri *Statues.* (Fig. 44.) These fetishes of the Pangwe tribe (Gabun) were not restricted to guarding the barrel containing the bones of the dead, as is generally stated. They also served as healing statues and were brought into the huts of the sick.

PREPARATION OF NAIL FETISHES

To assure the power of the nail fetish, certain rituals were required. Formerly, we are told, many slaves were killed at the felling of the tree used for the sculpture and their blood was mixed with the sap, thus combining their Nyama with that of the tree. According to another version, the name of a man was called out when the tree was felled, and he died in a day or two as his Nyama entered the log. The explorer Visser relates that an African who

FIG. 44. *Ancestor statue. Pangwe, Gabun. 17" high.* SEE PAGE 192

sought to own a nail fetish had to procure a human corpse, which he carried to a tree that he himself cut down. A sculptor then carved the figure under the future owner's personal supervision, which established his future mastery over the fetish. The corpse, meanwhile, was fumigated and rubbed with red wood powder. When the carving was finished, the same red powder was rubbed into it.

THE CONCEPT OF NAIL FETISHES

The nail fetish was a composite of varied forces, or rather desires, of the Africans. First, it was imbued with power by the deposit of magical substance in the cavity cut into the abdomen. The teeth of powerful animals, such as the leopard, were often included in the magical substance to impart the power of the animal. Secondly, the statue was endowed with outward powers —the mirror to reflect blinding sunlight against hostile spirits; the danger in the upraised arm; the defiant, protruding tongue. A third power was exerted by the user when he drove a nail into the body of the fetish at the moment of conjuration. All these powers were invoked by the user in order to have his particular wish granted. When the wish was expressed, the nail or piece of metal driven into the image drove the desire in deeply, thus concretizing it.

Probably the most widely known use of the nail fetish was for the purpose of having a sickness inflicted in turn upon whoever caused it in the current victim. The good offices of the medicine man and the persuasion of a proper sacrifice were used to induce the statue to act against the perpetrator, whom it was believed to know. Another purpose of the nail-driving was to injure thereby the evil spirit which caused the illness and, by thus reducing his power, to lessen the virulence of the disease. (When the illness was attributed to an ancestor's wrath, offerings were made to his statue to pacify him; the fetish was not used.)

The use of fetishes and other magical statues varied from tribe to tribe.

Peschuel-Loesche describes how a heated nail driven into a fetish caused an accused person to fall ill. After he had cleared himself, a process including payment of a fee to the magician, the nail was extracted and a cure followed. Nails were similarly driven into fetishes to bring about the destruction of enemies, also to kill the slaves of enemy tribes and thus weaken their power. Some nail fetishes were used only in the treatment of specific illnesses. Among other odd functions of nail fetishes was the tracking down of thieves, protection against dangers of travel, and other perils.

Sometimes the fetish was put to an entirely positive use. A nail might be driven into a fetish to solemnize an obligation undertaken toward another person. This is similar to our signature to a contract, or "nailing" someone to a deal. According to Vatter, the Loango tribesmen believe that driving the nail in stimulated the fetish to the desired action. (Conversely, the nail could be driven in to punish inaction.)

In the Bakhimba secret society of the Mayombe (Belgian Congo), the mirror inset in a statue was also used in taking an oath, the person who made the pledge licking the mirror.

ANALOGIES IN THE WEST

As in other primitive practices, parallels of the nail fetish may be found in the West. In the Hainaut Province of Belgium one may see a statue of St. Christopher studded with needles driven in by girls seeking marriage. In Germany during World War I, people paid to drive nails into a huge statue of Marshal Hindenburg, as a means of protecting a soldier at the front, or assuring his safe return if a prisoner. And a practice widespread in Europe in the Middle Ages was that of driving nails and needles into wax figures to injure enemies.

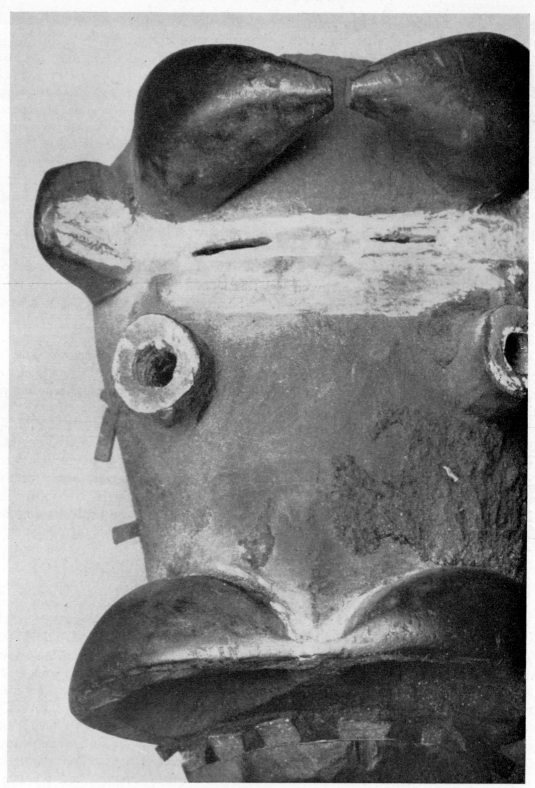

FIG. 45. *Animal mask. Guere-Ouobe, Ivory Coast. 10" high.*

FIG. 46. *Animal head. Baule, Ivory Coast. 10"
high.* SEE PAGE 170

B. Animal Carvings

When we consider the religious and cultural significance of the totem or mythological animal, plus the African tribesman's dependence upon animals for food, it is understandable that animal representation is evident in much of his art.

As mentioned earlier, the African practiced sympathetic magic on drawings of animals which he wished to kill in the hunt. Often, too, he tattooed his body with the images of his totem animal. However, the outstanding examples of this subject matter exist in the field of animal sculpture, where his subjects were either mythological or totem animals.

RITUAL OBJECTS USING ANIMALS

Let us examine four animal heads. The first (Fig. 46), from the Baule tribe on the Ivory Coast, represents a bull. Its head was used, not as a mask, but as a door guard for the house of a magician. Superficially it looks naturalistic, but in its simple, monumental form it is akin to Egyptian sculpture. The second (Fig. 45), another bull head, is from the Guere-Ouobe tribe. It is even less naturalistic. The nostrils are exaggerated and all the features of the animal's head are arranged in an artistic unity. The third (Fig. 48) is another Baule sculpture, this time of a cow. It is a further development in abstraction. It uses only the mouth and horn and exaggerates them.

A fourth (Fig. 49) is a stylized antelope *Koba,* from the Bambara tribe in the French Sudan. It is worn on the head in ritual dances.

The next group are *human figures or faces* to which a totem animal is added. The Baule mask (Fig. 47) represents a human face with a protective animal on top. In a large number of masks the main *human* feature is com-

FIG. 47. *Ancestor cult mask. Baule,
Ivory Coast. 16" high.* SEE PAGE 170

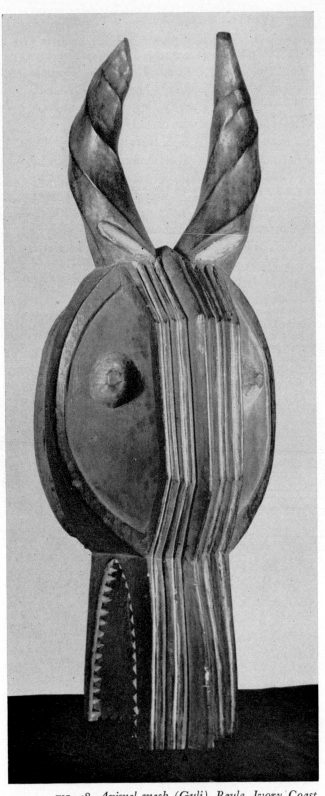

FIG. 48. *Animal mask (Guli). Baule, Ivory Coast.*
30" high. SEE PAGE 170

FIG. 49. *Antelope headgear. Bambara, Frenc*
Sudan. 30" high. SEE PAGE 15

FIG. 50. *Ancestor cult mask. Baule, Ivory Coast. 14″ high.* SEE PAGE 170

FIG. 51. *Antelope mask. Guro, Ivory Coast. 12″ high.* SEE PAGE 172

bined and intermingled with *animal features*. For example, there are the Baule mask (Fig. 50) or Guro (Ivory Coast) mask (Fig. 51) of human heads with animal horns, and another mask of the Guere-Ouobe people of the Ivory Coast (Fig. 52), all of which combine strange animal features with human characteristics. These are used in dances to invoke fear.

UTENSILS WITH ANIMALS

Many utensils carry carvings of animals, among them the weaving pulley of the Guros of the Ivory Coast (Fig. 53). Handles and lids of pots and jars are carved in animal forms (Fig. 29). These are believed to protect the food within and the persons to be fed from it. Animals carved on spoons have a similar role. Many musical instruments—drums, gong hammers, etc.—have animal ornaments. Animal figures on weapons are believed to protect the weapons and

FIG. 53. *Weaving pulley. Guro, Ivory Coast. 5" high.* SEE PAGE 172

the warriors who wield them. This probably has some psychological truth. Convinced that his weapon is protected, the warrior uses it with greater assurance and efficiency.

c. Masks

The use of masks as magical objects is universal, extending over all six continents and from prehistoric times to the present. They are to be found in the Swiss Tyrol, the Upper Rhineland, Ireland, and other European countries; in Tibet, China, Indonesia, Ceylon, Japan, and other Asiatic countries; in nearly all the islands of the South Seas; and in many sites on the North and South American continents.

In Africa, all territories covered in this book produced masks. They can be classified according to:

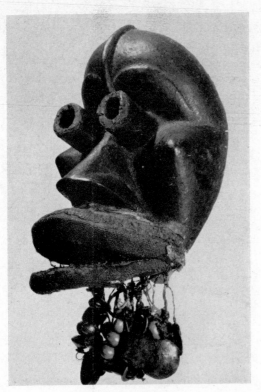

FIG. 52. *Initiation ceremony mask. Guere-Ouobe, Ivory Coast. 10" high.* SEE PAGE 172

Usage—cults (ancestor, initiation, magical, etc.), war, play, and nearly always in prescribed ritual dance.

Forms—varying from the crude to portraitlike naturalism to geometric or abstract stylizations, invoking specific emotions such as fear; and based on animal and human features, either singly or in combination.

Apparel—perforated masks, intended to be worn with a raffia, straw, or knitted costume, often including gloves; masklike objects to be worn above or below the face; masklike objects not to be worn; hoodlike masks completely covering the head; objects resembling headdresses; masks worn on ritual occasions, as badges of membership in a secret society or participation in a certain rite.

Certain masks, used for the dance, have holes on the rim for tying around the face but have no eye openings. These have been interpreted as masks for a dance symbolizing possession by a spirit. The staggering, sightless dancer would be unable to direct his movements, which for the African is a sign of being possessed by a spirit. In this case the spirit would be indicated by the mask.

FUNCTION OF THE MASK

Most masks are attached to a raffia, straw, or knitted costume which covers the dancer's whole body (Figs. 54 and 55). From this capelike garment the mask stands out with dramatic power. Without it the mask looks "nude" to the African. Instead of the complete costume, the dancer may use a shirt-like dress with a high neck, a hair net, ornaments on the chest, and arm and ankle bracelets, the latter often in the form of small bands.

In our exhibits the mask usually hangs on the wall or is mounted on a stand, static and isolated from its function. To the native, however, it is an inspiring object, inseparable from movement, whether used in

FIG. 54. *Masked dancer of the Poro Society. Liberia*

FIG. 55. *Masked Dancer. Boke, French Guinea*

FIG. 56. *Mask. Dan, Ivory Coast. 9" high.*

give the act and the catharsis a communal feeling. This is intensified by the powerful tones and vibrations of the musical instruments, mainly drums, and the curious annihilation of personal identity and substitution of a traditional identity in the wearing of the masks. All these elements combine to produce an exhilarating, ecstatic effect: unconscious powers are released, reality is obliterated, and what the African feels to be spirit power is assumed.

Different masks are used for different dances, depending on the aims of the dance. Some dances serve as the ritual for a boy's initiation into the tribe; some for the exorcism of evil spirits; some to invoke rain and fertility; some to communicate with the spirit of the dead and draw off his Nyama. Thus the function of the mask is close to that of the ancestor figure, though the motives may differ. The masker may seek to instill fear into enemies, raise his own courage, or repel evil spirits. For these purposes wild-animal masks may be used.

PHYSICAL ASPECT OF MASKS

Because the head represents the seat of wisdom, it is believed to be the last refuge of the Nyama before it is emitted from the body at the moment of death. Therefore most attention is paid to the face mask, which stands for the body as a whole and the spirit as well. Like the ancestor figures, a mask does not merely represent the spirit, it *is* the spirit.

This emphasis on the spiritual aspect of the face gives the masks rich expressiveness. They are masterpieces of facial sculpture rendered in stylized, abstract images. They have greater intensity than the faces of statues, where the emotion is distributed to all parts of the figure—the posture, the proportions of the limbs, etc. In the mask, all is concentrated on one surface. The mask is an *enlarged face*, dramatized to the utmost. Through forceful exaggeration the sculptor achieves an effect of spiritual intensity.

public or in rituals of a secret society. It is worn in a dance where gesture, rhythm, and singing hold significance and excitement for participants and spectators. Thus the mask has an intensity of radiation upon the African masses to which our reaction cannot compare.

The dancer, by his skill in carrying out the prescribed movements, evokes the spirit which the mask represents. Even without the mask, the dance affords physical release of emotional tensions. To this day in Africa dances are performed with strict and detailed adherence to precedent, which assures the desired effect. To this physical release through motion should be added the effects of the dancer's song, another release of tension. The singing in accompaniment and the clapping approval of the audience

As von Sydow expressed it, the masks are "loaded" with spiritual energy. And another German art critic, Carl Einstein, called it "the fixation of an ecstasy." This ecstasy is the result of a suspension of the rational faculties and ego controls. The sculptor was possessed (or obsessed) by an emotion so powerful that reality disappeared, and with it fear. For this release from anxiety the African willingly yields submission to the spirits.

Another reason for the enlargement of the face is the outdoor use of the mask, which must then be visible at a distance and to a multitude of people. The statues, on the other hand, are kept in sanctuaries and are used in close contact. The mask provokes excitement; the statue calls for contemplation. Because the mask is used as a "tool" in communal ceremonies, it possesses greater suggestive power.

The Dan mask (Fig. 56) has an expression of blissful detachment. Such masks aim at nirvanal serenity, release from the pressures of life, a "beatitude of death." Since death is not destruction, according to the African, its acceptance can be serene. The soul survives, the spirit triumphs over the body, the "idea" is more lasting than "matter." Most African sculptures are expressions of such ideas and emotions, not the reproduction of a physical reality.

PSYCHOLOGICAL SIGNIFICANCE OF MASKS

Through the ancestor figure the dead returns to the family, which thereby gains reassurance and peace. The ancestor statues have also an air of calm and repose.

Through the mask, worn in an ecstatic dance, the African seeks active communion with the spirit, to combat evil forces or to compel the spirit of the dead to act in his favor. Released from the limitation of everyday life, the masker and his audience are lifted into the superhuman and charged with fresh springs of vital energy.

The masker becomes the spirit itself, whether it be of the protective animal whose qualities he covets or the spirit which will heal sickness. He undergoes a complete change, a *transfiguration*. He loses his own identity and becomes the spirit. He fulfills his wishes for omnipotence.

In this the African achieves a simple and direct escape from oppressive reality—from the taboos and other tribal conventions.

FIG. 57. *Ceremonial stool. Ashanti, Gold Coast. 8" high.* SEE PAGE 173

FIG. 58. *Mask. Bobo, French Sudan, also Haute Volta. 10" high.* SEE PAGE 160

6. STYLISTIC FEATURES

PRIMITIVE arts include mainly sculpture by Africans, the South Sea Islanders, the American Indians, and the Eskimos. The unifying principles of primitive arts are animism and their common use in religio-magical exercises.

The term "primitive" is often misused and misunderstood. It is too often used synonomously with crudity, although the root of the word *primitive* means "original, primary, not derived." It is in this sense of an original, underivative art form that African sculpture may be called "primitive."

African sculpture is a sophisticated art—as Alain Locke put it, "culturally and technically so mature that it must be rated as classic in the best sense of the word," exhibiting a "completely successful harmony between the idea and its material embodiment." Its best examples can be rated with sculpture of the great periods in art history.

Each of the so-called "primitive arts" which, at first glance, seems so like the rest, exhibits marked stylistic individuality when carefully examined. On investigation we shall then have no difficulty in immediately distinguishing a piece of African sculpture from a South Sea or a Central American figure. Further acquaintance with African art will show that each part of West Africa and even each tribe has produced a quite typical and identifiably individual art style.

What distinguishes African art is its combination of architectonic immobility with calm serenity. By "architectonic" we mean that the masses of the sculpture are structural; the figure has a columnar effect. This architectonic quality characterizes most of the African statues. It gives even the masks a solid and sober quality markedly different from those of the South Seas. Their serenity suggests that the African had found peace in the world and within himself through cultural catharsis. In contrast, the art of the South Seas seems agitated and fantastic.

A. The Force of Tradition

In African sculpture, traditional stylistic characteristics are repeated in the work of each tribe. This enables us to chart what might be called a dictionary of style regions, defining the particularities of each. Such a "dictionary" has been assembled and can be found in the Appendix.

TRADITION

Unity of style marks each locality. We have only a limited knowledge of the origin and duration of styles, since exploration of these regions is less than a century old. But there are strong indications that styles had been handed down from generation to generation for centuries.

The anonymous sculptors who, at the genesis of African art, invented and produced the original styles which have since influenced many generations must have had a creative genius comparable to the greatest personalities of art history. In the primary reproductive sense of the word *genius*, these creative masters were able to reproduce vital formulations of the life of their community, similar in power to the achievements of religious and political leaders.

RELIGIOUS UNITY

How was it possible for such a strong style tradition to be produced by the African Negro? One answer is the overwhelming unity of *religious feeling and purpose* through the centuries. The sculptor shared the religious feelings handed down from the tribal ancestors. His art made him the spokesman of the tribe; through him the fears and desires of his people found expression. This made the expression more valid and intense than if it had conveyed only his individual feelings.

Imbued with the authority and conviction of a whole people, he acquired a sense of infallibility. This in turn produced the sure touch which gives African art its calm strength and certainty. There is no hesitancy; the sculpture radiates serenity and fulfillment.

DISCIPLINE

The style was handed down from father to son. The student spent many years acquiring this tradition, precept by precept.

This rigid adherence to tradition has another, a psychic, reason. The African is convinced that the traditional manner is good because it was effective in magical rites—it worked. Therefore it must be continued.

If there had been any change, who knows what the consequences might be? This fear of the consequences of change is behind his rigid traditionalism.

Moreover, he had to consider his fellow-believers. Each sculpture represented a well-known spirit, totem, or mythological personality, and its appearance had to be fixed for direct and immediate recognition.

This imposed a powerful discipline on the artist.

The rewards for such conformity, however, were substantial. They were assurance and serenity, reflecting social stability. Conformity was part of the artist's whole life pattern, as in his adherence to taboos and the other clan conventions. The tribal myths strengthened the hold of tradition. Precedent was regarded as having passed the test of efficiency. Thus everything in the artist's culture strengthened the force of tradition.

As soon as the social stability from which the tradition derives is disturbed, as occurred with the irruption of the Europeans into Africa, the indigenous art, deprived of its tradition, degenerates and frequently disappears.

EFFECT OF DISCIPLINE

Lack of creative liberty does not necessarily work to the detriment of art. Frequently it promotes intensity. In early Christian art, when painters followed strict prescriptions by the Church, their works achieved an unparalleled concentration of feeling. Similarly, the Buddhist sculptors of the Khmers, who established a powerful empire and a rich culture in the eleventh century at Angkor, in Cambodia, were also under a very rigid canonic discipline. The figures had to have a uniform dressing of the hair; the ear lobes were elongated in a certain way; and the head was held in a prescribed attitude. Nevertheless—and perhaps because of these limitations—Khmer sculpture is the most sublime manifestation of Buddhist art.

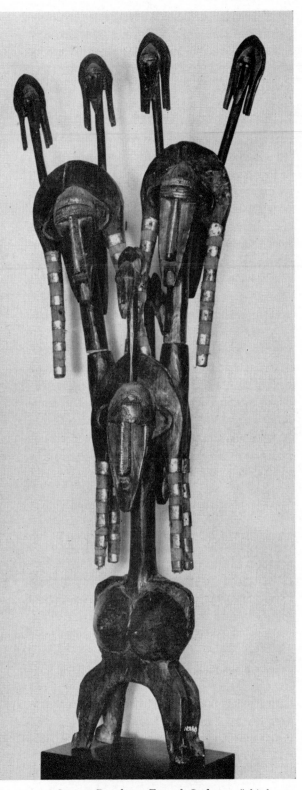

FIG. 59. *Statue. Bambara, French Sudan. 30" high.* SEE
PAGE 158

FIG. 60. *Mask with antelope. Bambara, French Sudan.*
15" high. SEE PAGE 158

The reverse can be seen in a case where foreign influence resulted in greater liberty for sculpture. At Gandhara in ancient Afghanistan, then a Buddhist land, Hellenistic Greek sculptors, not Buddhists themselves, were employed to carve figures of Buddha. Their work was refined and graceful, but it lacked the force, the penetration, the purity, and the simplicity of the later Khmer Buddhist sculpture.

INDIVIDUAL DIFFERENCES

It must not be thought, however, that African sculpture is without diversity and individuality. As we have seen, the traditional forms differ from region to region. And even in the separate style regions, the individuality of the sculptor breaks through the conventional form. This appears in the details where he ventures improvisations of his own. Thus Bambara antelopes or Bakota funerary figures will have a common form, but will differ in detail of the design.

The individuality of the artist is to be seen also in differences of *artistic quality*. Pieces from the very same tribe will differ in artistic quality. For, in spite of communal and traditional ways of thinking and carving, the *individual touch* still leave its mark.

INNER MECHANISM OF CREATION

A work of art may be considered from two approaches: its content and its form.

The emotion with which the content is charged originates in a perception of the artist, gained from an external impulse or from his inner self. This perception, as it sets up an interreacting complex of feelings, develops into a *conception*. Between the conception and the work of art that springs from it occurs a series of emotional processes. There may be frustration of desires; inability to crystallize the concept; a repression into the unconscious; a transformation in the form of sublimation; and so on.

These emotional processes cannot evolve without the artist's having "something to say." Ideas and feelings ripen into the conception. Ideally the emotions concentrated in the conception must be intense—so strong that no intellectual deliberation can distract the creator, and he coordinates directly those mediums of expression which alone will carry his emotion. When creation takes place in this manner, the medium of expression is chosen with spontaneous insight.

Picasso once told the writer that the act of creation is an overflow. Just as when too much water is poured in a glass, it overflows, so when one has experienced too much, there is an overflow which becomes the content of the work of art.

Creation is thus a coordination of this inner emotional reality with the artistic medium. If the emotion is strong, the artist's skill may become secondary. Even where little skill is involved, a forceful work of art may be produced. With an excess of skill, the artist may concentrate on virtuosity, and his work will lack forceful content.

African art at its best shows a rare coordination of skill and emotional tension.

B. Form and Expression

An inquiry into the form of African sculpture must concern itself with the materials, traditions, and techniques because of the limitations which each of these factors places upon the finished art work.

MATERIALS

Knowledge of the material used in a sculpture is important to its understanding. In many ways the material determines the nature of the statue. The sculptor knows that he cannot do anything *to* a particular material; he can do only that which is *in the nature of the material*. This the African intuitively recognized. Where the material was bronze, the objects were given a form not to be duplicated in wood. And when it

FIG. 62. *Mask with cowry shells. Bambara, French Sudan. 15″ high.* SEE PAGE 158.

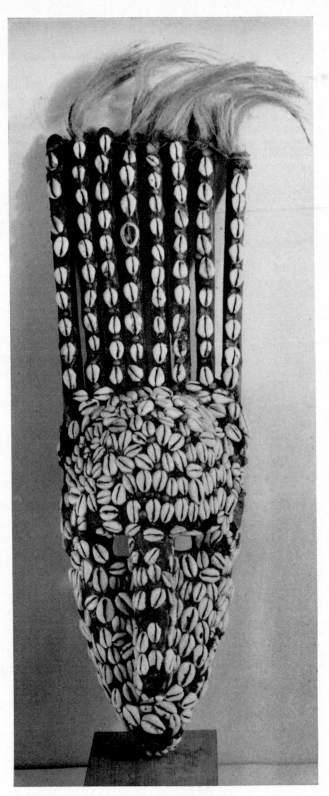

FIG. 61. *Handle mask (Ndemba). Bayaka, Belgian Congo. 17″ high.* SEE PAGE 218

was wood it attained that freedom of expression so characteristic of African art —greater than would have been possible in stone.

The actual selection of a material and the use made of it depend upon its availability. In Mexico, for instance, stone and clay predominate; in Alaska, bone. Mexican carving, therefore, is mainly in clay and stone; Alaskan carving in bone. African sculpture uses a great variety of materials, the most common being wood and the least common stone. We know of stone sculptures in Sierra Leone by the Mendi and in French Guinea by the Kissi tribes, some stone figures by the Bakongo (B. Congo), some stone heads in Northern Congo in the region of the river Uele, and the newly discovered stone figures from Esie in the Ilorin province of Nigeria.

Of ivory carvings, the best-known are the elephant tusks, armbands, a few statues, and the goblets from the Benin Kingdom. They are most abundant in the Belgian Congo (among the Warega, Wazimba, Baluba, Mossendjo, Basonge, Bakuba and Bapende tribes). Some new ivory and bone carvings are produced in Loango and also in Dahomey.

Because of its rarity, ivory was always highly appreciated, and constituted one of the chief exchange items traded to the Arabs. Most of the ivory pieces (armbands, amulet-like masks, figurines, etc.) were worn on the body, which contributed to the beautiful reddish-brown patina and smooth surface of old pieces.

As to metal, gold was used by the Ashanti, Aitutu, and Baule tribes, mostly on the Gold Coast, the Ivory Coast, and in Dahomey.

Of the bronzes, the most famous are those of Ife and Benin, and the Ashanti gold weights. In Nigeria, other tribes such as the Yoruba, Edo, Jabba, and Igara use bronze casts, as do the Dans and Krans in Liberia; the Tikar, Bali, Bagam, and Bamum tribes

in Cameroon; the Lobi, Degombe, Knkomba, Bobo, Killi tribes in the Sudan; and the Ewe and Ga in Togo. On the Gold Coast and the Ivory Coast, in addition to the Ashantis, the Baule, Anji, and Akan tribes have bronze casts. The *cire-perdue*, or lost-wax casting technique, is mainly used.

The last consists of making a model in wax over an earthen core. This is covered with fine-grained potter's clay, and when several layers have dried, the whole is enveloped in earth and baked. As the melted wax drains away through vents, it is replaced by molten bronze. When the cast has cooled the mold is broken. The emerging bronze cast exactly reproduces the original wax model. In the Benin Kingdom, extremely complicated plates, heads, etc., were cast in this technique, which experts rate as highly as that used for the Cellini casts.

We cannot say whether the West Africans discovered this technique or whether they borrowed it. It was used in ancient Egypt, Greece, and Rome; in India; and in pre-Columbian America. The fact remains, however, that the bronze castings achieved by the West African in the thirteenth to seventeenth centuries were never surpassed in technical perfection. If we presume an Egyptian origin, the learning must have fallen on very fertile ground; an amazing bronze art developed from it.

Other materials used in Africa are terra cotta, hammered-metal sheets to cover objects, clay, raffia and straw, palm fiber, and cotton thread.

Wood, which is available almost everywhere in Africa, is most commonly used. Another important reason for its use is its magico-religious significance.

THE MEANING OF WOOD TO THE AFRICAN

Africans worship the tree as the abode of supernatural forces. In Nigeria the tree is connected with human life. If a man falls sick or a woman wants a child, offerings are made to a particular tree. Some tribes be-

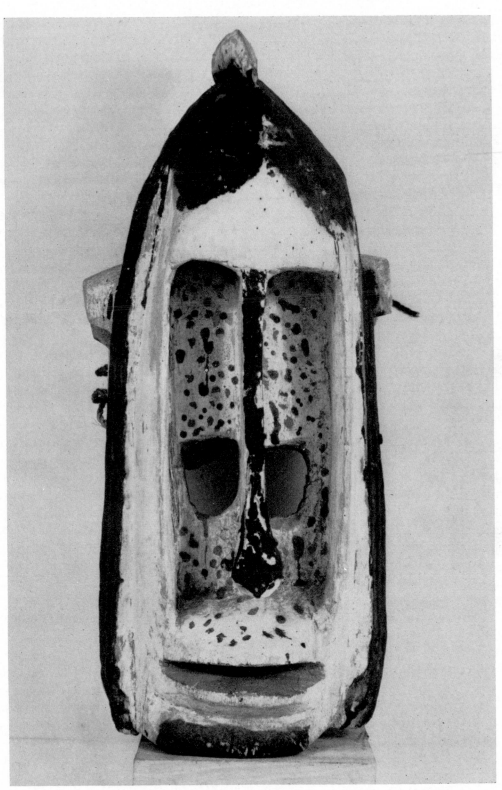

FIG. 63. *Mask. Dogon, French Sudan. 15″ high.* SEE PAGE 159

lieve trees are their ancestors. Trees are sometimes worshipped as mother symbols, since they produce and bear fruits.

The sacredness of trees associates them with the ancestor cult. The dead are buried in the holy forest; consequently the spirits of the deceased live there. Where the dead are buried near the village, a tree may be planted over the graves.

Belief in the sanctity of trees is found in all parts of the world. According to the Bible, God made his appearance to Moses in a bush. Zoroastrians held all plants sacred; the Greeks venerated Zeus at the oak of Dodona; Buddha found peace under the Bo tree. The instances could be endlessly multiplied.

Vestiges of this animistic belief in the life power of trees have been carried over in the present-day use by "dowsers" of hazel twigs to locate water. When we "knock on wood," we perpetuate an animistic belief: we summon the spirit of the tree to protect us.

SIGNIFICANCE OF POLES

The next development in tree worship is trimming the tree trunk into a pole. Early African explorers found large, roughly carved posts used as tribal fetishes. Today more elaborately sculptured house posts serve as guardian spirits of dwellings or commemorative statues of the deceased.

The word *pole* or *pale* in English is derived from the Latin word *palus*, the primordial symbol for phallus or *penis erectus*.

According to the Freudian system of dream interpretation, any long, hard object may serve as a symbol of the male genital. The Maypole dance (with the pole substituting for the tree) once had a phallic significance. This symbol is the elemental representation of vital force, of creation and fertility. The African columnar statue derives from the pale, or post, the primary form of the symbol. It has all the phallic

characteristics: the erect position, symmetry, etc.

The phallic symbolism of African sculpture is to be seen most clearly in the soapstone figures of the Kissi tribe in Sierra Leone or in the ivory carving (Ndugu) (Fig. 43). The oversize head of African statues is proportioned to the head of the penis. This is probably one of the reasons why masks, which are representations of the head, are also oversize.

A similar use of the pole to represent the human figure appears in Greek architecture. The early Doric column is the trunk of the male, abstracted into an aesthetic columnar unity, with the capital as an abstraction of the head (from which the word is in fact derived: Latin, *caput*, head). This symbolism was carried so far that the column had a standard measure of one foot (human-foot size) in diameter, and a height of six times this diameter, corresponding to the average male proportions. Later, for aesthetic considerations, the height was changed to seven times the diameter, and in the Ionic columns to nine times.

The caryatid is a decadent form of the same idea—a naturalistic illustration used to replace a forceful abstraction.

The Baluba stools with their supporting figures only apparently suggest the same caryatid idea. These stools might be representations of the ancient custom prescribing that the king sit on the back of a crouching slave, to symbolize his power (Fig. 66).

THE SPIRIT OF WOOD

Tree worship, with intermingled phallic symbolism, accounts for the African's deep attachment to wood. The ritual preparations for the sculpture reflect the mystical feeling toward the tree.

The part to be carved is carefully selected from either trunk or limb. When the tree is cut down, a magical ceremony is performed to cope with its spirit. This is pacified by

FIG. 64. *Initiation ceremony mask. Bayaka, Belgian Congo. 12" high.* SEE PAGE 218

FIG. 65. *Hood mask. Bena-Kosh, Belgian Congo. 15" high.* SEE PAGE 220

FIG. 66. *Chief's stool. Baluba, Belgian Congo.*
19" high. SEE PAGE 206

prayer or sacrifices, or more powerful spirits are invoked to provide protection against the spirit of the tree. Usually the log is left lying in the forest to give the spirit time to leave it, but sometimes it is immediately hauled to a secluded place, where the sculptor gives it a crude preliminary shaping. Among certain of the Congo tribes the man who ordered the sculpture from the magician had to participate in this ritual.

The feeling that the wood to be carved contains a spirit and has life contributed to the sculptor's deep feeling for his material. For him it was already endowed with power before he even began shaping it into a magic figure.

OTHER MATERIALS

For the African, metals too had symbolic power. In the Sudan, copper signified water itself and the rays of light reflected in water;

it was also considered the brother of gold. Even unshaped rocks were adored as manifestations of natural forces.

DOMINANT FORMS

An African sculpture is carved or hewn out of a single block of wood. The sculpture seems to emerge out of the mass of the material. The magical life that the block of wood is supposed to have seems to show in the massiveness of the wood and its beautiful grain, which the sculptor keeps intact. The contours follow the cylindrical form of the log, to which all parts are kept subordinate. Another, though subconscious, reason for retaining the natural outlines of the wood is probably to preserve its phallic suggestion.

This emphasis on the *vertical line* gives each statue a vertical *axis*, to which the different parts of the sculpture have an organic connection. If divided along this vertical axis, many African statues would separate into two symmetrical halves, an effect also to be observed in Babylonian, Egyptian, Archaic Greek, and Romanesque statues. It creates an impression of serenity and repose. Another example of this vertical symmetry lies in the deep, peaceful lines of the Gothic arch, as of two hands closed in prayer and raised toward heaven.

The majesty and serenity of African sculpture is also due to the wonderful coordination of the emotional and ideological attitudes of the African with structural principles. In its lack of bodily movement, Maillol compared Negro sculpture to the Egyptian, observing that the more immobile it is, the more it appears about to move. This latent movement, this anticipation of action, is an important element in its attraction to us. In our imagination we complete the indicated action. Maillol added that "Negro sculpture has reduced [synthesized] twenty forms into one." African sculpture is architectonic in the equilibrium of its masses.

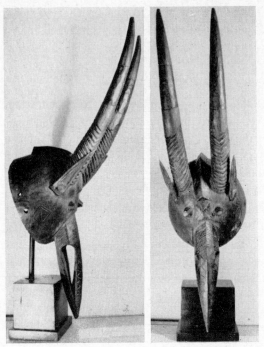

FIG. 67. *Animal mask. Bobo, French Sudan.*
25" high.

TECHNIQUE OF CARVING AND
ITS INFLUENCE ON FORM

In all works of art there is rhythm of forms, but it is so pronounced in African art as to become, in Elie Faure's words, "rhythmic reality."

Rhythm is elemental in all human beings, whose organic functions are carried on in regular pulsations; but this is truest, perhaps, of the African. His walk is markedly rhythmic. And rhythm is so important to the African that he even works to song. The sculptor swings his adze to cadences.

This rhythm, as Boas points out, becomes a "motor habit." Because tradition has imposed on the African a rigid manner of carving, his technique tends toward uniform, almost mechanical, operation. Although his tools vary according to region— axes, knives, and awls being used—the most common resembles an adze. The use of such a tool calls for chopping rather than carving. (The tool is used elsewhere for rough carving by ship carpenters, coopers, etc.) Since the blade is set at a right angle to the handle, the adze is swung from such a distance that precision is virtually impossible. Not creation of form but intensity of feeling is the sculptor's main concern. Like the violin virtuoso who transcends all kinds of technical difficulties and concentrates all his energies on forceful rendition, the African sculptor, sure of his form, concentrates on expression. That so many of the extremely fine carvings of Africa were done with this rough tool is a tribute to the skill of the sculptors, the sureness of their vision, and the coordination between tool and concept. As Mrs. Esther Warner put it: "The tool seemed a part of the artist's own body, an artery through which his soul flowed into the wood he was shaping."

The African sculptor acquired this rhythmical carving skill in many ways. To begin with, only one with a gift for carving became a sculptor. Usually he had a high standing in the community. Often magician and sculptor were one. In many instances the skill was handed down from father to son in a long and rigorous training.

The African sculptor possessed a vast amount of that commodity so essential to artistic creation—*leisure*. He could work on his statue until he was satisfied; and he got great satisfaction out of a well-made piece of sculpture. Love of the work is one of the reasons for its high artistic standard. Certain of his technical problems were difficult to solve, and he could have skimped or evaded the solution had his aim been merely to finish the sculpture quickly. Many statues have scarification marks in relief, which meant the chopping or carving of the whole block of wood to make these marks stand out in relief. Or, to provide for a small protrusion, an extremely large area of wood was cut away. The African sculptor would not think of omitting a detail to save time and work. Thus the Bobo (French Sudan) carver used a block of wood of about thirty by twenty by ten inches to produce the mask in Fig. 67. Had he shortened the horns

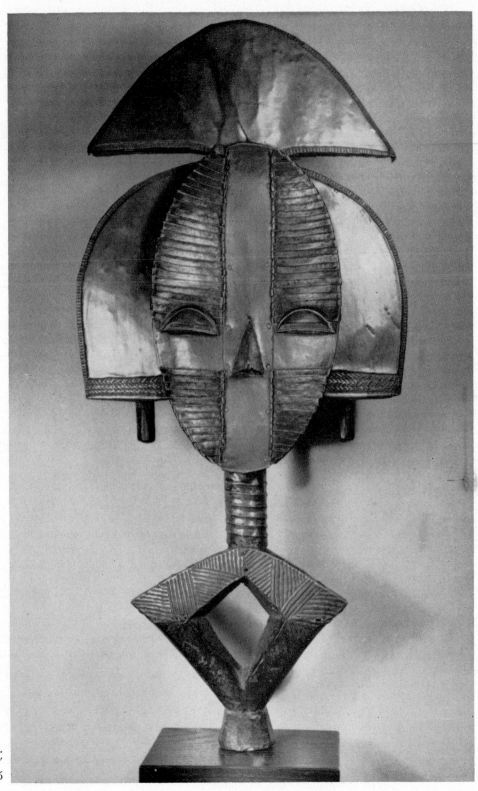

FIG. 68. *Funerary figure.*
Bakota, Gabun. 24″
high. SEE PAGE 186

or reduced their arc, he would have greatly simplified his task—but at a sacrifice of impressiveness and aesthetic values.

The surface of the completed statue appears to breathe its own life. The surface has a function in terms of light, gaining cadence from the reflection.

The sculptor identifies himself with the whole work. He participates in the ceremonies when the tree is felled, when dyes are applied, etc. Often he is the one who gives the magical substance to the statue in the ritual that consecrates it as a magic-working image.

ABSTRACTION

The most ancient forms of African sculpture are abstract. In the great period, abstractions were combined with semi-abstract features. Decadence came into African art when it turned to naturalism.

The majority of African sculptures show an interplay of round forms (Figs. 68 and 69). Exclusively *angular* shapes are rare. When angular abstractions are used, they are often surrounded with round forms. The resulting interplay creates a tension of interrelationship, like the interrelationships of organic life.

Abstract Forms. The most striking facet of African sculpture is exaggeration. Because the content of his work is spiritual, the sculptor chooses those forms which he feels intuitively. Since the culture in which the African sculptor's creative impulse has its source is marked by powerful abstractions, his work follows the same path. His objectivization of abstract ideas makes use of analogous abstract forms.

We know that all African sculptures, including ancestor figures, magical figures, and masks, had a magical meaning. All held potential mastery over the secret forces of nature, to be worked at man's command.

But it was more than that. The invisible idea of the ancestor spirit or the magic power was rendered visible and material in his sculpture. As Leonardo da Vinci said: "Inscribe in any place the name of God and set opposite it His image. You will then see which will be held in greater reverence."

The inspiration of the African artist lay in the collective belief in magico-religious animism. But the sculptor was also an individual, and he added something of his own. The question of individuality exists even in communal Africa, and personal differences are expressed in all African sculpture.

Animate nature, whether embodied in human, animal, or plant life, is manifested in visible forms. To order and subjugate them to his will, man deformed or transformed them into *invented* forms, products of his creative volition. This "will-to-form" (a phrase coined by Alois Riegl) turned to "denaturalized" forms to assert man's dominance and independence, and to express his individual personality and stamp it on his work. The forms became truly *new creations*, symbolizing man's presence on earth and his mastery over nature.

From the African point of view, however, the "new creation" or "inventive" form need be neither new nor invented, but a rendering imitative not of *visual* reality, but of *conceptual* reality. This primitive art provides images—indeed, true copies—of an intuitive concept, objectifications of an emotional reality. This emotional reality was a struggle against fear of the spirit forces. By overcoming his fear, he attained a feeling of superiority, controlling forces which hitherto had controlled him. Rank points out that first man felt himself a *creature* of nature and religious beliefs, eventually to emerge as a *creator* in his art activity.

Man's emergence as a self-asserting being developed another important attitude in him. Because of his inner ruling forces (which today we call "the unconscious"), he questioned the independent existence of visual reality. Natural forces, thunderstorms, fecundity, illness became real to him when he attributed their action to a spirit. Thus

FIG. 69. *Initiation ceremony mask. Geh, Liberia. 8″ high.* SEE PAGES 169, 172

natural phenomena were converted into imaginary forces to fit them into his inner reality.

The Revolt against Nature. From this *doubt* in the validity of reality came his revolt against nature's established order and his creation of the new order imposed by his will and conforming to his inner or conceptual reality. When he rendered something that in nature was short and round into something long and angular, this *symptomatic* action asserted opposition to nature's order.

In addition to the reasons given above, the African might have conceived his abstract or unnaturalistic form and realizations for a simpler reason. Let us turn from the mask in Fig. 70, which has all the Negroid features of naturalistic protraiture—short broad nose, thick lips, square head form— to a Baule mask (Fig. 50). Here the nose is thin and long, the mouth small, the head oblong. Every feature contradicts visual reality, has become an abstraction. This mask has been made the abode of a spirit. The ancestor spirit is obviously not a visual but a conceptual reality. It is abstract.

But being a true artist and understanding, or rather feeling, the inner mechanism of form within the creation, the sculptor did more than merely contradict. All forms are round, and their interplay creates a rhythm made more intense by the introduction of the unexpected, strong, angular, straight line. There is tension, but it has balance and therefore gives an impression of serenity and detachment.

All this, however, is on the unconscious level. When a natural form is transformed into an abstract one, it is the psychic *intent* —the drive—which counts. Because man's innate drives to power, to self-assertion, are so basic, the performance of this act, the creation of new forms, is carried on with great absorption and excitement, but governed by the strong, rhythmic design in which these impulses are coordinated.

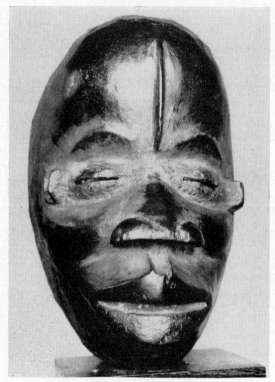

FIG. 70. *Initiation ceremony mask. Guere-Dan, Ivory Coast. 8" high.* SEE PAGES 172

To self-assertion is added the drive to assert an idea or fulfill a specific purpose; and this becomes the content of the work of art. Here the aim is man's protection. In African art the idea is animism; the purpose is to protect the beholder against malevolent spirits.

Abstract, exaggerated, stylized, unnaturalistic, or distorted forms occur in art whenever a dynamic expression of an idea takes place. When the pressure behind a dam becomes excessive the water breaks through; so, too, will the emotional pressure of a new and unified idea break through naturalistic forms.

Art, or style in art, is the expression of an ideology. Ideologies are subject to change; consequently art styles—resultants of such changes—are also subject to change.

Classification of Creative Art Activities. In Elie Faure's theory, the idea which is the content of a work of art should be projected or exteriorized in *expression*. When expression aims at *perfection* it uses the skill of the artist to attain maximum truth to nature—the hallmark of decadence.

When the Greek idea was strong and virile in its Archaic period, it achieved the most balanced, tightly formed statues, from which the idea radiated with great power. When the idea weakened and its emotional excitement died down, the artist—now having no deeply felt emotional need for expression—took the forms of his predecessors and tried to refine them and to do better, to achieve *perfection*.

Observing details and comparing them with nature, he arrived at the satisfaction of being more perfect (compared to nature) than his creative, explosive forerunner.

Thus *feeling*, the creative force, was replaced by *knowledge*. Maillol once remarked that Praxiteles had learned to make such fine, polished sculptures that they no longer possessed any character.

The Christian idea also produced unnaturalistic sculptures in the Byzantine and Romanesque periods, when it expressed a deep religious feeling. Later, especially in the fifteenth century in Germany, Christ heads were done with anatomical perfection and sculptured with tortured facial expressions, even with color to reproduce blood. In the early Romanesque sculptures the head of Christ, however, is serene, as if saying, "Forgive them, for they know not what they do." This is the Christian spirit; the imitation of physical suffering is not.

Our period, too, has its ideology, although it is more complex than any of the past. Whether based on individualism, anxiety, or any other elemental feeling, this ideology is vigorously expressed by great personalities, such as Picasso, who synthesized the spirit of the time and expressed it in forceful new forms. But their imitators, often quite unconscious of the influences they were responding to, did not understand the spirit and never felt the excitement of creative improvisations. They merely elaborated upon the already created forms, perfecting some (according to their own criteria); but their work was lifeless.

This can happen when an artist begins to imitate himself, as in the case of Utrillo. His early paintings were an expression of his loneliness. When his need to unload his intensity ceased he turned back to his own early inventions, repeated them, and they became lifeless.

The conflicting trends in art—the creative and emotional aspect as against the refining and intellectual aspect—have been given many different formulations. In Nietzsche they appear as the "Dionysian," or inspired and ecstatic expression, as against the "Apol-

FIG. 71. *Ceremonial cup. Bakuba, Belgian Congo. 12" high.*

FIG. 72. *Statue. Basonge, Belgian Congo. 5″ high.* SEE PAGE 212

lonian," or intellectually controlled expression. Scheltana called the two directions "Organic," when the drive stems from the inner need of the creator, and "Mechanical," when the expression merely uses and refines existing forms. Herbert Kuhn's terms for the two trends are "Imaginative" and "Sensory," with the imaginative leading to invented and, ultimately, abstract forms, and the sensory, deriving its inspiration from the visual, tending to become naturalistic. Max Verworn's terms are "Ideoplastic" as against "Physioplastic," one creative tendency working with ideas, the other with physical reality. E. von Sydow, in his psychoanalytical studies, called the two directions "Eros dominated" and "Eros dominating"—one dominated by libidinal (emotional) forces and the other dominating those forces.

Elaborating this, Otto Rank divides the directions into two groups:

I	II
Transformation of life into a personal experience	Makes use of other life experiences
Total participation of the artist	Partial participation of the artist
Self-justification of the individual, raised above the crowd	Justification by way of general recognition
Creating new forms to express his personality	Perfecting forms, using traditional materials
Driving to express an individual truth	Accepting generally adopted truth
Subjective; individual; personal	Objective; collection; social

Further divisions may be suggested, such as:

Psychological	Materialistic
Conceptual reality	Visual reality
Inventive	Imitative

Or they may be summed up as the expression of an inner reality, as opposed to the rendering of external reality.

Maillol said, "I use form to arrive at what is without form." The African, with innate artistic facility, has found forms to express his inner feeling and, in this way, to put order into his ideas—a process which may be called also the *spiritualization* of a work of art. The author gained a sense of this in a small church in Toledo, Spain, where hang several of El Greco's paintings. A priest who acted as guide was startled by the question: "What did El Greco's paintings mean to him personally?" After a while he answered: "They represent for me spiritualized reality."

Such spiritual realities are not confined to individual revelations. Animism for African art or Christianity for the Romanesque are collective ideologies for which the artist served as the expressive agent.

The individual artist expressing an ideology also has his own problem and inner realities. The formation of a style is thus the expression of ideologies through the "will-to-form" of the individual.

African art is similar to Egyptian or Romanesque art, simple and unified in idea as in individual expression. Like the idea of the cult of spirits, the personal problems were universal to Africans—fear, dependence on natural forces, etc. The uniqueness of a personality such as Michelangelo or Cézanne could not have developed in Africa because the personal problems were not unique but general.

DISTORTION OF THE BODY

In most African sculpture we find an overlarge head and a trunk too long for the legs. The same disproportion appears in the costumes of the maskers. Emphasis is placed on the head because in it the spirit powers are believed to reside (Fig. 72).

This is one phase of the soul concept. The soul has been variously located in the

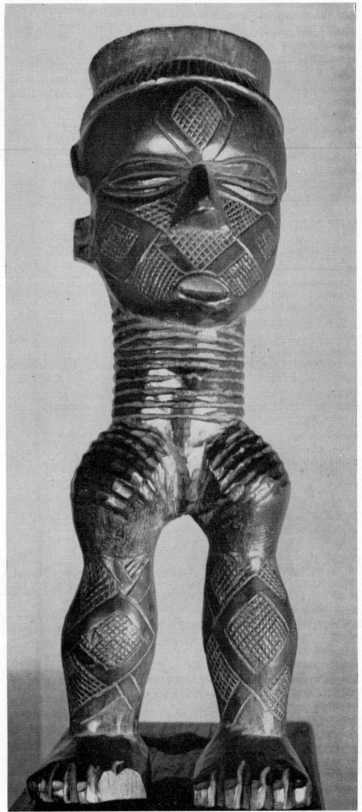

FIG. 73. *Ceremonial cup. Bakuba, Belgian Congo. 11″ high.*
SEE PAGE 200

stomach, the liver, and other organs of the body cavity, a variation of the concept of the womb as the origin of life.

The exaggeration of the head to the neglect of other parts of the body is best illustrated by the Bakota (Gabun) funerary statue (Fig. 68). The natives call such a figure *Mbulu Ngulu,* or "picture of the spirit of the dead." There is general agreement that these fetishes were placed in baskets containing ancestral bones (Fig. 23), but there is disagreement as to their function, some writers maintaining that it is to serve as watchman over the remains, others that these fetishes merely mark where the deceased lies.

The body of an African statue never appears "fleshy," but has a feeling of austerity and serenity. It shows no attempt at naturalistic resemblance. Although male and female genitals are often exaggerated, the purpose is never to evoke sensuous emotions, but rather to suggest the power, the procreative force (Fig. 71).

COMPARISON WITH CHILDREN'S DRAWINGS

The design aspect of African art has been compared to that of children's drawings. This can be of value only if we investigate whether the inner point of departure of the child's creative drive is close to that of the primitive African adult.

We find that children do not draw actual appearances. They reproduce a mental image. A typical children's drawing of a human being is a large head with large eyes, with the body frequently omitted and the limbs attached to the head. The child selects what seem to him the significant parts of the thing to be represented. With no concern for realistic appearance he expresses his symbolized concept. On this ground the child's concept meets the African.

The African, too, begins with an idea (a composite concept of feeling and mental image), whether it be of a spirit or a healing force. His conceptual image of this idea becomes his reality, which disregards visual sensations or realistic proportions. The sculptural forms with which he expresses it become conceptual symbols of his inner reality, his mental image.

To be specific, let us consider Fig. 73, a Bakuba cup, or Fig. 76, a Warega ivory statue (both Belgian Congo). Here we have the typical vision of the child—head and attached legs. The mask in Fig. 74, from the Ibo tribe in Nigeria, shows similar striking resemblances to the child's creation.

How basic is this instinct to present the essential is demonstrated by the oldest existing sculpture of the human body, the abstract, non-naturalistic Paleolithic "Venus of Willendorf." Its exaggerated breasts and buttocks are virtual ideograms of maternity, and comparable to a Kissi (French Guinea) stone figure (Fig. 75).

This would indicate that conceptual vision is inherent in man. Modern art—the expression of contemporary consciousness—is its latest demonstration.

The exaggerations in African sculpture touch upon and reveal in us, through the mechanism of identification, our own primary conceptualism, stored deep in us along with other values of our childhood. African sculpture reawakens early habits and sensations, plunges us again into the miraculous world of imagination.

The distortion of the head is not limited to its relative size. Often the forehead bulges out for further emphasis of mental power. Or emanations of the spirit are indicated by a nimbus of rays around the head. To the African this is no mere ornament or symbol—it is the spirit itself pulsing from the head (Fig. 68). As if to give a personal sense of each person whose spirit the fetish represents, the design of this radiation varies from figure to figure, a testimony to the sculptor's ingenuity.

FIG. 74. *Mask. Ibo, British Nigeria. 8″ high.*

Because the body, the earthly part of the deceased, no longer exists, it is only indicated, sometimes reduced to a lozenge form.

Frobenius suggests that the radiation of the Bakota figure may have another significance—that the head is also a symbol of the sun. Whether spirit of the dead or solar radiation, in any case its significance is spiritual and its expression is highly artistic. The same concept may be seen in the halos of Christian and Buddhist religious imagery.

The length of the trunk has a structural justification, as we saw when we discussed the relations of the form and the vertical axis. The subordination of body to spirit

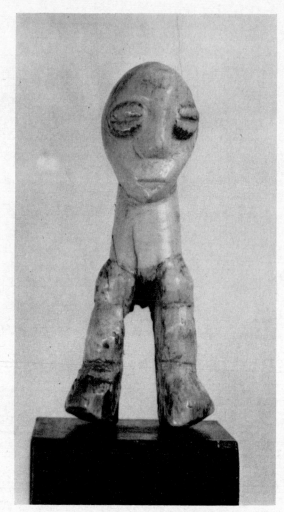

FIG. 76. *Ivory statue. Warega, Belgian Congo. 4½″ high.*

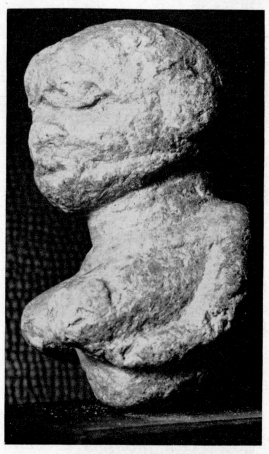

FIG. 75. *Stone funerary figure (Pombo). Kissi, French Guinea. 3½″ high.*
SEE PAGE 165

may have produced the simplification of the column-like trunk.

The legs, too, receive little attention, and often the feet are missing entirely. Arms are often attached in such a way as to accentuate the vertical. Exaggerated rendering of individual parts of the body in African sculpture may perhaps be better understood from this anecdote. An African, shown a photograph of a human being, had this reaction: "This is the nose"—pause—"This is the mouth. . . ." Having enumerated the separate features, he said, as if in surprise, "This is a figure."

PART III

AFRICAN ART
AND EUROPEAN
CIVILIZATION

FIG. 77. *Bronze plaque
(bird). Bini, Benin
Kingdom, British Nigeria.
17" high.* SEE PAGES 145, 181

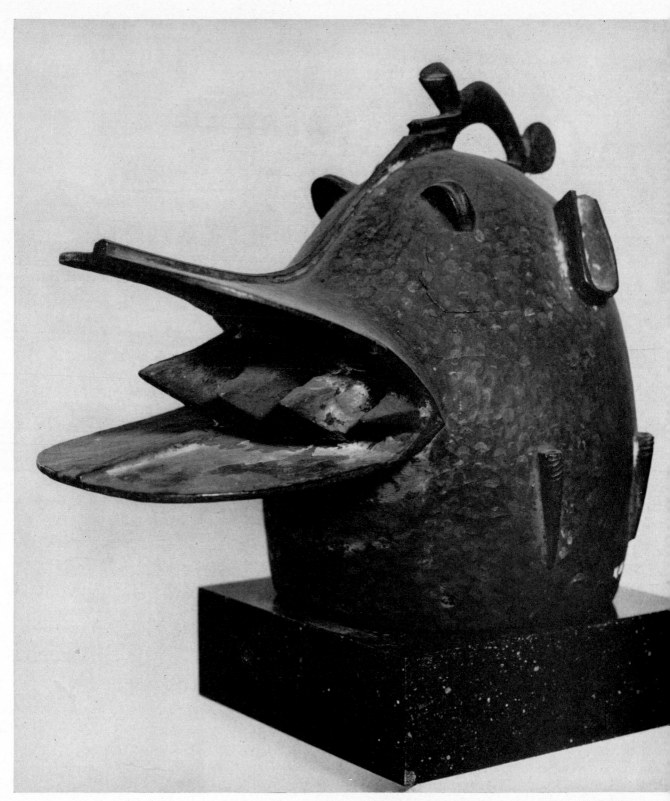

FIG. 78. *Mask. Senufo, French Sudan, Ivory Coast. 14" high.* SEE PAGE

7. OUR APPROACH TO AFRICAN ART

THE expression to which we respond in African art comes from its forceful emotional content. African sculpture is not *about* an emotional idea (it does not describe, illustrate, or represent), but it *is* the idea in immediate, uninhibited expression.

It may be said that the effect which African sculpture has upon us comes from its economy—every part being essential—or from the efficient coordination and functioning of its parts. It must now be clear that in our relationship with African art, we should not look for beauty in any conventional sense connoting naturalistic reality.

CONCEPTS OF BEAUTY

No satisfactory definition of beauty has yet been given; no usable measurement of it has been found. And concepts of beauty change according to time and place, and are not constant even in circles of the same class and background.

The African concept of beauty, considered comparatively, diverges from ours. For beauty's sake Africans undergo physical deformations which may seem monstrous to us. The Magandja women distend their lips with large rings and disks. Others use pressure to produce unnatural skull shapes, pierce the nose, from which they hang rings, tattoo the body, cut the skin to produce raised scars, file their teeth to points, and so on. Usually these marks of beauty are acquired at the cost of great physical pain. In some cases the marks have another use: tribal or secret-society identifications.

INTUITIVE APPROACH

Because what we look for lies in the realm of the emotions, we must be intuitive in our approach if we are to respond to it. In Schopenhauer's view, it is only through our intuition that a work of art can speak to us, or, rather, that we can comprehend its speech, which is untranslatable into the language of reason. Bergson adds that we must revive the feeling of reality obliterated by habits. Re-feeling, or *Einfuehlung*, as Worringer called it, suggests *empathy*, or sympathetic identification. We prefer Otto Rank's more literal translation of the word, "feeling oneself into" a work of art. We propose, as even more accurate, the expressions "intuitive projection" or "introjection" of ourselves to convey the idea of active participation in, and even projection of ourselves into, the emotion expressed by a work of art.

Such a personal projection occurs when a creative artist, using a communal concept, projects his own feeling into the work of art he bases on that concept. By projecting his own individualistic yet animistic feeling into the statue, the African artist achieves union with the communal animistic concept.

One might ask which came first, the community's or the individual's concept? The writer would attribute precedence to the communal philosophy, observing, however, that it fits into the artist's personal spiritual attitude. Otherwise the artist would not be in sympathy with it and would not be able to project himself into the work; hence he could not create it.

The observer's problem is to adopt an attitude that will enable him to relive this process, to do so through an understanding of the invisible through its visible signs. This requires projection or refinement of his perception beyond its normal range.

HOW TO SEE ANY WORK OF ART

In looking at any art, we first face the objects with a mind and eye as unclouded with other images as possible. To paraphrase Schopenhauer, we must first focus the whole power of our mind on *perception,* surrendering ourselves to contemplation of the object, according it our entire capacity for feeling, thus opening ourselves to the advent of something new. The French call this "depersonalization," and Worringer terms it "self-renunciation." A complete "opening" of our inner selves is necessary, but we cannot achieve this by a merely passive attitude. It requires an intuitive response and *projection* of our own feeling into the work of art. First we capture what the work says, then we project our reponse into the work of art.

Thus *perception* discloses within the onlooker a pent-up emotion (often on the unconscious level) which the observer will project onto the work of art.

We can see this in the reactions of an observer to the animism expressed in African sculpture. He projects intuitively his own inherent unconscious animism, awakened by the carving, back into it.

This is a process affecting the deepest reaches of the mind. As Elie Faure put it, the subject in any work of art is only the means of fixing our attention upon appearances and of inducing us to penetrate these appearances so as to penetrate to the spirit —or, as we would say, the unconscious.

What actually happens when one looks at a work of art may be understood through using the camera as illustration. Our eyes can be compared to the camera lens which has been ground to the required precision. They can be worked to comparable precision by looking at works of art and by applying basic viewpoints out of art books.

The image captured by the lens is deposited on the negative inside the camera. Good light, properly timed exposure, and especially the "speed," or refinement of the emulsion on the film, are necessary to get a satisfactory negative. This "speed" is comparable to our own inner sensitivity, and the extent to which it has been cultivated to absorb emotional reactions. The negative is then developed, printed, and "fixed" with the proper chemicals.

We similarly capture an image with our eyes and transfer it to our inner self; the print is our emotional concept, which may be very vague unless we have trained ourselves in each step of the process.

Those who can transform the first visual sensation into an emotional experience are few. The first image is usually captured by the intellect and related to conventional symbolic associations. This is not what we do when we react to music, which our training has enabled us to transform from a sensory perception (hearing) into emotion. We do not try to *understand* music; we seldom look for subject matter in it; we simply try to feel. But why cannot our eye, another sensory organ, also transform vision into an emotional reaction? Vision is also a concept-forming process. It develops images into ideas. Seeing paintings or sculpture differs little from hearing music.

Picasso once said that he uses his strong and startling forms and colors to give the onlooker such an emotional punch that intellectual deliberation has no chance to intervene. We should not merely *look* at a piece of sculpture (or any work of art), but *learn to see* it, which is far from simple. Bergson points out that the more pre-occupied we are with our practical life (rather, our mechanical life), the less we are inclined to see.

We may learn to see, to find the proper viewpoints, but our emotional enjoyment of a work of art will still depend upon our own inner life, upon the degree of sensitivity our psychological make-up has achieved and the life experience it has absorbed.

HOW TO SEE SCULPTURE

A statue being three-dimensional, it is impossible to see all of it at once. It can be seen from the front, the side, or the back; from below or from above; close up or far away; in strong light or dim light—and each time a new facet will be revealed. We can document this with a camera. A first full-front view of a statue (Fig. 80) gives us its overall rhythm, its position. On focusing and enlarging the head (Fig. 81) we perceive facial expressions which we probably missed before. A profile shot (Fig. 80) gives us still another aspect. A resourceful photographer can keep on uncovering new values.

Inspecting a piece of African sculpture in this manner, we soon discover that each side has its own life and latent movement, and an intense energy.

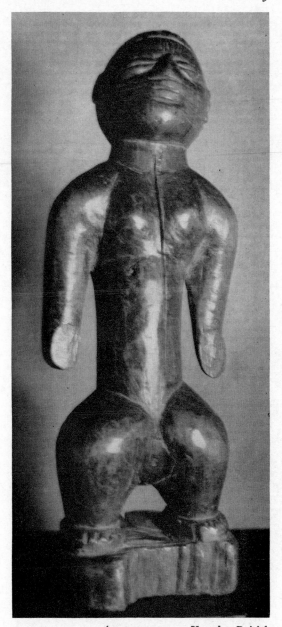

FIG. 79. *Ancestor statue. Yoruba, British Nigeria. 12" high.*

A Yoruba statue, for example (Fig. 79), gives such an impression of profound force that it appears ready to explode, though it is in repose and there is no indication of motion. Yet the forms are such, the coordination of masses is such, as to convey the feeling of immense energies held under severe control, but poised for energetic release.

Roger Fry placed the African among

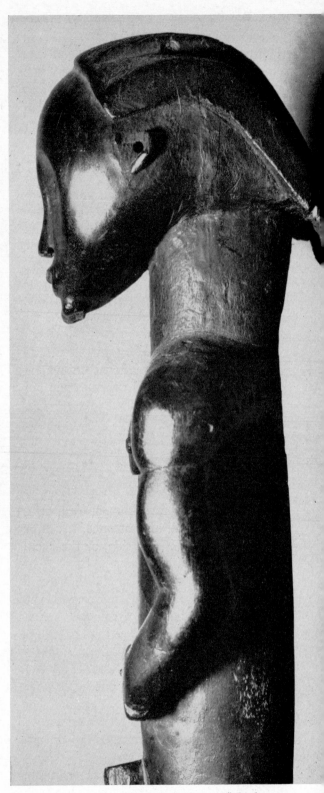

FIG. 80. *Ancestor cult statue. Pangwe, Gabun. 18" high.* SEE PAGE 1

FIG. 81. *Ancestor cult statue (detail of Fig. 80). Gabun.* SEE PAGE 192

the rare creative artists who "really conceived form in three dimensions," and had "the power to create expressive plastic forms."

All sculpture has three dimensions, but most is conceived in a relief-like manner, emphasizing the frontal view, so that the figures seem lifeless or meaningless from the back or the side. But the African created his vertically conceived statues so that all parts function in unity and each side flows into another. Any side suggests a continuity—that something is to follow. It invites our attention to proceed from the frontal view all around the whole statue —an exciting experience.

Touching an African sculpture provides an additional and unusual sensation. Close your eyes and concentrate on the sensations in your fingers; a new impression of delight is likely to result. Lines, planes, and volumes in African sculpture have so smooth a flow that your touch will record a living harmony.

This suggestion opens a new field of intersensory relationships, one aspect of the *Gestalt* psychology. Our simple vision is not a "simple sensation itself" (William James); "the totals themselves [in our case the sculpture] are different entities than the sums of their parts" (G. Hartmann). The experience of using one of our senses by touching the sculpture and adding this sensation to our visual perception is comparable to other sensory interrelations, such as "warm" (red, yellow, etc.) and "cool" (blue, green, etc.) colors; also "weights" of colors; and the "colors" of musical compositions. (A color piano has been constructed on the basis of the color sensations evoked by musical tones.) When we see a form its perception will depend upon the observer's position. And that which we see can be intensified by different stimuli— touch, smell, etc.

According to recent investigations of the phenomena of perception at Princeton, vision (mechanical reception of images) gives only cues to perception; the evaluation is made in terms of past experiences. Thus perception is seen as a subjective interpretation. Because each individual's associational material varies, perception must also be individual.

Unconsciously, then, a long process of Gestalt patterns takes place in us. Without our conscious knowledge, all our senses contribute, interrelate, and coordinate to form our individual inner perception.

The transformation of this perception into an emotional concept is the actual key to the "feel" of a piece of sculpture. We may add an everyday observation: our perception will depend, among other conditions, upon our daily changing mood and sensitivity, and upon our past experiences used as a reference material.

We may further add that the special "hitting power" that distinguishes sculpture among the arts is derived from the fact that it appears to have been the oldest of the plastic arts and from the impact of its direct three-dimensional form. It is the most primal of the plastic arts.

8. THE PLASTIC LANGUAGE

A PIECE of sculpture may be called a plastic structure. Since the forms of sculpture are expressive, they may be referred to as a plastic language.

There is a difference, however, between the plastic language of sculpture and verbal language. For we have a dictionary to define the meaning of each word in verbal language; there is general agreement as to what each word means. But we have no such accepted definitions of the meaning or psychological properties of the shapes which are the elements of plastic language. Yet we unconsciously associate certain emotional reactions with certain shapes or combinations of shapes. The sculpture which contains and integrates them imposes certain feelings upon us.

As an illustration, let us analyze possible psychological properties of primitive shapes. A flat surface may connote calmness; an angular shape, with its peaks, aggression; a curved form, something soothing; etc. It will be clear from this that the interplay of such forms (which is sculpture) will set up complex emotional reactions in us. And our response to the sculpture is the sum of the emotional responses it evokes from us.

The same principle applies in painting.

Colors, too, have inherent emotional values; and our reaction to the interplay of colors in painting produces reactions resembling our responses to sculpture. Wall colors for modern hospitals and other places where emotional tensions have to be given special consideration are carefully planned.

To use the plastic language of sculpture effectively, the artist must be possessed by a vital idea: he must start with "something to say." If the idea is big and urgently demands expression, the corresponding combination of sculptural forms will convey this power and intensity. The artist's plastic language will display a unity marked by simplicity, coherence, and vigor.

INVENTED FORMS

The matter becomes more complex in objectifying an inner reality when the artist *invents* forms outside the conventional patterns. It is this that causes many artists to be misunderstood in their day. Only when the *new form* invented by him becomes conventional does his unique personal concretization of an inner process become intelligible to the public. A further reason for difficulties in understanding is that the personal inner reality from which the urge

FIG. 82. *Statue. Senufo, Ivory Coast. 22″ high.*
SEE PAGES 160, 171

to create originates may be very deeply buried in the artist's unconscious.

THE EXPRESSION OF THE UNCONSCIOUS

The phrase, "The artist must have something to say," should not be understood as calling for anything analogous to a spoken or written statement. Artistic creation is the expression mainly of nonformulated ideas and unconscious feelings—the crystallization of an emotion.

Picasso once told the writer that if he knew, if he were conscious of what he intended to express in his work, he would not have created it. It is the tension of expressing the as yet unknown to him, but astir within his inner self, which drives the creator to action. The existence and importance of the artistic impulse are measurable only by the pressure within the artist and the urgency of the need to free himself of it in the work of art.

This statement does not mean that all the artist has to start with is this vague though pressing need. He will be conscious of a great variety of emotions: enraged protest, a desire for escape, the love for his fellow man, religious fervor, etc. Such emotional concepts fill him to such an extent that the need to express them in a work of art becomes imperative. But often subject matter serves as a vehicle, symbol, or occasion for introducing or concealing the real content: his unconscious feelings; the artist selects among innumerable available subjects the one which he feels can best carry his message. Soutine, for instance, chose gladioli to express his persecution complex; Picasso chose a bull's head to express brutality.

Not every artist, of course, has emotions of equal depth or complexity. Only *vital* artists—those who seek to do more than copy, who are moved to express basic human emotions—will plunge deep into themselves for the material of their art.

The process has certain similarities to

FIG. 83. *Mask. Simo (Boke), French Guinea. 25" high.* SEE PAGE 165

psychoanalysis. The analysand may start with a dream, but more significant are the free associations produced by pursuing the dream symbols. In the same manner, the "subject vehicle" is the artist's starting point, but the rhythm of creation introduces associations through which drives and impulses, hidden in his unconscious, slip into his works. We may say that the artist works with his fingers and the real content *slips* into his work *between* his fingers; just as in slips of the tongue or of the pen repressed truths slip into consciousness.

Much of art is *sublimation*. When the artist is unable to live out deeply rooted desires and drives, they are repressed. They can be permitted entry into consciousness in another, or sublimated, form, which may be the work of art. This sublimation will acquire a figurative, symbolic meaning. In the fantasy of his creation the artist frees himself, at least temporarily, from his conflict. Freudian investigation appears to show that most symbolic creations stem from repressed sex drives.

The African lives in fear; he is the prisoner of taboos; he must repress desires that conflict with the restrictions. He has all the characteristics of a neurotic. The mystery and power of the African artist's work come from the fact that during the rhythm of creation shaped by his animistic beliefs, he projects his unconscious into his work, thus freeing himself from his conflict.

We come now to the question: How can we recognize whether the work of art is a sublimation or a "straight" living-out of the artist's impulses, if such can actually occur?

It is only our own sensitivity that can tell us. From viewing the work of art we can get the excitement, the conflict, the feeling that during the creation something new was discovered by the artist and incorporated into his work.

Whether the point of departure was a sublimation or a direct statement, the sign of a genuine work of art is that it can stir us. This happens only when the artist has succeeded in projecting his excitement, in releasing an inner tension or emotion.

It is because this is rare that great works of art are rare.

INTERPRETATION OF PLASTIC LANGUAGE

The French sculptor Maillol, asked by the writer to explain the intent of a certain piece of sculpture in his studio at Marly, replied that he was more interested in knowing how the interviewer "deciphered" the very difficult language which is sculpture. We know that this deciphering must be done intuitively, through emotional associations. We know also that sometimes the subject hides the real meaning of the work. We know that our own unconscious may provide clues to the real content of the work. We know also that we have to learn how to see, how to open ourselves up, how to make ourselves receptive to forms of the plastic language so that they will speak to us. Only if these conditions are fulfilled shall we have an emotional reaction.

EMOTIONAL CONTENT AND
OUR REACTION TO WORKS OF ART

When we described the peculiarities of the African concept, we pointed out its similarity to our inner psychological make-up. We can experience only those emotions which at bottom are *our own*. We have an inner reserve of emotional experiences with which the work of art will react, permitting our participation, through their re-creation within ourselves, in the experiences which the work expresses. This participation is important in our artistic experience. In such manner we become ourselves the *creator* of the work, within ourselves.

We have produced a *resonance* or **vibration** in our inner selves with the content of the work of art. The participation, or resonance, is an *identification*. This identifica-

FIG. 84. *Steatite figure (Nomori). Mendi, Sierra Leone.* 7" *high.* SEE PAGE 166

tion is, however, possible only because the emotion expressed is one basic to all human beings (often on an unconscious level); and this feeling is not merely individual but *universal*.

FREE ASSOCIATION

The artist often expresses hidden, unconscious feelings, sometimes in a sublimated fashion, as in an uncontrollable, slip-of-the-finger manner. This is true not only for the artist in his creative activity, but for the onlooker in his re-creative activity.

The observer of a work of art, too, will receive initial stimuli; and through *free association* a chain reaction of emotional associations will take place. Past emotional experiences, sometimes on an unconscious level—images of the forgotten past—will erupt within his inner self. The emotions thus evoked will be projected into the work of art. This is "feeling oneself into" the work of art.

EMOTIONAL CONTENT OF AFRICAN SCULPTURE

More specifically we may ask: what are those emotions which are expressed in African sculpture and resonate in us?

First, an expression of the compulsion to unload an intense feeling.

What we feel intensely may be fear or flight from reality; and not only fear and escape into the unreal, but fear of the unknown as well—of the panic and anxiety that can paralyze our faculties. Just as fear elsewhere has created the concept of the protecting God, it may well have created the African statues and masks as objectifications or concretizations of fear. Our own search for communion, a relaxation within a unified faith that relieves us of panic and terror of the unknown and the responsibility of action, might have been the same as the search which produced African sculpture.

It may be that African sculpture awak-

ens some primeval fantasies latent in us since childhood, something connected with our human beginnings, murmurs from an ancestral background, a longing to revert to the primitive and escape from the complexities of civilization, or a response to elemental rhythms felt in all of us. Or the "divine spark" struck off by the impact of the artist's faith may light up depths of our own experience. Or our insight may enable us to see into the working of a creative will.

In the previous paragraph some possibilities of identification or association, all of which on analysis are seen to be elemental human drives, have been indicated. They are not the complicated civilized or intellectual problems of a Rembrandt, a Michelangelo, a Cézanne, or a Picasso. They are ancient impulses and emotions which still live in us, although in a repressed or dormant stage. We recognize their power only when our inability to cope with them produces a neurosis.

The deep significance of African art lies in its incorporation and expression of the emotional states of man at the stage of his awakening as individual. Through them we can rediscover and set in vibration, with an organic, emotional shock, our own dawning impulses as a human being.

It is not important to be conscious of what we feel; it is enough just to feel, to feel with intensity. If we do, we may experience an urge to express these feelings which, unless we can live them out, demand the creativity of an artist. Therefore our real interest in an art work is often that, in our imagination, we re-create or complete the work of art.

We know that African sculpture is religious and its significance for the natives is that they have *faith* in it. Whether they be one or many, the common denominator in the worship of all gods and spirits everywhere is faith. This is the universal constant. It is within us and it can be reached

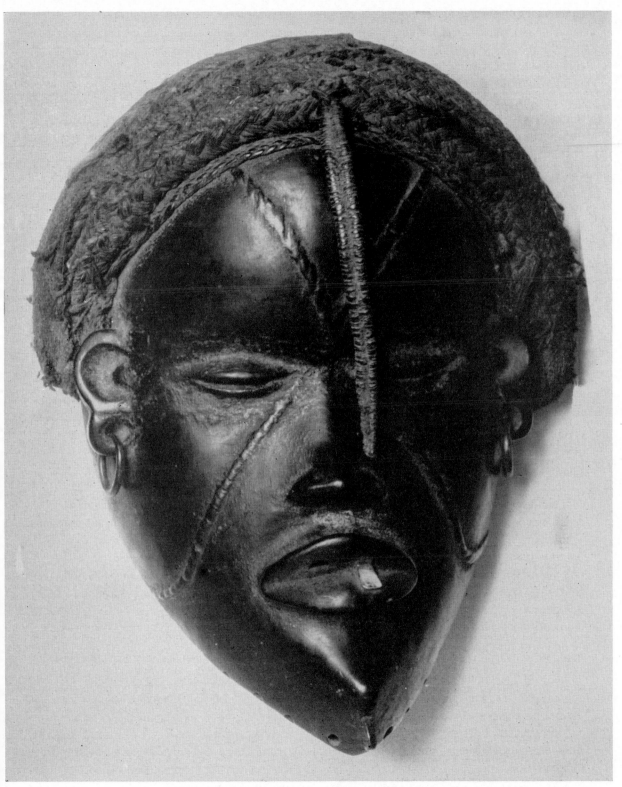

FIG. 85. *Initiation ceremonial mask (Poro Society). Mano, Liberia. 8″ high.* SEE PAGE 167

by a work of art. This is the explanation why works of art, even though they are five thousand years old, still stir us. It is this that assures immortality to genuine works of art of all ages. It is thus that African sculpture becomes our own, as if we might have created it; we relive it on our own terms.

It is a valid question whether or not we respond to the same emotion that the Africans expressed. But knowing the African concept will help us to localize or channel our own reaction. This knowledge will give the observer a direction. After having seen a number of African works he will be able to place his reaction.

Experience has shown that individuals with approximately the same artistic and intellectual background, with a refined inner sensitivity accumulated through experience, have this in common: they have learned how to *see*. They have developed a "code" which organizes their educated reactions in a similar way. Spectators of this type will all find a Braque still life "subdued and poetically calm," a particular Picasso painting "emotionally explosive."

Because African sculpture speaks such a suggestive plastic language, the same standards of inner reaction will apply for those who have learned how to "see." Even where our reactions may differ from others, the important fact is that we have had an emotional reaction. That African sculpture can provoke a multiple and varied reaction is proof of its richness.

AFRICAN AND EUROPEAN ART WORKS

African art at its best is aesthetically comparable to the products of the best periods in the history of art. Where African and Western art differ is in the *level* of their emotional content and in their form of expression.

The greatness of Negro art is that it ex-presses *basic* human emotions—fear, faith, etc.—and may evoke in us the same emotions, though sometimes on a subconscious level.

Western art at its best may also go back to basic compulsions, but the emotional content will be more complex because the inner life of the Western artist is under more control. The artist is less able to "let himself go" and express himself intuitively; he must consult his intellect, must resort to artistic discipline to arrive at artistic creation. In an analogous but simpler process, the African artist submits to the dogmas of the African concept, and to the forms of tribal style.

Although the content of the African work is more direct than the complex work of a Maillol, for instance, yet appreciation of the latter will be easier for the Western art lover. For the plastic language of a Maillol is more *conventional* than the daring, "strange," semi-abstract African forms. We have to overcome a *resistance* against them; we have to forget the naturalistic-conventional-symbolic associations to which we have become accustomed, and take the forms of African art at their intrinsic worth.

But it takes strict concentration to capture the meaning of purely plastic language and thus penetrate to the content of a work of art.

The forms of African art are not symbolic, or descriptive, or comparable to other forms. They are direct, intense statements of the emotions of their creators.

CHART OF CREATION AND PARTICIPATION

As we have seen, the emotional participation of the onlooker in a work of art resembles, and is as complex as, the creation activity of the artist. To summarize this resemblance and simplify its understanding, the reader may find the following chart helpful (page 125).

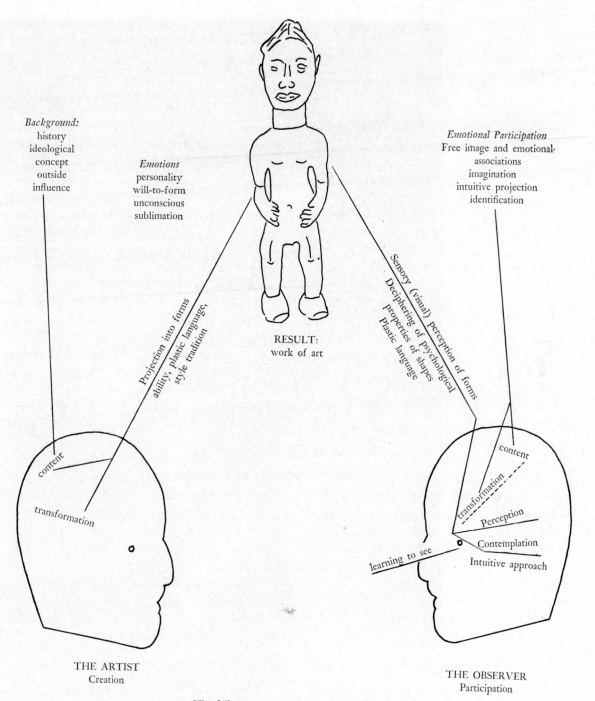

Background:
history
ideological
concept
outside
influence

Emotions
personality
will-to-form
unconscious
sublimation

Emotional Participation
Free image and emotional
associations
imagination
intuitive projection
identification

Projection into forms
ability, plastic language,
style tradition

RESULT:
work of art

Sensory (visual) perception of forms
Deciphering of psychological
properties of shapes
Plastic language

content

transformation

content

transformation

Perception

Contemplation

learning to see

Intuitive approach

THE ARTIST
Creation

THE OBSERVER
Participation

The following general thesis could be indicated:

The Artist	Expression	PRODUCT:	Perception	The Observer
Content:	in forms:	THE WORK	interpretation	Content:
emotional	creation	OF ART	of forms	Emotional
experience				experience

FIG. 86. *Mask. Dan, Ivory Coast. 9" high.* SEE PAGE 171

9. AFRICAN ART AND MODERN EUROPEAN ART

DURING the late nineteenth and early twentieth centuries, so-called "intellectual" circles in Europe, especially in Germany, developed a passion for exotic objects and started indiscriminate collecting of curios. Their interest was neither ethnographic nor aesthetic, but romantic. They were chiefly motivated by flight from reality.

This pull toward the exotic was evident also in late nineteenth-century painting. It was part of the general aesthetic revolt against academicism. We are familiar with the influence of Japanese prints on the impressionists. Gauguin went to Tahiti; Pechstein to the Pelieu Islands; Barlach carved copies of African statues. Exotic objects were also used as subject matter by many German artists, but were treated academically, with little understanding of what they stood for.

Gauguin's and Pechstein's stay in the South Sea Islands enriched their palettes, but their work shows no inward grasp of primitive arts. A more direct influence appears in the work of James Ensor, the Belgian artist, who was inspired by Congo masks. Also, certain masks with a distinctive polychrome design element exhibit characteristics similar to those found in the works of Paul Klee. And although when Klee lived in Munich he had several African masks of this type in his studio, it is by no means certain that these parallels indicate an African inspiration. In neither Ensor nor Klee was there, as yet, any profound contact with the spiritual qualities of African art.

In the early years of this century primitive sculptures, especially from Africa, began to evoke responsive understanding in Western artists.

Cézanne, who was probably unfamiliar with African art, once wrote to his son that what he wanted was to treat nature in terms of cylinders, spheres, and cones, in such a perspective that all sides of the objects would be oriented toward a central point. Cézanne's idea was to decompose the elements of nature into simple forms with which to create a *pictorial architecture*. A painting was to be a construction with simplified forms taken from nature, not a copy of nature.

This, actually, was the approach of the African artist. He made use only of elements of nature (mostly the human body) and created a true *sculptural architecture*.

Cézanne's ideas, as realized in his canvases, were a great inspiration to modern artists. These ideas germinated and reached full bloom in cubism. A further development inspired the creation of abstract art.

When painters like Modigliani, Picasso, Braque, Vlaminck, and the German *Bruecke* and *Blaue Reiter* groups began, about 1907, to collect the works of primitive peoples, mainly African objects, they felt an instinctual affinity with those works.

The French cubists and the German expressionists differed, however, in their approach. The former were concerned with forms; they recognized the architectonic character of African art; they were chiefly interested in *how* the expression took place. The expressionists were attracted toward the emotional content, the *what*, mixing romantic-mystic notions of their own into their interpretation.

Masks similar to the Dan mask from Ivory Coast (Fig. 87) might have been seen by these artists. The anonymous African sculptors, modeling a face, used perfect triangular shapes to indicate nose and cheeks, and formed mouth and chin in cubist planes.

This was at the opposite pole from naturalism. It was cubism in spirit and rendition.

But before analyzing the daring artistic creations of the African and their relationship to modern art, let us examine the reasons why African sculpture was rediscovered as art at that particular time, after having been buried for many years.

THE SPIRIT OF THE AGE

The beginning of the twentieth century was a period of insurgence. Artists were open-minded and disposed to accept new ideas. The École de Paris united artists of different nationalities: the Spaniards Picasso, Gris, Miro, Picabia, Gargallo, Dali, etc.; the Russians Chagall, Zadkine, Kandinsky, and the Lithuanian Soutine; the Poles Lipchitz, Kisling, etc.; the Italians Modigliani, Chirico, de Pisis, Severini, and others; the Dutch Mondrian and Van Dongen; the Romanian Brancusi; the German Ernst; the Bulgarian Pascin; the Swiss Klee. All contributed to the most vital art movement of the century. And such was the public's participation that more contemporary art was bought than in any previous period in the history of art.

The French, traditionally conservative, accepted these artists because this was the period of search, of renovation, mixing and amalgamation of new ideas and artistic styles. This spirit made them welcome the anonymous African artist into the family of the École de Paris; and his contribution was merged into the dynamic art forms of this creative evolution.

FORMALISTIC "INFLUENCE"

Little attention has been paid heretofore to what actually happened in this contact between modern artists and African art. Because certain simplifications similar to those of African art appeared in a few of Picasso's paintings, this was described as "African influence."

It was the Grenoble Museum which first had the daring and the imagination to show African art side by side with modern art. The Museum of Modern Art in New York exhibited Negro sculpture in their show "Cubism and Abstract Art" in 1936; and was followed by the Institute of Contemporary Art in Boston in 1939, in its exhibition "The Sources of Modern Painting." In 1948, the Institute of Contemporary Arts in London organized a comparative exhibition entitled "40,000 Years of Modern Art."

If African sculpture is placed next to cubistic paintings, an obvious formal affinity appears. But it would be misleading to imply that the very profound effect of African art is limited to such accidental similarity of forms.

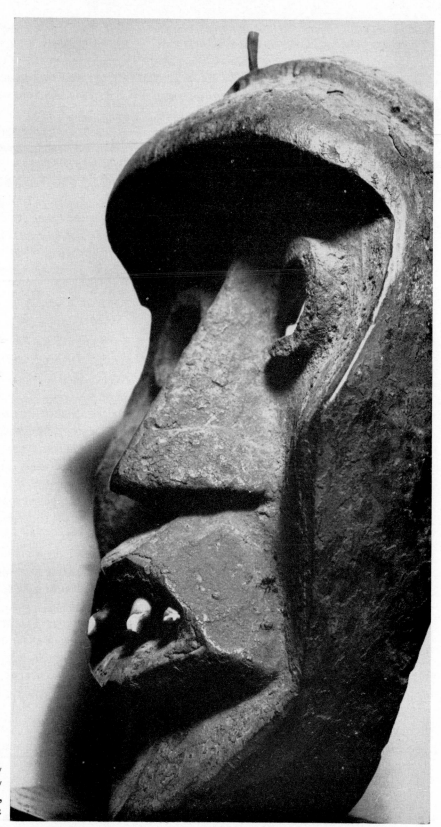

FIG. 87. *Initiation ceremony
mask. Dan-Guere, Ivory
Coast. 8" high.* SEE PAGES 169,
172

It was the *spirit* of that African sculpture, its content, its inner drive, which was captured by the modern artists. The fact that they collected African sculptures meant that these moderns lived with them sufficiently to absorb the sculptures' radiance, and not merely to "borrow" forms. They did not divide the form from the content, any more than the human body can be separated from the mind. It was an "influence," if one wishes to use the word; but an influence of the *content* which was first digested in its essence by the artists, and then re-created by them.

THE INNER CONTACT

The artists, naturally, considered African sculptures only as works of art and not as ethnological objects. They felt that, by its very presence, African sculpture had an existence in space, independent of conventional comparisons. The sculpture had validity not because it did look like, but because it did *not* look like, an object or model known to us. It was *itself*, a creation in a sculptural medium. This was the very essence of what the cubist painters were aiming at. Picasso defined cubism as an art dealing primarily with forms; when the form is realized, it is there *to live its own life*.

Both the African and cubist works existed through their own invented and co-ordinated forms, used for their own meaning and not to copy natural objects. The resulting interplay of forms (the sculpture) had its own inner life. By "invented" we mean that each form was something new, never seen before, something particular to the artist, his own. If the forms were new, never seen before; if their interplay was new, the results also became new. The work of art had a new existence.

There are different realities; one we can see, another we can feel, and still another —the inner life of an art creation. The fact that it carries a message of the artist makes this reality the more exciting. But without the suggestive power of the plastic coordination we could not perceive what the artist wanted to convey.

Unlike the signs in other languages, there is no general agreement on the meanings of signs in the language of art. Yet each has its strong, suggestive power for us to feel and grasp.

The discovery that each artistic object can have its own plastic and emotional reality helped the understanding of African art. It also helps to explain why we admire, why we can "feel" African art products. This discovery brought a new influence into modern art.

AFFINITY OF IDEAS

First: We have to recall here that the transformation of natural forms into abstract forms is a symptomatic action of man's basic unconscious compulsion; his self-assertion, his drive for power; his revolt against and control over natural forces. Since, on basic human issues and compulsions, there is no difference between primitive man and civilized man, the same psychological compulsion is behind the endeavors of the modern artists to abstract nature.

The "will-to-form," the desire to express a personal experience, to search for individual truth, and to create imaginative, inventive works motivated modern art to a much larger extent than African art. Because this age is dominated by the cult of the individual, all art activity, with full cognizance of the role of the unconscious impulses, became a glorification of individuality.

The creative will-to-form has another dramatic significance today in the age of anxiety. The will to assert oneself, to invent new forms, is an unconscious reaction to the fear of life; it seeks to prove, to justify one's own presence and existence in the world.

FIG. 88. *Mask. Senufo, Ivory Coast. 11″ high.* SEE PAGE 171

The aspect of *doubt of reality* should here be emphasized. If the African questioned reality, so did the modern artist. Their respective points of departure, however, were different. This was the time of Freud, who introduced a new concept to evaluate human behavior; of the Curies, who produced new values in terms of the elements; of Einstein, whose theory of relativity revolutionized our viewpoint of the universe; it was the time when prophecies of changes were confirmed by world wars and revolutions. All this was reflected in art. The artist's doubts were translated into cubistic painting. A bottle (representing reality) was decomposed into parts which lost their identity with the bottle, were used by the artist as new elements in paintings that became a new reality, the product of the artist's invention. Later, in this inventive creative process, forms were no longer borrowed from naturalistic reality, but were purely the products of the artist's imagination. The result was independent, abstract works of art.

Second: Throughout history, artists of great personality and imagination have reacted against the prevailing schools. Giotto freed himself from the rigidity of Byzantine art; El Greco invented pure designs in revolt against Renaissance formalism; the Impressionists revolted against the classicism of David; the *Fauves* (literally "Wild Beasts") rebelled against the established patterns of Impressionism, "inventing" realities by the use of bold, unnaturalistic colors and brush strokes.

Our modern artists have carried this process further. In addition to the revolt against the accepted, conventional art styles, they have sought expression of the *inner self;* not only liberation from conventional art forms, but from inhibitions as well. This search coincided with the recognition of the fact that African artists had already produced works in such complete freedom.

Third: Modern art, like African art, seeks to "express" an idea or an emotion instead of "perfecting" the medium through which this expression takes place. The African has the same urgency of expression as the modern. In his case, too, the object, or the subject matter, is only a vehicle for the idea. Cézanne said that the subject is only a pretext for expressing a sensation or a vision.

Fourth: The African and the modern artist both aim to express a conceptual image, instead of a visual image.

Fifth: Modern artists abandoned representational ideas or symbolic imagery for direct statement. The work of their art seeks to be *itself*, to move us directly, rather than merely to *look like* something. From this aim of avoiding conventional associations comes the invention of abstract forms.

In the case of the African, his belief that an inanimate object has life (animism) is comparable to the modern artist's determination to produce art that has an existence of its own. The painting is achieved, said Picasso, when it is there "to live its own life."

Thus we can see that the creations of both the African and the modern artists were a logical outcome of viewpoints and volitions differing from each other but reducible to common denominators. The criterion for the moderns was whether or not the work was a genuine expression of the artist's personality. The painting became *organic* with the inner self of the artist, just as African sculpture was a functional expression of the African concept. To the African, a piece of sculpture was "good" or "bad" depending on whether it was effective or not. Effective meant, to the African, whether it gave results in his magical rites. The idea of beauty or ugliness in sculpture did not occur to him. This led to a disregard of any forms except those essential to carry the message. This also characterized modern art and led, in both cases, to exaggeration, with unnatu-

FIG. 89. *Mask. Dan, Ivory Coast. 10″ high.* SEE PAGE 171

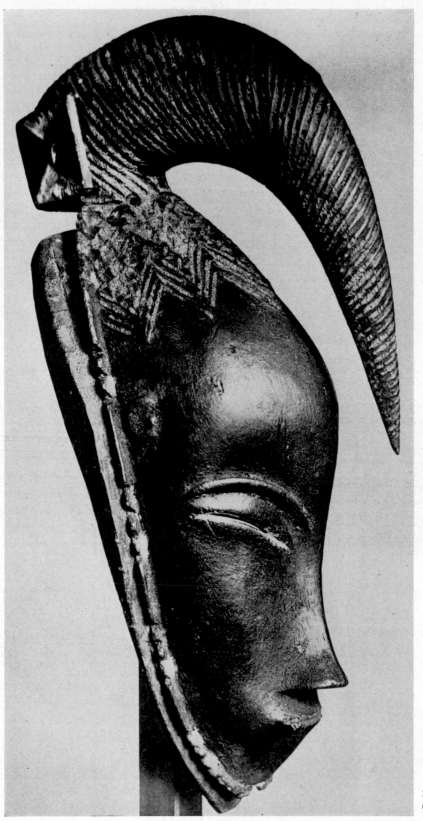

FIG. 90. *Mask. Guro, Ivory Coast. 9″ high.* SEE PAGE 172

ralistic forms developing into abstract forms.

The real meeting ground, however, between African art and the moderns is on a deep emotional level. It must be emphasized that the influence which modern art derived from African art, whatever its extent, was more subtle than a mere copying or adaptation of African forms. The points of contact were the mutual inner compulsions. As Cézanne said, "the realization of the sensations" was the problem, and here the African showed examples of complete plastic integration. Because of the similarity of artistic directions of the African and the European artists, *independently of each other*, the writer believes that this period of modern art should be seen as the coincidental meeting of two directions, rather than as a time when Western art fell under African "influence."

Considering the unconscious to be the real source of inspiration, some modern artists practiced "automatic drawing" (drawing with closed eyes). Other artists, experimenting in direct, spontaneous expression, sought other ways to exclude intellectual control and create from "soul to hand" or "from unconscious to conscious action."

It is understood that only the intent is indicated by the expression "soul to hand," for the intellect could not be excluded. The African was disciplined by his tradition and his unconscious compulsions, yet in direct expression of primary emotions he had the advantage of living in them. They constituted his habitual level of feeling and acting. And he had the added advantage of *not* being self-conscious about being an artist.

The modern creative artist, on the other hand, is conscious of being an artist. He has to overcome this self-consciousness to produce a state of mind in which he will be free to "let himself go." He must use an intellectual effort not to be intellectual. To overcome this handicap, he has to produce such an intensity of emotion or conviction

that the urgency to express it will "blind" him and force him to disregard (or rather overcome) imbedded, established tradition.

From the viewpoint of the public to whom the work of art is addressed, the African artist used traditional symbolic forms, simplified abstractions known to all the natives. Thus the meaning of his work was clear. His audience shared the same background and beliefs. The forms were not created for aesthetic quality, but for direct emotional communication. Because emotion was felt deeply and communicated directly, it proved aesthetically acceptable everywhere.

In contrast, the contemporary Western artist is too much of an individualist, being the product of his atomistic time, as the African was the product of a communal ideology. The Western artist's "abstract language" is his own, and often alien to his public. This is why the interpretation of a modern abstraction varies with each beholder. In Africa, artist and audience are in rapport. The outlook of the artist and that of his public is the same.

There is a difference, too, in the basic intent, the need to create, of the African and the modern Western artist. The latter seeks new forms and artistic values as a *revolt* against tradition, while the African artist is in accord with his tradition.

The need to change, the drama of "becoming," to quote Bergson, is felt in all modern art. But, at the same time, there is perceptible a struggle to be one with the product, to make it integrally, organically, an expression of the artist. In this, however, he was too often handicapped by the emphasis on "individuality" and by the intellect that could not be excluded from his work, which often reflected theories and "isms."

With the greatest ease the African artist "arrived" at a realization which radiates serenity. He was able to reduce a multitude of complex feelings, fears, and dogmatic or

FIG. 92. *Mother and child. Yoruba, Brit[*
Nigeria. 20″ high. SEE PAGE ▮

FIG. 91. *Mother and child. Yoruba, British*
Nigeria. 15″ high. SEE PAGE 177

stylistic limitations into a synthesis exhibiting a nirvanal calmness and fulfillment.

When an idea or emotion projected under uniform social conditions has been so universally accepted and imbedded in the soul of a people for a long time, it can be realized aesthetically with an astonishing unity of form. A similar fulfillment was seen in Egyptian, Greek, and Romanesque art. The Cathedral of Chartres is a magnificent work, produced by several generations and for many thousands of individuals. Yet it shows a unified style and radiates a sober dignity.

If we knew nothing of the history of any of those people, if we were to excavate their works out of the earth, we would at once be struck by their tremendous unity and we would conclude that that particular period must have had an all-embracing unity of idea. If, after a thousand years, works of art of our period were to be unearthed, our descendants would be struck by their difference; their common denominator would be their *lack of unity*.

Our time lacks religious unification. And no compensating overall spiritual idea has appeared. Modern man and the modern artist have failed to create a synthesis or unification of their problems. In our "age of anxiety," with each individual artist seeking to express his own multitude of problems, we can find no counterparts of the "conclusions" of African art.

But the aim, the search for expression, was the same. And here they met.

FIG. 93. *Animal mask.*
Bamum, Cameroon.
10" high.
SEE PAGE 184

FIG. 94. *Bronze cock. Bini, Benin Kingdom, British Nigeria. 8″ high.* SEE PAGES 145, 181

10. THE COLLECTOR'S POINT OF VIEW

Ethnological museums (or museums of natural history) collect African objects to illustrate the life of particular ethnic groups. The art collector's viewpoint is aesthetic. Most collectors of African art are drawn to it by its similarity of feeling to modern art. Additions to their collections are sought in order to renew the emotional experience of the first acquisition. They seek in it aesthetic and emotional satisfactions.

The collector's interest grows as his knowledge of African art develops, and he is soon eager to form a comprehensive and representative collection. In a short time he becomes aware of the rarity of certain objects. He learns that Ife heads have become virtually unobtainable; that the Benin ivory tusk is more unusual than the Benin bell, a Warega ivory mask less common than a Warega ivory statue, a Pangwe head rarer than a Pangwe full figure; that there is a greater variety of Dan masks in other styles than in the cubist style from Liberia; and so on.

Those collectors who content themselves with a few pieces as shelf ornaments or other decor use them for their astonishing harmony with modern paintings, furniture, and interiors.

The largest collections are in the museums. In Europe many of these collections have been assembled for the study of the use of African sculptures in the dance, religion, magic, medicine, and psychology. Of course, not all of these objects satisfy aesthetic standards; not all were used in religious rites or produced by carvers of talent.

AGE OF AFRICAN SCULPTURES

It is probable that, from the beginning of their occupation of West Africa, the Negroes there have carved sculpture for their religious rites. Documents of the fifteenth and sixteenth centuries mention their idols.

In only a few instances can we set the date of African objects. The Ife terra-cotta and bronze heads and the Benin bronzes and ivory sculptures can be safely dated from the fifteenth century on. We can date the famous Bushongo king statues to the reign of Shamba Bolongongo (the ninety-third *Nyimi*, or sovereign of divine origin), around 1600, who instituted the custom of

FIG. 95. *Bronze figure. Bini, Benin*
Kingdom, British Nigeria. 14″ high.
SEE PAGES 145, 181

FIG. 96. *Ivory pendant mask. Bini, Benin Kingdom, British Nigeria. 9½″ high.* SEE PAGES 145, 181

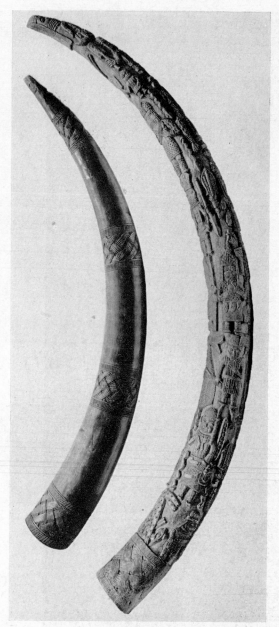

FIG. 97. *Ivory tusks. Bini, Benin Kingdom, British Nigeria. 48" high.* SEE PAGES 145, 181

Other objects may be three to four hundred years old; but there are no data to guide us.

The majority of African wood carvings are not older than one hundred fifty years. Moist heat and termites and other insects have destroyed the wood of which most were made.

Furthermore, objects were protected only as long as they were used. Having fulfilled a certain function, they were discarded or destroyed. A magic statue that failed to "give results" was destroyed. We have reports of statues burned on pyres; and the traditions of certain secret societies called for the destruction of masks after their use.

The destruction of what must have amounted to millions of sculptural objects is a great loss. Yet this very fact must have contributed to the dynamic quality of the work, to the continuity of a strong sculptural tradition, and to the honorable and socially integrated role of the sculptor, for whose work there was a constant demand, since the destroyed work was continually being replaced.

Although we cannot date the sculptures, we may safely make a distinction between objects produced *before* and *since* the European penetration of Africa. The *Pre-European Period* is the intensely religious period, when refined tools were missing, when outside influence had not yet corrupted the vision of the African.

The *Post-European Period* is marked, on the one hand, by the loosening of the deep belief in the power of the spirits. The missionaries warred upon the animistic cults. While the native concept still flourishes in many regions, new social conditions, including certain features of industrialism, are eroding the old way of life, and the African's religio-magical faith is losing its intensity.

European influence was strongest in the coastal regions, where art activity was very high. Consequently, the isolation necessary

carving a wooden image of the ruler (Fig. 2). We know of seventeen such king statues, of which twelve can be dated and identified. The survival of the Ife and Benin objects is due to their material, which was not wood but bronze, pottery, and ivory. The wooden Bushongo king statues survived because they were preserved in the palace.

FIG. 98. *Ivory leopard. Bini, Benin Kingdom, British Nigeria. 33″ high.* SEE PAGES 145, 181

FIG. 99. *Ivory double gong. Bini, Benin Kingdom, British Nigeria. 14" high.* SEE PAGES 145, 181

for the continuity of the African art tradition was impossible to maintain. Finally, appreciation of this type of art has become quite undiscriminating. Virtual sweatshops have been set up in Africa to produce wood sculptures for the tourist trade.

Some governmental agencies have established schools to encourage the native handicrafts, but they have concentrated on objects of decorative use. Because the former emotional content is lacking, these objects

are lifeless. In Nigeria, a well-known native sculptor was engaged to teach in one of the schools. It was not long after he became an "artist" that his work declined to the level of the tourist-trade objects.

PRESENT-DAY PRODUCTION

Most present-day production can be classified as:

(1.) Useful decorative objects for the tourist trade: bookends, ashtrays, bowls, animal figures, small statuettes, ivory letter openers, etc. (2.) Copies of traditional masks and sculptures. (3.) New creations.

The useful objects are generally of good execution, applied art forms without aesthetic pretense. Between masks and statues in the traditional style a distinction must be made. There are regions where the secret societies maintain a strong foothold, as in the Liberian hinterland, and the masks used there are of great artistic merit. Elsewhere, particularly among the Northeast Yorubas, the Ibibios and Ijaws of Nigeria, the Baules and Guros of the Ivory Coast, and the Dogons of Sudan, very talented carvers continue the tradition, and their work is of excellent quality. Here it is the talent of the individual sculptor that counts, and the works are to be judged in that sense. But work done under European influence is extremely ugly—figures in European garb, painted with commercial colors, with hats, sticks, or guns in their hands, etc.

Concerning contemporary copies of objects of traditional designs, we have a first-hand account from Himmelheber, who interviewed some native sculptors on the Ivory Coast in 1933. Now, he said, they carve to make money. They seek to become famous because this will bring higher prices. They consider carving hard work (harder than agricultural labor) because it demands thinking. They feel no pleasure in the act of creation. They win their place by training rather than by talent. They copy old models over and over.

But it is still the magician who prescribes the fetish for the client, and the image is still intended for magic use; certain woods are still avoided because their spirits are evil; other woods are still preferred as enhancing the power of the statue; a cock is killed to consecrate an object, etc.

About the present-day condition, the anthropologist Herskovits reports that to obtain a sculpture in Dahomey required the following procedure: the collector had to propose an exchange to the owner, who then consulted the diviner. If the auspices were favorable, the woodcarver was commissioned to make a copy. A sacrifice was offered at the shrine when the old image was removed and again when the new one was installed. The collector paid all the costs plus a gift to compensate the owner.

The old objects have been collected for the past century by different expeditions. Even at the beginning these perishable statues were few, and it is now extremely difficult to find genuine old pieces.

RARITY OF ANTIQUE PIECES

It is true that certain expeditions undertaken in the last ten years were still able to uncover, in the hinterland, a small number of ancient objects. But their very limited number and the high cost of procuring them means that the African source is exhausted. The French, British, and Belgian African governmental agencies have recognized this fact and have prohibited exportation of objects considered antique.

In Nigeria, where the Benin bronzes originated, only about fifty pieces exist in the State Museum in Benin City, compared to the approximately three thousand pieces in Europe and America. Felix von Luschan, in a book published in 1919, listed two thousand four hundred pieces, mostly in museums. Two plates lately exhibited here in the African city of Lagos had been bought in London. The Nigerian Government has appropriated £25,000 for the purchase of Benin bronzes in Europe, to be brought back to Nigeria.

BENIN BRONZES

No African art objects have undergone as thorough an investigation and study as the Benin bronzes. Major works (see Bibliography) have been devoted to them, describing the method of casting, chasing, use, nomenclature, and periods of production, and analyzing the form.

From a collector's viewpoint, the best objects are of the *High Period* (1500–1575). They are of complex construction with elaborate chasing and a warm greenish, reddish, or dull-black patina. In objects of the *Declining Period* (1691–1819) the

FIG. 100. *Ivory figure. Bini, Benin Kingdom, British Nigeria. 8" high.* SEE PAGE 181

FIG. 101. *Bronze head. Bini, Benin Kingdom, British Nigeria. 11″ high.* SEE PAGES 145, 181

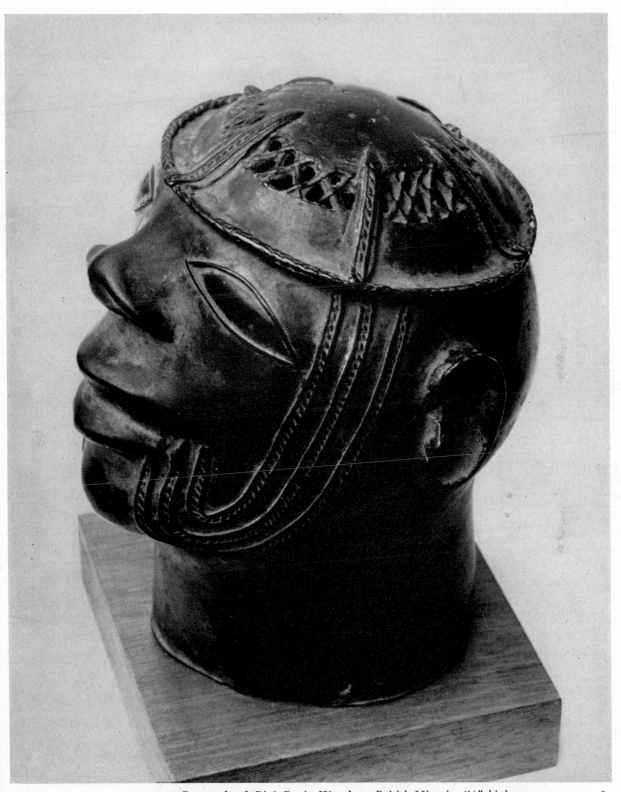

FIG. 102. *Bronze head. Bini, Benin Kingdom, British Nigeria. 6½″ high.* SEE PAGES 145, 181

FIG. 103. *Bronze head. Bini, Benin Kingdom, British Nigeria. 14" high.* SEE PAGES 145, 181

more conventionalized heads larger than life, adorned with necklaces of broad, cylindrical pearls (Fig. 103); large elephant tusk holders ornamented with numerous figures; branched, so-called "fetish trees"; plaques with bas reliefs of groups of natives (Fig. 104); warriors, hunters or dignitaries (Fig. 109) etc.; plaques with single figures (warriors, dignitaries, musicians, Europeans, messengers etc.); ritual plaques; animals and animal heads (fishes, birds, snakes, crocodiles, panthers) (Fig. 77); and other large pieces. Smaller objects include figurines, often in groups; small animals (Fig. 105); ceremonial maces; pendants with figures (Fig. 106); small masks worn as buckles or other dress accessories; bracelets and armlets (Fig. 107); bells (Fig. 108), vases, wood heads, boxes, carved coconut shells, etc. (See also p. 181.)

THE VALUE OF AFRICAN SCULPTURES

In spite of the high artistic quality of African objects and their place as products of a virtually ended creative period, their market value is not high as compared, for example, to Egyptian sculpture. Thus far, only a minority of highly developed connoisseurs are aware of the intrinsic beauty, power, and rarity of African art. The available objects can therefore be purchased at comparatively reasonable prices.

Art auctions show that objects of good quality range in price from $150 to $500. Extremely rare sculpture may cost over $1000. The Benin bronzes, of which there is still a limited number on the market, may go above $1000.

HOW TO RECOGNIZE THE STYLE OF AN OBJECT

After having seen a large number of sculptures the collector will recognize certain stylistic marks (described in the Appendix). The beginner will find books on African art helpful when he compares the object with illustrations and identifications given in their pages. Similar comparative

execution is rough, often without chasing or with the chasing rudimentary. These still have the traditional spirit, but the work has lost the strong yet sophisticated and refined execution of the High Period.

In order of rarity of Benin sculptures, come large figures of dwarfs in the round; bronze figures (Fig. 95); richly carved ivory panthers (Fig. 98); ivory tusks (Fig. 97); ivory masks (Fig. 96); ivory rattles (Fig. 99); also ivory figures (Fig. 100), goblets, and armlets; large bronze figures of flute players, dignitaries, etc. in the round; animals (panthers, roosters) (Fig. 94); portrait-like, life-size heads (Figs. 101 and 102);

FIG. 104. *Bronze plaque (warriors). Bini, Benin Kingdom, British Nigeria. 17″ high.* SEE PAGES 145, 181

FIG. 105. *Bronze bird. Bini, Benin Kingdom, British Nigeria. 5" high.* SEE PAGES 145, 181

FIG. 106. *Bronze pendant. Bini, Benin Kingdom, British Nigeria. 7" high.* SEE PAGES 145, 181

study can be made with objects in museums and private collections. The sculptured forms differ according to the style regions. For example, the Pangwes favored round, refined, smooth shapes; the Bayakas' taste was more rugged.

Although objects from the same tribe are in the same style, the sculptor's individual touch makes each object a unique piece. In the very same style of mask, for instance, the interplay of different volumes will produce a different facial expression; each will radiate a slightly different mood or attitude.

Few sculptures are pure in style—that is, few conform to the established characteristics of a particular style region. Most objects are of a mixed style. In some cases the mixture is the result of migration into a new style region or the influence of a neighbor tribe with a strongly marked style. Thus the statues of some Batshioko tribes settled in Bakuba country show the intense Batshioko facial expression and headdress, while

the body is in the Bakuba style. Also, as tribal tradition slackened, the carver introduced individual innovations to produce a "hybrid" style.

In the mixed or hybrid examples, the loss of classical style sometimes so weakens the carving that it is utterly without character. In others the traditional style, exaggerated to very bold forms, gained an added "character" of its own. Such statues and masks, by their bold abstract quality, can be very exciting to Westerners (Fig. 19).

In estimating the collector-value of an African sculpture, purity of style will carry greater weight with those who look for classical work; boldness of style, with those who look for carvings close to modern art.

HOW TO RECOGNIZE A GENUINE OLD CARVING

First, an antique carving can be recognized by its artistic unity, apart from purity of style. Artistic unity is a universal quality of good art. The artistic sensitivity of the collector will tell him immediately whether

FIG. 107. *Bronze armlet. Bini, Benin Kingdom, British Nigeria. 5" high.* SEE PAGES 145, 181

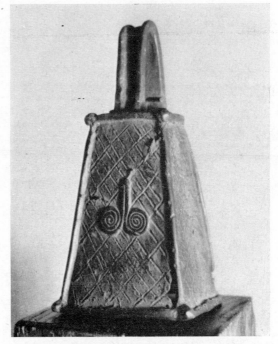

FIG. 108. *Bronze bell. Bini, Benin Kingdom, British Nigeria. 5" high.* SEE PAGES 145, 181

or not an object has it, by its power to stir him. That indicates whether the coordination of the inner emotional tension has been expressed forcefully. Mrs. Esther Warner commented on her impressions of a sculpture she saw in Africa: "I felt infected with its implications, as though the emotions of the carver were readily contagious. I had 'caught' them by looking and running my fingertips over his work." This quality is self-evident in a genuine piece.

Other criteria are technical, such as *the condition of the wood*. Many old pieces are damaged, some by termites, some by rotting or splitting through exposure. The wood is mostly white, occasionally brown; it is never ebony, which has only lately been used in Nigeria and only for the tourist trade. The white wood is generally stained black, to adhere to tribal tradition.

A mask used only once in an initiation ceremony and cast aside suffered quick deterioration. However, if it was picked up by an explorer in time and brought to Europe, it may be in perfect condition to-

day. Objects used inside the house (such as family ancestor statues) or cherished by the tribe for their artistic quality, as among the Bakubas and Baules, were frequently protected against humidity with beeswax and are well-preserved.

Edges are worn smooth in the old pieces and the interflow of the shapes contributes to their unity. Incisions have been almost obliterated by wear or filled in by earth, or the magical substances smeared over the surface. If holes were used on the masks (to attach them to raffia cloth), these are often not round (drilled), but have been gouged out. The rubbing of the raffia cords may also have affected their shape.

COLOR AND PATINA

Most statues are split because the sculptor avoids seasoned wood, the green wood being easier to carve. The statue splits on drying. To prevent this, the sculpture in some regions is smeared with sesame oil, palm oil, or butter. In the Sudan, the statue is often finished with a hot iron to give it

FIG. 109. *Bronze plaque (Oba of Benin). Bini, Benin Kingdom, British Nigeria. 18" high.* SEE PAGES 145, 181

brownish tint through use. Some Pangwe figures treated with a certain dressing appear oily, and "sweat" under certain climatic conditions. Ivory fetishes or masks acquire a brownish-red patina from contact with the body. The carving and incisions are worn away, leaving a very smooth surface.

Polychrome objects carry layers of vegetable and earth colors, having been repainted each time they were used. The cracked paint has left an uneven surface. On recent objects with only one layer the color is uniform, and often of imported ready-made oil paints. Despite the evenness of the surface, the effects are usually inartistic.

PRESERVATION OF OBJECTS

Many objects are split. If the crack is small, it could be left as it is. If it is large, it may be advisable to plug it with a wood inset cut to fit exactly.

Termites, wood worms, or beetles may still be in the wood. They can be traced by the white wood dust that appears from time to time around the little holes that mark their burrows. Drops of carbon bisulphide in each hole will dispose of them. If not checked, the insects will destroy the sculpture.

The ritual use of the sculpture led to an accumulation of substances which often contribute to the surface texture and appearance but sometimes mar it. This is especially true when sacrificial blood has been poured over the object. When mixed with earth, this blood coats the sculpture with a heavy layer. In such cases, we face the object as a restorer faces a discolored oil painting or a damaged faience. Extreme discrimination should be used to decide how much of the earth-and-dust layer should be removed. Complete removal would give a "new" look that would spoil the effect. Judicious cleaning will restore the original beauty of the piece with no in-

a slightly carbonized surface, which later is colored and acquires a patina through use.

The color is always vegetable or earth color, often mixed with magical substance or sacrificial blood. Sometimes latex or gum is added to this mixture. As in the carving, the application of the color to the sculpture is accompanied by ceremonies to insure its magical efficiency.

Subsequently, the statue is exposed to dust, earth, and the smoke of the hut in which it is stored. These overlay the original color and produce an inimitable patina that has the uneven warm tone of bronze.

Some masks and fetishes have a glossy surface because a wax substance has been added to the color which, when rubbed, polishes to a lacquer-like finish. Vandenhoute mentions the "mud bath" technique used by the Dan tribe, which consisted of burying the mask in a mud substance that contained color. Where sculptures have not been colored, the wood, especially when hard, may acquire a high polish and a warm

ASHANTI.

Figures of cast brass; given by
Major F.S.Parry,1876,A.W.Franks,Esq.,1882,
Capt.F.C.T.Ewald & Rev.G.Pole-Carew, 1909.

FIG. 110. *Gold weights (brass). Ashanti, Gold Coast.* SEE PAGE 173

jury to the patina of age and use. This viewpoint guided the cleaning of Benin objects found on the Juju altars in Benin City, which had become unrecognizable under layers of coagulated sacrificial blood and earth.

No wax, varnish, or polishing material should be used, for this would destroy the patina. Metal-plated or bronze objects, particularly, should not be washed or polished, for their patinas (green, black, red, etc.) are a part of the quality of the object.

It is advisable to mount objects on stands. This makes for more effective display and for greater safety. Masks are often mounted on walls, but mounting them on stands is preferable. By presenting them as statues we come a little closer to their use as part of a costume. Another advantage is that they can then be turned around or viewed from different angles, allowing the many facets and the three-dimensional quality and richness of forms to emerge. Similarly, Benin plates should be nailed directly on the wall, as was done originally in Benin City.

EXHIBITIONS OF AFRICAN ART

Private ethnological collections of African sculpture began in Germany. The first collections as *art* began in France about forty years ago. This was followed in Belgium, England, Holland, and again in Germany.

In the United States, the first exhibition of African art was held in 1914 in Alfred Stieglitz' Gallery "291"; in 1916 Marius de Zayas organized a show in the Modern Gallery and published what was probably the first book in America on African art. In 1922 the Brummer Gallery, and in 1927 the J. B. Neumann Gallery, held special exhibitions on African art.

Many art museums, which are supposed to include the art of *all* ages and cultures, are without African collections. Chaldean, Hittite, Luristan or Egyptian sculptures are represented, but no Benin or Bakuba examples are shown. This is true also of products of such high cultures as the Maya, Zapotec, or Nahua periods of Mexico and Central America. These, along with African sculpture, suffer from the antiquated notion that their chief interest is ethnological.

This anachronism is disappearing as special exhibits of African sculptures in art museums become more common. In this country such showings began with an exhibit at the Brooklyn Museum in 1923, others at the Cleveland Museum of Art in 1929 and the Detroit Institute of Arts in 1930. Exhibitions followed in the Fogg Art Museum in Cambridge in 1934, at the Museum of Modern Art in New York in 1935, at the University of Minnesota in 1940, at the Baltimore Museum of Art in 1946, and at the De Young Memorial Museum in San Francisco in 1948.

Some art museums, however, continue to ignore African art. Because today no new production in Africa compares in quality with antique works, the available objects are limited to those assembled in the last forty to fifty years in private collections in Europe and the United States. The first large private collection in the United States was formed by the late Dr. Albert Barnes in Merion, Pennsylvania. Dr. Barnes found "African sculptures . . . equal in artistic value to the great Greek, Egyptian, or Chinese sculptures, and as difficult to obtain."

The last five years have witnessed an upsurge of interest in African art. Not only museums and educational institutions, but increasing numbers of private collectors as well, have formed collections. They have opened new vistas of art experience with an unlimited range of emotional responses.

APPENDIX: STYLE REGIONS

BIBLIOGRAPHY

LIST OF ILLUSTRATIONS

INDEX

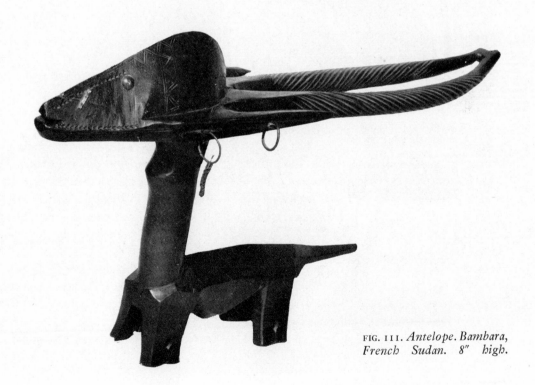

FIG. III. *Antelope. Bambara, French Sudan. 8" high.*

FIG. 112. *Initiation ceremony mask (Maji). Ibo, British Nigeria. 19"high.* SEE PAGE 177

APPENDIX: STYLE REGIONS

Assembling a "dictionary" of West African style regions is a difficult task. In the Belgian Congo alone there are over a hundred tribes, many with individual styles. A complete list would probably involve a nomenclature of a thousand tribes.

The ideal would be to use illustrations pointing out the special characteristics of each style, and the varied uses of the objects illustrated. We can only attempt here to list and describe the best-known, and to use as many illustrations as the scope of this book permits.

TERRITORIES

Although the arts of East and South Africa are related to those of West Africa, we have limited our scope to the latter, because of its predominant Negro population, its unity, and the abundance of its art activities.

Proceeding from north to south on the West Coast of Africa, we find the following countries:

French Sudan
Portuguese Guinea
French Guinea
Sierra Leone
Liberia
Ivory Coast
Gold Coast
Togo (or Togoland)

Dahomey
Nigeria
Cameroon
French Equatorial Africa
Belgian Congo and Angola

It should be noted that these boundaries were established by the European conquerors in complete disregard of tribal frontiers.

To this handicap in identifying a style region is added the fact that some tribes are found in several geographical areas. Before the European conquests the tribes were in continual movement. Overpopulation, or the search for water and salt, produced continual migrations. Each tribe carried its own stylistic tradition into the new location, where it influenced and was influenced by local traditions. Only in the case of a mass migration, or when the tribe occupied a new, uninhabited territory, did it conserve its own tradition intact.

Thus we find the Dan tribe both on the Ivory Coast and in Liberia; the Senufos both on the Ivory Coast and in the Sudan; the Yorubas in Nigeria, Dahomey, Togo and on the Gold Coast; the Pangwes, in Gabon and in Cameroon; the Ashantis, both on the Gold Coast and in Dahomey, etc.*

* English, French, and German usage differs in the transliteration of tribal names. Preference has been given here to the English forms except in the case of the Belgian Congo, where we have adhered to the spellings established by the *Musée du Congo Belge*, Tervuren.

FRENCH SUDAN

BAMBARA

Ancestor and fecundity *statues* in geometric shapes. Angular contours; facial expression severe; a superstructure like a crest, delicately carved, often descending on both sides of the head; arms held away from the body; scarification marks frequently cover entire statue (Fig. 59). Also statues to protect the child (Fig. 113).

Horned *masks* (Fig. 114) (often with several horns). Some surmounted by a human figure or an antelope (Fig. 60); some decorated with cowrie shells (Fig. 62).

Stylized antelopes showing great inventiveness and artistic merit; the body sometimes small in proportion to the large and intricate horns (Fig. 49). These headgears are called Tchi-Ouara (also Tji-'Wara) and symbolize Dadje and Songoni (the great and small antelopes). They were worn as ceremonial headdress called Songoni-Kun, in ritual agricultural dances imitating the leaps of the antelope.

Although they can be classified into several distinct groups, the variation within each group is so great that none of the known examples are similar. One group is characterized by simple rendition of the antelope's body with the two horns stretching horizontally in a bold manner. The second group has a daring vertical form: the body of the animal small and the mane a simple design tending to follow the vertical line of the animal (Fig. 111). The third type is of similar style, except that the mane is very elaborate and broad (Fig. 49). In the fourth group the antelope's body is large and instead of the broad mane a smaller animal is standing on the back of the main figure. The fifth group has an elaborate body and the mane is in close unity with the body; this type is found with four horns as well as with two (Fig. 115).

These sculptures, which are extremely graceful and show great skill of workmanship, are considered masterpieces of West African art.

Also: carved wooden *crossbolts* for doors (Fig. 116); small *pottery animals*.

FIG. 113. *Protective statue. Bambara, French Sudan. 9" high.*

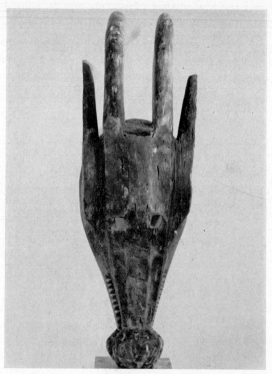

FIG. 114. *Animal mask. Bambara, French Sudan. 25" high.*

FIG. 115. *Antelope headgear. Bambara, French Sudan. 19" high.*

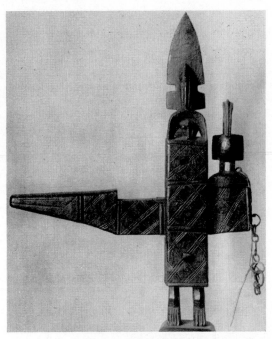

FIG. 116. *Cross bolt. Bambara, French Sudan.*

DOGON *or* HABE

Statues. Severe-looking figures. Some bearded, some hermaphrodite; some in double form; some seated. In all, the arms are in angular positions. Except that they lack crests, they are close to the Bambara statues in feeling (Fig. 117).

Masks were used for initiation ceremonies, burials, and rituals connected with mythological ancestor ceremonies. Each clan had a Great Mask kept in a secret cave for use on special occasions. Examples of this mask are topped by a plank twenty-five to thirty feet long, which extends vertically into the air. Smaller masks are of wood or fiber knitted into a hood and ornamented with cowrie shells. Most masks represent animals (totemistic or mythological origin)—antelopes, lions, monkeys, birds, snakes, crocodiles, etc. (Fig. 119). Human beings, old men, old women, priests, hunters, healers, etc., are also represented.

Wooden masks are generally abstract in design, of broad, simple volumes, and usually in polychrome, triangular patterns; hood form with the back part open, a short wooden stick inside, holding it in position. Eyes cut into the mask in quadrangular or triangular form (Fig. 120), nose a long slit or a long wooden piece, sometimes dividing the face into two parts; mouth a conic construction or absent (Fig. 63).

A large number of animal masks represent antelopes, with an amazing variety of horn formations: two flat horns with serrated tips; straight, tubular horns, two or three times the size of the mask; four or five horns in a straight line; two horns bent backwards in a daring arc and demanding a great block of wood for their construction. Some masks are surmounted by animal or human figures.

Another Dogon mask has a Cross of Lorraine superstructure twice the size of the mask, with arms attached to each bar (Fig. 118). The cross form frequently evolved into abstract patterns. Both types are ornamented with multicolored triangular patterns.

Most Dogon masks—many are in the Musée de l'Homme in Paris—are of recent origin, but are nevertheless quite rare, and of superior artistic quality. The native culture resisted inroads until very recently, and the purity and forceful abstract design of the sculpture was maintained.

FIG. 117. *Statue.*
Dogon, French Sudan.
26" high.

FIG. 118. *Mask. Dogon,*
French Sudan. 40" high.

Rock pictures created by the Dogons are unique in West African art (Fig. 121). The style is not in the realistic vein of the prehistoric rock picture of Altamira (Spain) or Dordogne (France), nor does it resemble those of the rock paintings of North Africa (Atlas and the Libyan desert) or of the Bushmen of South Africa. These are symbols reduced to the most essential concept of an idea or of an object, rather than a visual rendition. They show striking resemblances to modern abstract paintings, some being so "abstracted" that they require painstaking research to reveal their meaning. They are painted on rock and in caves where the masks are stored or where circumcision ceremonies are performed. Most are multicolored (ocher, red, white, black). Most have a religious significance. It is difficult to estimate their age, since they have been repainted continuously. Subject matter includes masks of different style and use, dancers with masks (Fig. 121), animals, genii, and utensils or other objects.

The Dogons also have *doors* carved in relief (Fig. 122); wooden *locks* decorated with human and animal figures; carved *stools;* sacrificial *bowls* surmounted by a bearded horseman.

BOBO

Statues. Ancestor figures.

Large polychromed *masks* with abstract design (Figs. 58, 128); masks in the form of animal heads (Fig. 124); carved *stools;* also small bronze *casts, jewelry.*

SENUFO (SENOUFO)   *This tribe also appears on the Ivory Coast*

Statues. Fecundity fetishes (Fig. 82) given to young girls; double fetishes for twin children; statues with protruding chin; statues with helmet-like hairdo; scarification marks on the face and body.

Masks combining human and animal features; masks similar to those of the Ivory Coast Senufo, surmounted by the Kono bird, the tribal totem and used by the Do dancers. Some masks covered with copper plate. Varying from the well-known Senufo mask style is one characterized by large animal head (up to two feet high) with great open mouth and strong teeth, often with a superstructure. Those without superstructure are in two styles, one (Fig. 78) constructed in round forms, the other (Fig. 123) with all features angular. The mask style with superstructure has large teeth

FIG. 119. *Mask of a hyena. Dogon, French Sudan. 15″ high.*

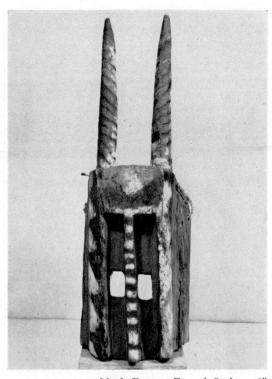

FIG. 120. *Mask. Dogon, French Sudan. 18″ high.*

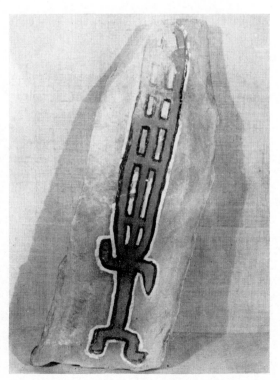

FIG. 121. *Rock picture (dancer with mask). Dogon, French Sudan. 15″ high.*

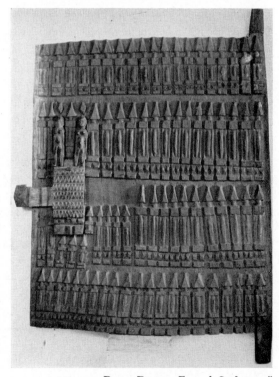

FIG. 122. *Door. Dogon, French Sudan. 32″ high.*

FIG. 123. *Mask. Senufo, Ivory Coast. 16" high.*

FIG. 124. *Mask. Bobo, French Sudan. 18" high.*

FIG. 125. *Mask with horns. Senufo, Ivory Coast. 29" high.*

FIG. 126. *Mask. Mossi,*
French Sudan. 43″ high.

FIG. 127. *Mask. Malinke,*
French Sudan. 24″ high.

FIG. 128. *Mask. Bobo,*
French Sudan. 10″ high.

and horns combined with animal figures (Fig.
125).

Also carved *drums*.

MOSSI

Statues. Figures less angular than Bambara and
Dogon.

Totemic *masks*, with abstract or human figure superstructure, over six feet in height,
used in the Wango ritual dances. The superstructure, including antelope horns, is often
five to seven times the height of the actual
mask (Fig. 126).

MALINKE

Animal *masks* with powerful mouth and horn
ornaments similar in concept to the large animal-head mask of the Senufo tribe (Fig. 127).

MANDINGUE

"Kita" *masks* with horn and cowrie-shell decoration.

PORTUGUESE GUINEA

BISSAGOS ISLANDS (BIJAGO *or* BIDJUGO)
A matriarchical society in which the
women select their men

Mostly female ancestor *statues*, legs wide apart,
carried on the back like children; body long
and thin; some grouped figures with oversize
heads, similar to the Baga style of French
Guinea.

Also busts, heads, and animal sculptures.

Few *masks* and only with animal heads.

Bowls with carved human and animal figures.

FRENCH GUINEA   *Guinea in the*
Baga language means "woman"

BAGA   (*Rivière du Sud*)

Statues on round columns, called Tambaane,

Tsakala, or Kelefa. Extremely large heads, compressed on both sides, in angular, stylized construction; jutting nose; arms without hands, or hands resting under the chin; kept in round huts by the Simo secret society (Fig. 130).

Bird figures in cubistic design.

Also polychrome animal figures.

Masks. Large heads, similar in style to heads of statues (see above), called Nimba (Fig. 129), mother of fecundity, protector of pregnant women; with attached fiber costumes; worn by ritual dancers. Masks combine human and animal features, some with horns. A few are

FIG. 130. *Statue. Baga, French Guinea. 31"* *high.*

FIG. 129. *Head (Nimba). Baga, French* *Guinea. 30" high.*

FIG. 131. *Funerary figure, steatite (Pombo).* *Kissi, French Guinea. 6" high.*

known to have been covered with small polished copper plates. Face masks, used in circumcision ceremonies of young girls.

Carved *drums* supported by four human figures with large heads.

KISSI

Soapstone *statues,* called Pombo—"image of death"—resembling the Nomori statues of the Mendi tribe in Sierra Leone (Fig. 131, also 75). Mostly in round, columnar, phallic-symbol form with small head (sometimes oversize heads); produced by past generations. When these soapstone statues were first discovered in the fields by the Kissi tribesmen they were identified in dreams as images of an ancestor, were swathed in cotton, set on altars and consulted as oracles.

SIMO (BOKE)

An exceptionally large type of *mask* (Fig. 83) with polychrome design and often elaborate superstructure of intertwined carving, is identified by the Musée de l'Homme, Paris, as a Simo mask, although the Colonial Museum in the same city ascribed them to the Baga, while the Institut Francais d'Afrique Noire at Dakar ascribed them to the Boke (both in French Guinea).

GUERZE AND KONO

These tribes, dominated by the Poro secret societies, produced *masks* of the same type as those discussed under Liberia and the Dan of the Ivory Coast. Fig. 132 is Guerze and Fig. 133 Kono (both from the Institut at Dakar). These illustrations show that a style tradition established by an intertribal secret society was maintained by different tribes, over a great expanse—in this case, from French Guinea through Sierra Leone and Liberia to the Ivory Coast.

SUSU (SOUSOU)

Masks with large forehead used in harvest and burial ceremonies.

FIG. 132. *Mask. Guerze, French Guinea. 8"* *high.*

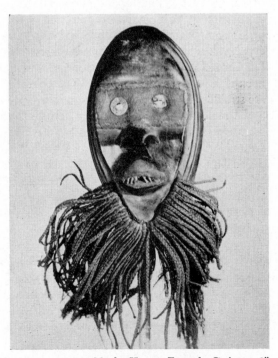

FIG. 133. *Mask. Kono, French Guinea. 8"* *high.*

FIG. 134. *Oracle figure. Mendi, Sierra Leone. 8″ high.*

FIG. 135. *Initiation ceremony mask. Landa (Toma), Sierra Leone. 18″ high.*

SIERRA LEONE

MENDI (MENDE)

Statues. Fecundity fetishes. Heads have large, domed forehead with face depressed underneath; groovelike line for the eyes; extremely small mouth; chin indicated but not developed; complicated hairdo showing great variety. Neck is long with numerous bulbous ringlike forms. Body is slender with large breasts; neck thin in proportion to head. The thin legs are straight, arms and hands close to the body. Some male figures, but most are female. Female figures were used as oracles by the Yassi women's secret society (Fig. 134). The figures called Minsereh were anointed, through which they acquired their magical power. The woman leader (Ya-Mama) of the society deposited them beside the secret tribal medicine and then fell into a trance. On awakening, the statue was anointed again, then held in her hands, and from its motions during a dance the answers to questions were construed. Stone figures of steatite (soapstone), called Nomori (Fig. 84). Style entirely different from the wood figures. The idiom is free. The large head has a narrow forehead (as opposed to the broad ones of the wood statues); curved nose, large froglike eyes, large lips, facial expression often portraitlike. Position is also varied: standing, kneeling, sitting, etc. Statues were found in graves and in the fields. Offerings were brought to them; and if they failed, they were flogged.

Masks. Hood- or helmet-like heads, carved from the full trunk of a large tree. Worn over the entire head, with rims resting on the masker's shoulders (Fig. 26). Have characteristics similar to the heads of statues, but exaggerated. Forehead is more than half the size of the entire head, and ends in a point; face is depressed; eyes, mouth, and chin small, and hairdo elaborate. Used by the Bundu (or Sande) women's secret society. Some have one, two, or four faces. The mask is colored black on the outside. A costume of black fiber covering hands and legs was worn with the mask in rituals. This mask, called Min or spirit, has been written of as a devil mask. Girls are ad-

mitted into the society at puberty or after
and are educated in marital duties. Prospec-
tive husbands often pay the initiation fee.
"Fat" rings on the hood masks are thought to
be symbolic of the fattening of the girl into
a woman. The graduates of this training receive a new name.

(The Poro secret society is also strong in
Sierra Leone and is affiliated with local societies. Its ritual objects found also in this area
will be discussed under Liberia.)

One of the men's secret societies has produced unusually free, rather abstract types of
masks, among them the so-called Landa mask,
an extremely large, oval mask with eyes and
nose roughly carved in the upper third of the
surface, leaving the lower part blank (Fig.
135). This was listed as a Toma (French
Guinea) mask by the Musée de l'Homme in
Paris and as a Bambara (French Sudan) by
the Colonial Museum in Paris. Either this type
has a wide distribution or further clarification
is necessary for a definitive identification.

Another mask, called Nyangbai, makes a
design of the eyes—two small rings, and nose
in a straight line; rest of face patterned in
straight lines; the whole surmounted by a
crownlike structure. This type represents a
spirit or demon.

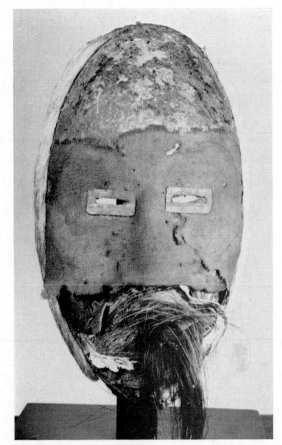

FIG. 136. *Initiation ceremony mask (Poro
Society). Mano, Liberia. 9" high.*

LIBERIA

Most of the ceremonial *masks* were produced
for the powerful men's secret society, Poro,
and the women's secret society, Sande. Both
were under hierarchical rule and controlled
the religious and social life of the tribes, imposing capital punishment and keeping the
tribesmen in constant fear. Each mask, being
itself the spirit ("ge") had a special name, the
belief being that it was the mask, not the man,
which performed the specific ritual function.

The chief tribes, each dominated by a Poro
society, are the Mano, Geh, and Gio. Several
minor tribes, among them the Kra and Konor.
Masks fall into six general types: (1) Finely
carved masks in simple columnar form, portraitlike, with spiritualized facial expression;
small eye slits; scarifications carved vertically
from forehead to nose (Fig. 85); (2) Same

FIG. 137. *Initiation ceremony mask (Poro
Society). Mano, Liberia. 9" high.*

FIG. 138. *Initiation ceremony mask (Poro Society). Geh, Liberia. 9" high.*

FIG. 139. *Initiation ceremony mask (Poro Society). Geh, Liberia. 16" high.*

FIG. 140. *Ancestor statue. Baule, Ivory Coast. 15" high.*

type with applied hair and beard of woven hair or raffia; eyes indicated by white or red paint or colored strips of cloth (Fig. 136); (3) Protruding tubular eyes; forehead often richly ornamented with carvings (Fig. 137); (4) Beak-mouthed masks (Fig. 139), some with movable lower jaw (Fig. 138); (5) Over-size masks, cubistic in design, eyes in large triangles (Figs. 69 and 87); (6) Small replicas of large masks, two or three inches in size, carried on the owner's person or kept at his home. Descriptions are based upon Dr. Harley's paper, "The Poro in Liberia." Masks similar to those described, found on the Ivory Coast, are attributed to Dan and Guere-Ouobe tribes.

The Sande women's secret society masks resemble the hoodlike masks of the Bundu women's society masks (Fig. 26). (See Sierra Leone.)

DEY (DE)

Masks similar to the Mendi of Sierra Leone, but eyes indicated in small swellings without openings.

VAI (WEI)

Same *masks* as Dey, but some are given distinctively masculine features and some are colored white and red. Used in initiation ceremonies. Also postlike figures with roughly carved human features.

GOLAH (GOLA)

A few wooden *sculptures;* some steatite figures.

Mendi-style *masks,* with human teeth inset into the mouth.

BASSA (BASA)

Large-headed *statues* with face planes and small round forehead meeting at a forty-five degree angle; small, snout-like, protruding mouth placed under the broad, projecting nose.

Also, three-inch *masks,* replicas of the above.

FIG. 141. *Mask (Guli). Baule, Ivory Coast.*

three sections. Some masks combine human and animal features. Some human-face masks are surmounted by stylized horns (Fig. 50), or an animal (Fig. 47), or a human figure. Many have a sophisticated beauty; some, though contemporary products, are in perfect traditional form. Masks also represent animal heads—elephant, bull, ram, antelope (Fig. 46)—the best-known being the cowhead in rather abstract design (Fig. 48) representing the spirit of the dead and called Kakagye or Guli. Masks of great beauty with animal and human features combined in perfect harmony. Animal heads often represent spirits from the Baule mythology. One Baule mask varies sharply from the traditional style, a round face with eyes shaped like inverted drops, straight mouth, no nose and arched horn on the head. This mask, called Goli, is a simple abstract design (Fig. 141).

Carved *utensils* include weaver's pulley, spoons, hammerlike musical instruments, all with artistic human- or animal-head ornaments, drums, wooden bowls with human figures, gold-dust weights of Ashanti origin, wooden boxes with grill-like base similar to Ashanti Kuduo brass caskets.

Small gold *pendants* in the form of a ram's head or human face are worn (Fig. 142).

IVORY COAST

BAULE (BAOULE)   *One of the rare tribes where sculpture is also produced for aesthetic appreciation*

Ancestor *statues*, male and female, carved with pedestals; sophisticated elegance, and strongly marked, traditional style (Fig. 140). Statues are usually slender, face delicate, forehead high, nose long and thin, rounded chin, almond-shaped eyes with finely carved eyebrows and lashes over half-lidded eyes, mouth broad and finely cut. Tribal hairdo highly stylized, done with elaborate, fine, parallel curving incisions. Scarification marks on neck, face, and body skillfully done in relief. Some statues have long, stylized beard. Arms with long fingers, part of the body. Legs balanced, finely carved, bulbous in form.

Masks. Sensitive frontal dome; attenuated face, elongated nose, arched eyes with emphasized lids, small stylized mouth; ornamental patterns around the face (often like sideburns); hairdo in fine ornamental incisions, often in

FIG. 142. *Gold pendant mask. Baule, Ivory Coast. 3½" high.*

FIG. 143. *Statue. Senufo, Ivory Coast. 10"*
high.

Wooden house *doors* carved in relief, representing animals. Also gold weights similar to Ashanti casts (Fig. 110).

ST. ANDRÉ *or* SASSANDRE REGIONS

Masks in flat planes, with small projecting noses; protruding cylinder eyes; block or cylinder-type mouth, domed forehead, similar to Dan masks. Eyes indicated by swellings without openings.

SENUFO (SENOUFO)

Statues. Long scarification marks on face and body, helmetlike hairdo, protuberant abdomen, hands often neglected (Fig. 143, also 82). Also equestrian figures.

Masks have scarification marks on the face, double horn ornament on top, ornamental side carvings, and leglike parts (Fig. 88). Two-headed masks produced in the region of Korhogo; others surmounted by animal figures, mostly totem birds; wooden masks with horns, covered with hammered brass; animal-head masks; small animal masks with human features.

Carved *doors.*

DAN (YAKOBA)

(The range and development of style forms in this region, particularly in masks, has inspired extensive studies. Since Vandenhoute's research is based on field study and covers the largest area, we shall adopt his classification.)

(1) The *classic* Dan style characterized by an idealized realism of the human face, executed usually in a smooth, polished manner, with high domed forehead; sensitively carved mouth, sometimes inset with human, animal, or metal teeth; eyes either completely round (Fig. 86), slanted (Fig. 89), or rectangular. Some masks have a hairdo and some a beard woven of black raffia or hair. Others have one or several incised grooves on the rim of the mask (Fig. 89), a stylized representation of the tattoo marks of the Diomande tribe. Or the face is stylized into two flat planes with eyes at the meeting of the planes of the brows and cheeks.

(2) *Masks* with beaklike mouth, produced in the region of *Bafing.* This beak may have a movable lower jaw (Fig. 138) or be covered with hair.

FIG. 144. *Initiation ceremony mask.*
Guere-Ouobe, Ivory Coast. 10" high.

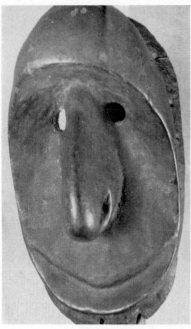

FIG. 145. *Mask. Koulime, Ivory Coast. 7″ high.*

FIG. 146. *Statue. Alangua, Ivory Coast. 18″ high.*

(3) The *southern* Dan style, characterized by more stylized forms with a vertical scarification mark on the forehead, often continued on the nose; pointed chin and forehead flatter than classical Dan, with slant eyes or slits.

(4) The *Guere-Ouobe* style marked by an audacious combination of human and animal features (Fig. 52), forehead and chin thrust forward in a massive and dramatic manner, enlarged mouth and nose, eyes tubular, horn-like structures on the face. Between the protruding parts are hidden slits used by the masker to see through (Fig. 144).

A type of *portrait mask*, with the most realistic Negroid features to be found in African masks (Fig. 70).

(5) The *Dan-Guéré* substyle, with two main mask types. First, most amazing, cubistic construction; not only the eyes but nose, mouth and often the planes of the face, all in triangular patterns (Figs. 69 and 87), set off by a contrasted, hemispherical forehead, with the ears, in some, enlarged into flanking masses. Second, masks with pointed chins, protruding, tubular eyes, and carved ornaments on the forehead, a stylization of small antelope horns.

(6) The so-called *Flanpleu* style, named after a village which developed a style marked by heavy eyelids, protruding mouth, tilted upper lip, bulging forehead, and small antelope-horn ornament.

(7) The *Koulime* style marked by overdevelopment of some important part of the face; mask may be nothing but an oversized beak-like mouth and a forehead with slits for eyes (Fig. 145).

In the region of *Man*, human heads in terra cotta, with head feathers.

GURO (GOURO)

No *statues* are known.

Masks. Long, narrow, human face, refined features, long narrow nose, oval eyes; prominent forehead; chin with frequent beardlike extension; hairdo often in elaborated geometrical patterns, surmounted by horns (Fig. 90) or totem animal. In some the nose forms an animal-like beak, similar to those of the Poro society; or the mask is an entire animal head (elephant, open-mouthed antelope (Fig. 51), ape, etc.).

Weaver's *pulley* decorated with carved human and animal heads (Fig. 53).

FIG. 147. *Funerary pottery figure. Agni (region Krinjabo), Ivory Coast. 16" high.*

FIG. 148. *Brass casket (Kuduo). Ashanti, Gold Coast. 7½" high.*

ALANGUA

Statues. This tribe has produced an interesting style, different from the usual Ivory Coast figures. The arms and legs are in bulbous form (similar to the Baule), but the arms are raised toward the head and are holding an ornament. We know of standing and sitting figures (Fig. 146).

KRINDJABO

Statues. Excavations in the region of Krindjabo, along the southwestern Ivory Coast, bordering Togo, turned up astonishing pottery figures dating from the sixteenth and seventeenth centuries, probably used as funerary statuettes (Fig. 147). Their style shows some similarities to the Sao pottery figures (see French Equatorial Africa, p. 193).

GOLD COAST

ASHANTI

Ashanti- and Akan-speaking people on the Gold Coast were organized into a confederacy about 1700. Their Golden Stool was then introduced by one of their rulers to symbolize unity of body and spirit. First a state symbol, stools were adopted by the middle class, as embodiments of ancestor spirits. The spirit of the owner of a *stool* was believed to enter into it after his death, thus becoming his shrine.

Statues. The best known Ashanti figures are the Akua Ba, worn by expectant mothers. The figures have a round, disklike face, cylindrical body, and outstretched arms. There are also small wooden figures; stools (Fig. 57), some supported by human figures; clay heads; and wooden utensils with repoussé metal decorations.

Small bronze, brass or copper figures (Mrammuo), produced in the *cire-perdue* technique and used as gold-weights (Fig. 110), fall into three classifications: (1) Single human and animal forms or groups depicting some legend, proverb, or scene, the latter sometimes rendered in a vivacious manner and representing such everyday happenings as two old men walking arm-in-arm, a man climbing a tree, a mother holding her child, etc.; (2) Inanimate objects, plants, seeds, fruits, weapons, utensils, etc.; (3) Gold-weights of beauti-

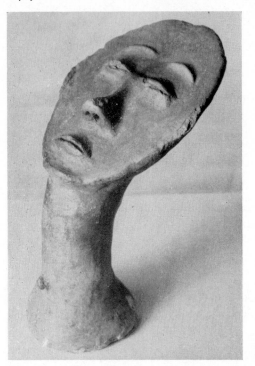

FIG. 149. *Funerary pottery head. Ashanti (Akan), Gold Coast. 28" high.*

ful abstract designs in geometrical forms which probably had symbolical meaning, later also used as jewelry. Produced only since the eighteenth century, their use spread to the Ivory Coast. Most of the weights found among the Baules are of Ashanti origin.

Gold *jewelry*, also in the form of small masks, shows inventiveness and careful craftsmanship (Fig. 142).

Other objects include richly decorated bronze *boxes* for gold dust; animal *figures* in metal, of later origin; bronze *vessels* (Fig. 148), called Kuduo, vaselike in form, richly decorated with chasing or animal figures in relief with a grate base, probably for burnt offerings to the ancestor spirits. Found in burial grounds, filled with gold trinkets or beads.

No *masks* are known.

Interesting terra-cotta figures (Fig. 149) similar in style and function to those found on the Ivory Coast (see p. 170).

BRON (BRONG)

We know only of two magnificent bronze *masks* recently excavated (Fig. 150).

GRUNSHI

Animal heads in *mask* form, often combining several animal features, mostly in polychrome (Fig. 151).

TOGO

EWE

Statues. Legba clay figures used as tribal or family fetish. Of phallic form, crest of cock feathers representing the spirit of fecundity and generative power, goat hair as beard. Aklama statues, roughly carved out of wood, representing the protective spirit. Ibeji twin fetishes (Fig. 40), to protect survivor after death of twin. Animal figures in black clay. Copper figures in *cire-perdue* technique representing animals and small masks.

PORTO NOVO

This region of the Togo coast is the origin

FIG. 150. *Man's head in bronze. Bron, Gold Coast. 6" high.*

FIG. 151. *Mask. Grunshi, Gold Coast. 58"
high.*

of many of the Ewe works. In addition:

Life-size royal *statues* characterized by a monumental naturalism.

Wood *carvings*, in relief of decorative patterns with human and animal figures.

Large *thrones*, supported by kneeling or erect human figures. *Bowls* supported by human figures.

Animal *figures* recently produced.

DAHOMEY

YORUBA

(The Yorubas live here but also in Togoland and along the Gold Coast, while the majority, numbering about three million, live in southwest Nigeria. We shall therefore discuss their art under Nigeria.)

ABOMEY

Statues. Small brass figurines, often in groups, in *cire-perdue* technique, of recent production, mainly of a repeated, traditional pattern. Fine old wrought-iron and brass figures, now rare.

Equestrian figure of the mythological god Obathalla, Legba clay statues. Animal figures representing mythical gods and demons. Alligator symbol of the sun-god Lisa. Lizard symbol of the national god Togbodonou.

Carved wood or clay *wall-reliefs* composed of figures, animals, and plants. Crude, massive, caplike masks, colored with commercial, imported colors (Fig. 152).

House posts in the form of human figures.

FON

Statues with sword in hand, with animal heads, or with arms outstretched.

Animal-head *masks* surmounted by a human figure.

NIGERIA

YORUBA

Nigeria's chief art productions come from the Yorubas, its ancient inhabitants, with Ife their religious center. Yoruba *statues* and *masks* show a traditional tribal mark, three parallel lines on both cheeks and often one on the

FIG. 152. *Mask (Egun). Yoruba, Dahomey.
17" high.*

FIG. 153. *Mask with mounted warrior.
Yoruba (Ekiti district), British Nigeria.
40" high.*

FIG. 154. *Mask (Gelede). Yoruba, British
Nigeria. 9" high.*

FIG. 155. *Statue (Ikenga). Ibo, British Nigeria.
19" high.*

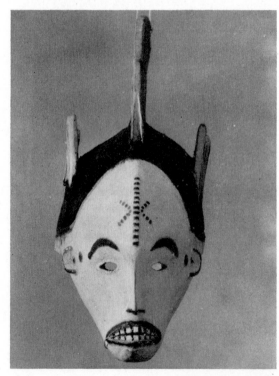

FIG. 156. *Mask (Agboko). Ibo, British
Nigeria. 12" high.*

forehead. These, according to legend, are the claw marks of the panther Agassou, totem animal of the royal family. This panther is, however, not an object of worship, but rather a symbol of power.

SOUTH YORUBA

Statues. Clay tribal fetishes (Legba) decorated with feathers, considered either as fecundity spirits or as malignant invisible companions of victims of accidents. Also polychromed horsemen, sometimes used as supports for bowls; horsemen with entourage, some with complicated superstructure of several figures or masks (Fig. 153). Small wooden statuettes of children carried by bereaved mothers. Mother-and-child groups (Fig. 91 and 92). Ibeji twin fetishes (also called Oricha) with rather oblong head, high hairdo, large pointed oval eyes (Fig. 40). Also figures with European dress and accessories.

Masks. Polychromed hoods or caplike masks surmounted by an animal. Head masks with domed high forehead, open eyes, slightly curved nose, large lips, closed mouth, protruding chin, stylized triangular ears, large hairdo, were used at burial ceremonies by the Gelede society (Fig. 154). Many caplike masks are recent, have strong Negroid features, with typical tribal marks, and are polychromed in commercial colors.

Ritual *stools* (Azeinkpo) supported by one or more standing or kneeling human figures, some in the form of mounted or armed figures.

Iron and brass works of recent origin, including single or grouped human and animal figures (similar to those of Abomey), mostly of stereotyped popular designs, made in *cire-perdue* technique.

Fabric dolls.

Doors carved in relief.

Bowls and *divination vessels* supported by human and animal figures.

NORTHERN YORUBA

Masks. Most of these represent mythological personages. They come in sets of sixteen, one for each god, the color for each varying and having a specific meaning. Great variety of postures (standing, sitting, kneeling, crouching). Also Ibeji twin statues (Fig. 40).

IBO

Statues. House fetishes (Ikenga). About twelve inches high; human figure, with head surmounted by backward-curving horns (Fig. 155), sometimes by a bird figure; seated on a stool, some smoking a long pipe. Used as healing images and by young men as luck fetishes.

Masks with deformed, fantastic features, many in polychrome (Fig. 112). Ram masks of the Ayaka secret society. Headdress masks, in human or animal form, used in the Agbogo secret society initiation ceremonies (Fig. 156). Also masks worn horizontally on the head representing water spirits (Owu) of the Obukele secret society, and in forms of animal heads or animal and human features in combination (Fig. 157). Used by waders who, walking immersed in water up to the neck, gave the impression that the mask was propelling itself on the surface. Polychromed figures surmounted by a superstructure of an animal group. Also tribal or village statues.

IBIBIO

Statues. Contrary to the African principle of carving the sculpture out of one block of wood, parts of Ibibio statues and masks are *movable*—arms, legs, jaws, and superstructure. Seated female statues. A large number of wooden statues called Ekpu by the Oron

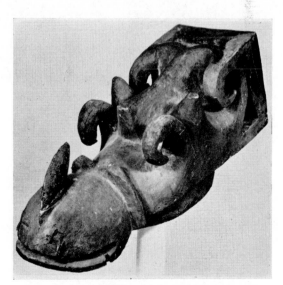

FIG. 157. *Mask headdress (Obukele Society). Abuan-Ibo, British Nigeria. 24" high.*

FIG. 158. *Ancestor figure (Ekpu). Ibibio (Oron Clan), British Nigeria. 42" high.*

FIG. 159. *Horned mask. Ibibio, British Nigeria. 14" high.*

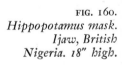

FIG. 160. *Hippopotamus mask. Ijaw, British Nigeria. 18" high.*

FIG. 161. *Mask. Ijaw, British Nigeria. high.*

FIG. 162. *Mask. Ijaw, British Nigeria.*
15" high.

tribe were recently discovered in the Calabar region (Fig. 158). They differ from the present Ibibio style; elaborately carved male figures, some bearded, very large lower body, and unshaped feet.

Masks in abstract forms, similar to the Ibo masks, head with bulging forehead, arched nose, small pointed mouth, generally large features (Fig. 159). Some masks with calm expression, polychrome headdress in the form of a human figure with abstract ornaments, animal-head masks, naturalistic horned wood heads covered with skin, eyes plated with metal, used by the Ekpo secret society and similar to the Ekoi heads.

IJAW

Statues in strong geometrical design, with large outthrust cylindrical eyes and square mouth. Wax figures used in secret magical rites.

Masks and *mask parts*, abstractly ornamented, often in strong abstract manner (Figs. 160, 161, 162) frequently based on animal features, some with bird forms. Many hood-like, Janus-type two-faced masks worn over the head.

SOBO

Columnar *carvings* with elaborate motifs.

Statues of Europeans with commercial colors, of later origin.

Masks. Naturalistic human-face masks with superstructures of elaborate abstract design, often in animal forms.

Stools supported by human or animal figures.

OWO

Heads. Owo was probably under the influence of Benin, sixty miles away. But the Owo style possesses greater fluidity and freer abstraction, as can be seen in the magnificent ram's head (Fig. 32) and the horned man's head (Fig. 163), both types probably used in an ancestor cult.

MAHIN REGION

Masks. Caplike, worn on the head, with long-beaked animal heads turned upward. Some, with horns, represent mythological water spirits.

FIG. 163. *Man's head with ram's horns.*
Yoruba (Owo region), British Nigeria. 17"
high.

IFE

Heads. Terra-cotta heads of naturalistic tendency, with fine incisions on the face, were
discovered in 1910–12 by Leo Frobenius. In
1936–38 bronze heads (also a pure copper
mask) with greenish patina in a strong naturalistic style, reminiscent of Roman heads,
were excavated—nineteen pieces in all, of
which sixteen are in the possession of the
Oni (King) of Ife, and one is in the British
Museum (Fig. 30). The heads are mostly
life size, some smaller. In 1949 another series
of terra-cotta human and animal heads were
excavated in Abini, near Ife. All the bronze
heads were cast in the *cire-perdue* technique,
with such technical delicacy as to surpass all
other casting. Most of the bronze heads, which
are similar in style to the terra-cotta heads,
have fine parallel incisions covering the whole
face, probably scarification marks. Rows of
holes along the hairline on the forehead and
the line of mustache and beard must have
held human hair. The tradition survived in
the Ekoi (Cameroon) skin-covered heads.

To the Yorubas Ife is the source and spiritual
center of their nation. It had a flourishing
culture long before Benin. Its position resembled that of Delphi in Ancient Greece.
It was the home of the Yoruba Oracle. As
early as 1172 the Benin elders are said to have
applied to Ife for a ruler. Bronze casting was
introduced into Benin from Ife during the
reign of Benin Oba Oguola (about 1280).
However, although the earliest works show
the influence of Ife heads, the Benin artists
rejected the classic, naturalistic Ife style. An
extremely large variety of objects were produced in Benin differing from the unique
naturalistic head style of Ife and more in the
prevailing West African tradition of rendering a conceptual reality, resulting in an abstract quality. Another enigma is that, without any slow development, at least according
to our present knowledge, we witness the
summit of a most accomplished artistic form
and technique which suddenly came to an end,
showing no survival or further development.
(We must suppose that such an eruption of a
new style as that of Ife must have been the
effect of foreign influence, probably a direct
Mediterranean influence.)

FIG. 164. *Stone figure (detail of Fig. 34). Esie,
British Nigeria.*

TADA AND JEBBA

Statues. Only a few years ago the most astonishing bronzes were found in the Nigerian
fishing village of Tada. One was a two-foot-
high seated figure with a strong resemblance to
the early Egyptian "scribe" statue (Fig. 33),
and closer to the Ife bronzes than to other
West African sculpture. Another figure with
clasped hands is different in style and poorer
in workmanship. A third figure (Gago) (Fig.
31), about four feet high, has a tunic similar
to that of the Coptic Nubians or Egyptians
of the first century, was found at Jebba Island.
Another larger, nude figure was found along
with a warrior statue.

With these discoveries new vistas open in
the history of Western Africa.

ESIE

Equally mysterious and exciting in implica-
tion are the seven hundred and fifty stone
statues found in the sacred grove near Esie,
Ilorin Province (Fig. 34), seventy miles northeast of Ife (Fig. 164). Most of the figures
are seated (some on a mushroom type of
stool). They average twenty-two inches in

height. Two types of facial expression can be distinguished: one, a northern type, with swelling forehead, straight nose and pointed beard; the other, a Negroid type, with broad nose and thick lip. Judging from the richness of facial expression, they were portraits, not ritual objects. They show a highly developed style, but not as sophisticated as that of the Ife heads. They appear to have originated in the Nupe Kingdom (founded about 640), part of which extended along the Niger River, said to have once included Ife and Benin. It was later conquered by the Yorubas, probably in the eleventh or twelfth century.

NOK

Seven or eight years ago, at a depth of twenty-five feet, some terra-cotta *heads* were unearthed at Nok, in the northern provinces (Fig. 165). Their estimated date is the latter half of the first millenium B.C. As yet we have no data for this culture and its possible connections with Nigerian archaeology.

BINI (BENIN KINGDOM)

(Best known among the Negro empires, discovered by the Portuguese in 1472 and described in documents by Dutch travelers in 1670 and 1700.)

Bronzes. The discovery of the Benin bronzes dates from 1897, when a British punitive expedition stripped the city of Benin of about 2500 to 3000 objects, which were carried to London. A Dutch traveler's description describes the city as it was in 1668 and dilates on the splendor of the king's palace, where bronze plates decorated its rectangular pillars. This went unmentioned, however, in a later Dutch description (1701). The English in Benin found many buildings in ruins and the art objects scattered around or heaped in storerooms. What happened between 1668 and 1701 can only be conjectured. In all probability the decline of the slave trade and continuous tribal warfare contributed to the downfall of the kingdom. It is to be noted that, contrary to the extremely delicate execution of the plates, rough nail holes are found on most. It is possible that originally the plates were mounted in grooved recesses on the

FIG. 165. *Terra-cotta head. Village of Nok, British Nigeria.* 7½" *high.*

pillars, without the use of nails, and that during one of the tribal invasions, probably between 1668 and 1701, the plates were ripped down; which would account for their damaged or broken condition. During the eighteenth century those plates must have been nailed up, later to be torn down again by other invaders and left in their present marred state with rough nail holes, in which the British found them. Felix von Luschan's book *Die Altertuemer von Benin* lists about 2400 objects, mostly in museums. Today only about fifty pieces are in Nigeria, in the home of the Oba of Benin.

A nomenclature of the great variety of objects produced, mostly in bronze, is given on page 138. (Figs. 94 to 109) Benin art has given rise to a large literature; certain art periods have been established:

Archaic period		1149–1360
Old	"	1360–1500
Great	"	1500–1575
High	"	1575–1648
New flourishing period		1648–1691
Late period		1691–1819

Unfortunately, our limited space does not permit detailed descriptions of the great variety of art works and the origin and use of each object. The casting was of a two-to-three-millimeter thickness, a feat still unmatched by modern techniques. Also produced were steel tools of such hardness as to mystify modern steel makers. It is calculated that with the advanced methods used today approximately six months of work would be needed to produce similar work. Von Luschan declares: "Cellini himself could not have molded better, nor anybody else before or after him."

CAMEROON

Three large style regions are to be distinguished in this territory:

1. *The Cross River region* (extending to Nigeria). Typical are carved wooden heads in naturalistic style, covered with skin (Fig. 144).

2. *Grassland.* The statues, masks, and utensils of this region are free, elastic, and bold in execution, and sometimes on a grandiose scale, with an effect of strong vitality, and a peasantlike lack of sophistication.

3. *The Coast region* or *forestland*, with smaller statues and masks.

Cross River Region

EKOI

Skin-covered wooden *heads* and *masks* of a demonic naturalism in three sizes: smaller than life, life size, and twice life size. Earlier skins of slaves, later skins of antelopes were used. Human hair went into the hairdo. It is presumed that all masks represented ancestors. They were used in burial ceremonies by the Egbo (or Ekpe) secret societies (Fig. 166). Janus-type, two-faced masks, having mythological significance: one face (black) representing Father Heaven; the other (white or yellow) Mother Earth. (Black signifies male, white female.)

Statues. Rough in execution, emphasizing the expressive head. Also skin-covered seated figures.

BOKI

Sculpture in human and animal form.
Skin-covered *heads*.

ANJANG (ANYANG)

Statues. Unique seated figures, head resting on the right hand; large, with high, broad forehead, arched nose, open toothless mouth, protruding chin; the expression intense and brutal. Also skin-covered statues and *masks* with a savage expression.

BANJANG (BANYANGI)

Skin-covered, antelope-head *masks*.

Grassland

BANGWA

Statues. Some about forty inches in height, of monumental construction. Mother-and-child groups. Large carved human heads. Animal sculpture. Roughly carved dramatic female statues. Skin-covered heads. Seated figures holding bowls.

Masks. Large, dramatic; of human and animal form.

Food *bowls* with lids carved in the form of animals.

BALI

Known for their clay *pipe bowls*, mainly derived from the Bamessing, Bamileke, Babungo, and Bamum tribes. The variety is large, the most common in the form of a seated human figure with oversize head (Fig. 167); several heads with arms and legs attached (Fig. 168); some with human body and animal head.

Footstools with human and animal figures as ornaments of supports.

BAFUM

The products of Bafum are dramatic in effect.

Statues. Some heads have extremely high hairdos and flat, high foreheads; human and animal figures. Some large figures are entirely encrusted with beads and cowries.

Masks. These are more important. Their exaggerated but original forms show an almost brutal force, mainly human in feature

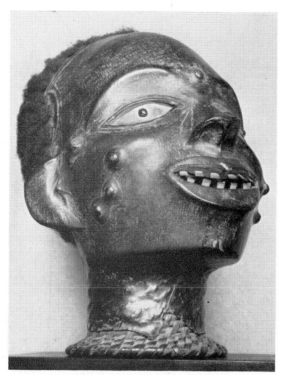

FIG. 166. *Skin covered head. Ekoi, Cameroon.*
7" high.

FIG. 167. *Clay pipe. Bamessing (Bali),*
Cameroon. 6" high.

FIG. 168. *Clay pipe. Bamileke (Bali),*
Cameroon. 12" high.

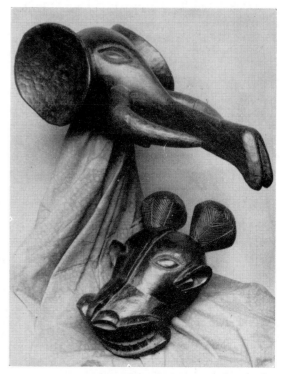

FIG. 169. *Animal head. Bali, Cameroon. 28"*
high. Animal head. Bamessing, Cameroon.
18" high.

and sometimes surmounted by a human figure. Also animal forms with a bulky, expressive vitality, worn over the head, the rim resting on the shoulders of the dancer.

BEKOM

Statues. Some life-size, naturalistic figures covered with pearls or metal plating, supporting thrones.

Masks. Monumental masks (some over twenty inches high) (Fig. 4) with half-open mouth, teeth distinctively carved; with a high hair superstructure, sometimes with pierced effects; eyes framed by a lighter color than the mask itself. These masks are often classified under Bamum and Bamenda, and it is possible that they were used by all three tribes.

BAMUM (BAMOUN)

Statues. Large figures encrusted with beads and cowries.

Heads. Noteworthy elephant heads cast in bronze.

Dance *masks* in the form of a long head on a high neck, also in animal-head form (Fig. 93).

Footstools and *thrones* decorated and supported by animal or human figures.

Bowls in animal form, or carried by human figures. Some in strong, cubistic design; some soft and round in form.

A great variety of *pipe bowls* in clay and cast bronze (*cire perdue*) in the form of a seated figure with oversized head.

TIKAR

Masks. Carved of wood with a broad collar made of raffia, called Ngiga; used in mask play, and reserved for men. The face forms a flat surface with outthrust cylindrical eyes and mouth a cubistic oval.

Also bronze-cast *pipe bowls* in the form of human and animal heads.

BAMESSING

Masks in the form of animal heads (Fig. 169).

Pipe bowls of red clay in the form of a human face with bulging cheeks (Fig. 167).

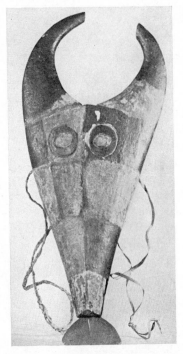

FIG. 170. *Animal head. Bamum (Dualla), Cameroon. 28" high.*

BANGO

Heads, over life-size, with puffed cheeks and bulging eyes.

Forest Land   Coastal Regions

BAFO

Statues. Individual and group figures, varying in size, both standing and seated. Busts. Figures of animals.

Bird-head *masks,* many in polychrome.

BAKUNDU *or* BALUNG

Janus-type, two-faced *statues* supported by six small figures. Musongo or Mosongo figures, used when taking an oath. Figures are roughly carved.

Also carved, skin-covered wooden *heads.*

DUALLA

No *statues.*

Rich variety of polychrome *masks;* some animal-headed, some with horns (Fig. 170). Polychromed bovine masks used in the Ekongolo secret society, and also by the Bajong tribe.

Elaborate *dance-scepters* and *carvings* for oar banks on pirogues (native boats).

NGOLO

Headdress *masks;* human head resting on a high, conelike neck realized in a simple, naturalistic manner. Single and two-faced masks, some with horns.

Wood *panels* carved in relief in cubistic style.

BASSA

Headdress *masks.*

Round human and animal *figures* used by the Koso secret society.

BAKOKO

Masks in the form of hemispheres.

FIG. 171. *Mask. Adoumas, Gabun. 6" high.*

JABASSI

Figures in geometrical forms.

BATAUGA

Masks in human form.

Other Regions in Cameroon

ISSANGILLI

Statues.

ABU

Statues.

Masks. Unusual face patterns in statues and masks; eyes and mouth quadrangular.

BODIMAN

Horned antelope *heads.*

MBANG

Statues. Life-size figures used by the Koso secret society.

FRENCH EQUATORIAL AFRICA

Studies of this large territory are incomplete and sometimes contradictory.

In the south, called Moyen Congo (Middle Congo), bordering the Belgian Congo, the main tribes are: Bateke, Babembe, Ambete, Bavili, Balumbo, Bakuele, Kuyu, Machango; in the middle region called Gabun, the Pangwe, M'Pongwe, Bakota, Bangiri, Nkomi, Eschira, Nitsogo; in the north up to the border of Cameroon, the Pangwe and Bakota extend, plus such tribes as Boulou, Ngoumba, etc. (The Pangwe tribe extends also into the southern Cameroon.)

ADOUMAS *or* BADOUMAS

This tribe is located in the Ogowe region.

Abstract design *masks* sometimes classified as Okondje masks, made of simple planes. Some have a jutting forehead continued in the line of the nose (Fig. 171).

FIG. 172. *Ancestor statue. Babembe, Moyen Congo. 6" high.*

FIG. 173. *Statue. Babembe, Moyen Congo. 5" high.*

BABEMBE

A section of this tribe is located in the Belgian Congo and is called *Babwende* (*Babuende*). Their proximity to the Bakongo accounts for the realism in facial expression of their sculpture and also for their use of shell or ivory inlay for the eyes. (The Bakongo also use fragments of mirror.)

Statues. This tribe produced distinctive statuettes of about five to six inches, sometimes called Sibiti figures (after the name of the principal village). They are finely carved in natural brown wood and have a high patina (Fig. 172). They are considered house fetishes, representing the ancestor and are adorned with distinctive scarification marks on the abdomen (usually carved in relief). They are often bearded and seated (Fig. 12). Because their expression has a superficially Egyptian appearance certain writers have assumed an Egyptian influence. Some figures carry a gun, knife, or stick in the hand (Fig. 173); some carry a child.

BAKHAMBA

Female and male *statues* with arms raised to the back of the head.

BAKOTA (So-called Bakota statues are also produced by ONDUMBO, ADUMA, OBAMBA, OKANDA, AMBETE)

Statues. Wooden funerary figures plated with hammered copper and brass, or both, often in strips (Fig. 68). In some a human face is centered, sometimes with protruding forehead, convex brow indicating male, concave brow, female. Abstract ornament surrounds the head; lozenge-shaped body. Some have two faces, front and back. According to one theory, the round forms have a solar symbolism; according to another, they represent the radiation of the dead man's spirit. The body is merely indicated because after death it no longer exists. Their names, Bengala or Mbulu Ngulu, mean "image of the spirit of the dead," and would bear out the theory that the ornamental part represents the surviving spirit. It may be, however, that these nimbus ornaments are stylized renderings of a hairdo, as in the case of M'Pongwe masks, since this tribe is the western neighbor of the Bakotas. These figures are kept in baskets containing skulls or bones of the deceased. They serve as memorials (or tombstones—Fig. 23), but are also used as ancestor figures whose spirits the

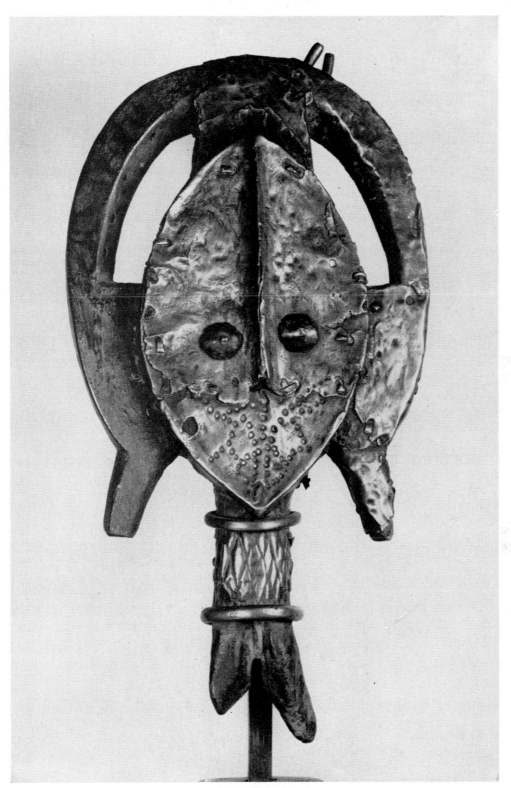

FIG. 174. *Funerary figure. Bakota, Gabun. 12" high.*

FIG. 175. Mask (Bakosi).
Benjabi, Gabun. 12"
high.

FIG. 176. Mask. Bakouele (Bakwele),
Gabun. 38" high.

FIG. 178. Mask. Batanga,
Gabun. 12" high.

FIG. 177. Funerary figure. Bakota (Ossyeba), Gabun. 20" high.

FIG. 179. *Head. Benjabi, Gabun. 12″ high.*

was produced by a Pangwe subtribe, the Ossyeba. More simplified than the traditional Bakota statues, the head formed the entire superstructure, eliminating the side and upper ornament (Fig. 177), and was attached by copper strips (lamelles) to the wooden base.

BAKOUELE

Animal-head *masks* of great simplicity (Fig. 176). Also masks of completely abstract design.

BATANGA

Seated female *statues*.
  Also vividly colored *masks* (Fig. 178).

BENJABI

Masks, called Bakosi, with large white face, large black eyebrows, often fused with the nose, in a strong black design (Fig. 175).
  Heads in the same style, some with intricate, abstract hairdo (Fig. 179).

petitioner summons by clapping his hands.
  From these basic forms or designs there are many variations. Seldom are two Bakota statues the same. The flat form affords greater range for phantasy. The sizes show a similar diversity. The smaller are about thirteen to fifteen inches high (Fig. 174) and are quite rare; the majority are larger, about twenty-five to thirty inches high. As to the ornamental part of these figures, there are two basic designs, occurring in the smaller as in the larger sizes. One type has the side parts independent from the top ornament (Fig. 68); the other type has the side parts formed into a unity with the top form (Fig. 174). Those figures which have the face covered with strips of copper combined with flat hammered-brass sheet metal are considered rarer than those where the combinations of metal are made only in hammered metal.
  The lozenge-shaped underpart of many Bakota statues is broken or damaged because, being placed among skulls or bones, the figures were exposed to friction and decay. One of the rarest forms of these funerary figures

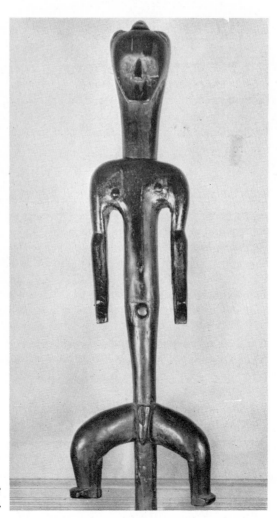

FIG. 180. *Ancestor statue. Pangwe (Jaunde), Gabun. 23″ high.*

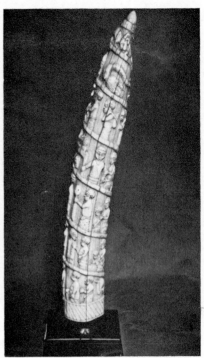

FIG. 181. *Mask ornament. Kuyu,*
Gabun. 24″ high.

FIG. 182. *Statue.*
Kuyu, Gabun.
27″ high.

FIG. 183. *Ivory tusk. Loango*
(region), Gabun. 14″ high.

BULE (BULU)   *A sub-tribe of the*
                                    Pangwes

Mostly *masks* in the form of human faces, some with horns.

Geometrically formed human *heads*, mostly colored white and black.

JAUNDE

Statues. Pangwe-style so-called "dancer" figures. (Fig. 180). Akaba sticks with carved human and animal figures.

Masks. Strongly marked: the surface is flat, the upper part round, the lower part square; the forehead domed; very long nose; eyes and mouth quadrangular holes.

KUYU *or* BABOCHI

Clublike polychrome wood carvings, used in snake ceremonial dances called Kebe-Kebe, sometimes used as crest ornaments on *masks.* Most are of very recent origin. With few exceptions—such as Fig. 181—they represent a low level of African statuary.

Only one Kuyu statue is known (Fig. 182).

LOANGO

Loango is the name both of a region and of a seaport on the Atlantic in southernmost French Equatorial Africa. It has been mistakenly used by some authors as a tribal identification. The sculpture-producing tribes of this region include the Kakongo, Basundi, and Mayombe. Their sculptures are in the style of the Bakongo in the Belgian Congo, and the majority of the objects formerly attributed to Loango should be classified under Bakongo. Many small *ivory tusks* in serpentine shapes, carved with figures in European dress, some carrying bundles and hammock. These carvings are done for sale to foreigners at a price calculated on the number of figures in the carving (Fig. 183).

MABEA

Statues. Ancestor figures.

Masks. Both ancestor figures and masks are carved in long triangular shapes with two triangular eye openings.

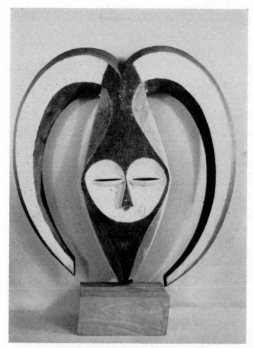

FIG. 184. *Mask. Majabi, Gabun. 17"
high.*

FIG. 185. *Initiation ceremony mask. M'Pongwe,
Gabun. 15" high.*

MAJABI

A variation of the white-faced Bakosi *masks*,
with hornlike ornaments (Fig. 184) frequently
classified as masks of the Ogoue region. Abstract designs of great beauty.

MBETE

Statues. Probably ancestor figures, painted
white, roughly carved, with simple facial
structures.

M'PONGWE

(In their migration to the coastal region, the
M'Pongwe carried the art tradition of the
inland Ishongo, Nkomi, and Bapuno tribes.)

Statues. The salient features of some are the
metal (copper) eyes and metal tongues.

Masks. These are the best-known M'Pongwe
carvings (Fig. 185). These have a highly
elaborate hairdo in black, white face with slit,
Oriental eyes and red mouth, and sometimes
highly stylized scarification marks on forehead, temples, and cheeks. The scarification
marks usually indicate a sub-tribe. The hairdo
follows the tower-shaped chignon of the
Ishongo women which is built up on a frame
of old grass cloth.

The white color (a paint made of kaolin)
represents the spirit or "ghost," the word
often used by western commentators to whom
the ancestor spirit had a spectral connotation.
To the African it is natural for a spirit to re-
main active; there is nothing of the "spook"
in their concept. For this reason we prefer
the word *spirit*. Because spirits appear only at
night, they can be seen only if they are white,
hence the color association. The red of the
mouth also has significance; red repels evil
spirits. After the funeral, powdered redwood
is rubbed on the cheeks or red paint is smeared
on house walls to keep off evil spirits.

The still inconclusive state of our information on this region may be seen in the diver-
gent reports on the use of the M'Pongwe
masks. They are variously reported to identify the leader of a women's secret society
and membership in two different women's
secret societies, the Okuwe (or Okuki or
Yasi) and the Mukui.

NGUMBA

Statues (called Ngwun Malanda). Most of them
have head covered with feathers, head and body

with metal appliqué; some have pipes in their mouths. Kept in Bieri containers, like the Pangwe (see below). In times of sickness, offerings are presented.

PANGWE

(In most French documents called Pahouin, although this is said not to be an indigenous name. Other names used by authorities include Fang, Panwe, Fan, M'Pangwe, etc. Said to have come from the Upper Nile region about 1834 and settled along the Ogowe River about 1860, spreading to the coastal regions about 1870. Another theory presumes a Sudanese origin, Haute Sangha region, and their migration about 1800.)

Statues. The Pangwe have three styles of ancestor statuary. Heads on short or long necks (Fig. 14); half-figures (Figs. 80 and 81), and full figures, standing (Fig. 15) or seated (Fig. 44). The first two styles are comparatively rare and are favored by French collectors. The Pangwe statues are carved with extreme simplicity, dignity, and plastic freedom, in curved lines, with smooth surface. Calm facial expression often accented by the folded arms. Eyes are mainly metal pieces. The remarkable hairdo follows the line of the head. A derivation of the above style is the "dancer" figure (Jaunde) with strong, stylized movement (Fig. 180).

The full figures are called Bian (Medicine), or Bian Malan, or Malan. These and the sculptured heads are placed on containers, called Bieri, about forty inches high, holding skulls (five to twenty in number) of the deceased. The Bieri are usually kept in the family dwellings but sometimes in a specially constructed hut. They are used also as medicine figures, the sick being placed beside them. The Bieri is considered a protector of the ancestor's spirit. Other Pangwe figures, up to forty inches in size, called Niamodo, are not kept in Bieri containers but are secretly stored away from the women. The Pangwes also carve animal figures, elephants, boars, lizards, etc., which often hang from community houses. They also mold clay figures seven to ten feet long, used in the Ngi cult.

Masks. Oblong with prominent noses (Fig. 186); some have feather ornaments; some are surmounted by small figures. They are col-

FIG. 186. *Mask. Pangwe, Gabun. 22" high.*

FIG. 187. *Mask. Bavili (Loango), Gabun. 16" high.*

FIG. 188. *Pottery figure. Tago (Sao Kingdom), Tchad region, French Equatorial Africa. 7" high.*

ored white (the hue of spirits) but the features of some of them are outlined in black (Fig. 187) and are also attributed to the Bavili tribe. They are used by the secret societies.

SAO

Recent discoveries (1948) were made in the plains of the Lake Chad region which, politically, is part of French Equatorial Africa. Pottery figures excavated here (Fig. 188) from the ancient Sao empire are of great artistic merit and were probably used as ancestor *statues*. Tentative datings range from the ninth to the sixteenth centuries.

BELGIAN CONGO

The peoples of the Belgian Congo have produced a great variety of statuary in wood, ivory, cloth, shells and other material, and in a great range of color and design. Amazing artistic talent was shown by certain tribes (Bakubas or Balubas) and a great diversity of styles in individual tribes (the Bayakas had seven styles of masks alone). In general the styles show boldness in concept and execution.

Because of this abundance of styles and the extent of the region (roughly a million square miles), varied classifications have been made by authorities.

We prefer the classification system of Professor Frans M. Olbrechts, director of the Musée du Congo Belge, who distinguishes four major style regions:

1. *Lower Congo*, including the Bakongo, Babuende, Bateke, Bayaka, Bambala, Basuku, Bapende, Bambunda tribes;

2. *Bakuba*, including the Bashilile, Basongo-Meno, Dengese, Bakete (or Basala-Mpasu) tribes;

3. *Baluba*, the Basonge, Balunda, Bena Kanioka, Batshioko, Wabembe tribes;

4. *Northern*, including the Azande, Baboa, Bambole, Ngbandi, Ngbaka, Mangbetu, Bangala tribes.

The southern tribes, those below the fourth parallel, were the major art-producing peoples. Their figures have a wide range of attitudes, their forms are opulent, and the modeling is subtle.

The northern region, with twice the area, produced little in art. Such work as was produced is rigid in form and crude in execution, the arm held away from the body and clumsily carved.

Here we shall limit ourselves to the simple enumeration of the major tribes and their most typical art works.

We have used the names adopted, after thorough study of first-hand explorers' accounts, in the excellent book *Les Peuplades du Congo Belge, nom et situation géographique*, by J. Maes and O. Boone, published by the Musée du Congo Belge.

As already noted, the prefix *Ba* in many tribal names means "people." Thus *Baluba* means "the people of Luba." Since Luba is said to have been the name of a chief, this can be extended to mean "the people of the great chief Luba." The prefix *Mo* or *Mu* signifies an individual. *Moluba* or *Muluba* therefore means "member of the Baluba tribe."

Hyphenation has been proposed to simplify the nomenclature—Bu-Shongo, Wa-Rega, A-Zande, Ma-Ngbetu, etc. Most published

FIG. 189. *Throwing knife (Shongo). Azande, Belgian Congo. 18" high.*

FIG. 190. *Hood mask. Babindji, Belgian Congo. 13" high.*

material, however, uses the unhyphenated spellings which, for that reason, we use here.

AZANDE (*Also* BSANDE, BAZENDA, ZANDEH, ADYO, BADJO, IDIO, NIAM-NIAM)

Sande or *Sende* means "the earth." In this connotation it means "the people who possess much land." This goes back to their history as conquering warriors famous for their iron throwing-knives in elaborate abstract designs (Fig. 189). Simple abstract design and pale colors characterize their *masks*. Other *carvings* include boxes and harplike musical instruments with a human head carved on top.

BABEMBA *or* WABEMBA (*Not to be confused with the Wabembe*)

(Also called Wawemba, Babemba, Bemba, Ayemba, etc. groups, also live at the south end of Lake Tanganyika. The name means "people of the lake.")

Statues. Heads of male statues are flat, and broad-bearded. Seated female figures hold bowls. "Fetishsticks." Nonritual male and female figures in costumes, used as decorative objects.

Carved wooden *heads*.

Masks. Some are in the form of human and animal heads and are characterized by very small eyes; others are of abstract forms.

Stools with supporting figures, similar to the Baluba stools.

BABINDJI   *Southern Belgian Congo, near Angola*

Masks. A remarkable type of woven fiber mask, used as a hood, very similar to some American Indian masks (Fig. 190). Another type, a wooden mask (sometimes in polychrome), is characterized by a pointed chin and is carved in broad volumes (Fig. 192).

BABOA (*Also* ABABUA, ABABWA)

Masks with wood rings in place of ears, in striking black-and-white color contrasts. Polychrome masks of abstract design (Fig. 191).

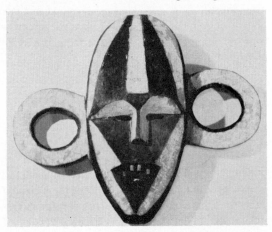

FIG. 191. *Mask. Baboa (Ababua), Belgian Congo. 13" high.*

FIG. 192. *Mask. Babindji, Belgian Congo. 12" high.*

BABOMA   *Situated close to Lake Leopold*

Statues. An interesting and distinctive sculptural style, with a crownlike hairdo, and angular arms (Fig. 193).

BABUNDA

Small magical *statues* containing magical substance. Also a few mother-and-child groups.

Also *scepters* with carved figures on the knobs.

BABUYE *or* BABUI

Statues and *busts* resembling the Wabembe work.

BAHOLOHOLO *or* BAGUA

Statues. Two-faced half-figures, breasts on both sides. Statues with long sticks in the hands, hairdo formed in three braids.

FIG. 193. *Statue. Baboma, Belgian Congo. 5″ high.*

FIG. 194. *Ivory pendant. Bahuana, Belgian Congo. 2½″ high.*

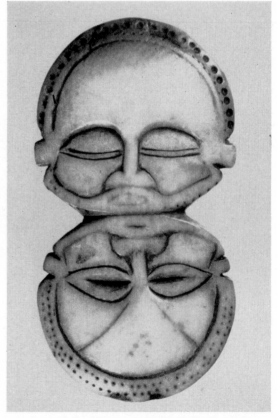

FIG. 195. *Ivory pendant. Bahuana, Belgian Congo. 2½″ high.*

FIG. 196. *Statue. Bakete,
Belgian Congo. 5" high.*

FIG. 197. *Mask. Bakete,
Belgian Congo. 13" high.*

BAHUANA

Statues. Mother-and-child groups.

Mahembe *masks* used at chiefs' weddings. Two heavy horns arched back, low forehead, large round eyes, short flat nose.

Some unusual types of *ivory carvings;* one a stylized human-figure pendant shaped from a flat strip of ivory (Fig. 194); another, two human heads (Fig. 195). Also small ivory figurines.

BAKETE

(Southern neighbors of the Bakubas with whose statues and masks Bakete works are often classified.)

Statues. Marked by protruding eyes and broad noses (Fig. 196).

Masks. Eyes with a polychrome pattern; small, colored triangular patterns line the face. This characteristic can also be found in many masks of the Bakubas, northern neighbor of the Bakete. The mask forms vary; some have V-shaped chins, some resemble the Bapende masks, some are horned or surmounted either by a geometrical form or a figure (Fig. 197).

These masks were also found among the Bapende and Batchioko tribes, and often at-tributed to the first tribe. They probably were used in the circumcision ceremonies. It is not yet clarified whether these masks were actu-ally made in the other territories and imported from the Baketes.

BAKONGO

This tribe is not to be confused with Bas-Congo (Lower Congo), in which they live. The regional name is Kongo, the tribal name *Bakongo* means "people of Kongo." An indi-vidual tribesman is called *Mukongo*. A numer-ous people whose sub-tribes include the Baso-longo (Muserongo), Bawoyo, Basundi (both in the Mayombe region), Bambata, Bazombo, Bavili and Bakuni. The attribution *Mayombe* frequently used for their work is incorrect. Mayombe is the name of one of the regions they inhabit.

Statues. In a great variety of attitudes. Faces are flat-nosed and expressive and many have indications of teeth. The Bakongo style is characterized by unusual realism.

The Konde, Pezu, Na Moganga fetishes from this region have been described under Magical Statues (pages 71 to 75).

Of great beauty are the so-called "mater-nity statues" (Figs. 17 and 198) which rep-

FIG. 198. *Maternity statue. Bakongo (Mayombe region), Belgian Congo. 11" high.*

FIG. 199. *Initiation ceremony statue (Thafu Malungu). Bakongo, Belgian Congo. 13" high.*

resent women, kneeling or seated, holding children in their laps. The facial expression is naturalistic. Elaborate geometrical patterns occur on the pedestal or the body, where they may be mingled with fine scarification marks. The figures were used to ward off danger from mothers during delivery and to protect the health of the child. Their effectiveness depended on the dignity of the figure and its youth (shown by the firmness of the breast) and the jewelry which augmented her beauty and status.

A very unusual type of sculpture produced in this region is made of soapstone (steatite). It has a strong Romanesque feeling. Some represent a seated figure, resting his chin on his hand; others represent a mother and child (Fig. 16).

There are many other statues and *scepters* covered with intricately carved figures, some seated, some holding chin in hand with calm, meditative facial expressions.

A very unusual figure is the "Thafu Malungu," representing Mbumba Luangu, a serpent spirit connected with the rainbow, and

used by the Bakhimba men's secret society (Fig. 199). The objects hanging from it possessed magic. It was credited with great power, the clan magician and his assistants devoting three weeks in the forest to its sanctification.

Masks are not generally known; however the Belgian Congo Museum has two interesting specimens (Figs. 200 and 201), both from the Mayombe region.

BAKUBA *or* BUSHONGO

According to Emil Torday, the name *Bakuba* is a Baluba word meaning "people of the lightning," a probable paraphrase of the word *Bushongo*, which means "people of the throwing knife." The shongo was a weapon unknown to the Baluba until they came in contact with the Bushongo whose battle weapon must have struck them as having the effect of a lightning bolt. This knife was later adopted by the Azande (Fig. 189). Though some authorities vary in the use of the name, we follow the usage of the Belgian Congo Museum which prefers *Bakuba*.

We owe our knowledge of the Bushongos

FIG. 200. *Mask. Bakongo (Mayombe region),*
Belgian Congo. 18" high.

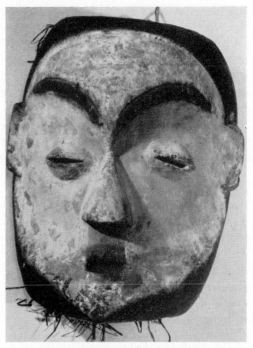

FIG. 201. *Mask. Bakongo (Mayombe region),*
Belgian Congo. 11" high.

to the publications of Torday. Their line of
120 kings, called Nyimi, were held to be of
divine origin. One of the most famous was
the ninety-third king, Shamba Balongongo
(1600–1620 A.D.), who introduced the custom
of carving a wooden image of the ruler. His
statue is now in the British Museum (Fig. 2).
The royal statues, representing the king wearing a caplike crown, seated on his haunches,
were mounted on a quadrangular pedestal.
One hand is on his shin, the other holds a ritual sword. At the foot of the pedestal is an
object emblematic of royal authority—a drum,
an anvil, a cup, a human or animal figure.
These statues are the product of a court art
similar, in its unique place in African art, to
that of the Benin Kingdom. Technically refined, this sophisticated, conventional art form
shows marked naturalistic tendencies. The
royal attitude implies reflection and will power
and aristocratic aloofness. We know of seventeen extant pieces and the names of twelve
rulers are recorded. The figures vary little
from each other; apparently, the carving of
the successors was modeled after the first.

The Bakubas, due to favorable agricultural
and climatic conditions, enjoyed a prosperity
favorable to artistic activity and appreciation.
Their villages were well organized, and clean.
Special sheds were provided for the artisans
whose work was greatly admired.

In spite of this unique appreciation of art,
comparable only to that of the Baule tribe of
the Ivory Coast, most of the objects served a
ritualistic purpose. Often a seemingly decorative, geometric pattern on an object had symbolic meaning.

This love of form, knowledge of materials,
skill in execution and appreciation of quality
is best seen in the number and variety of *gob-*
lets and cups, mostly for drinking palm wine
and restricted, among the Bashilele, to initiated
men. There are reports—not confirmed—that
these cups might have been used in the poison
ordeal. Among the Bakubas, as among other
African tribes, death is never attributed to
natural causes, but to malevolent spirits or to
witchcraft. The person suspected of using
witchcraft must drink poison from such a cup.
If he vomits up the drink, he is declared inno-
cent. On the other hand, his death proclaims
his guilt and constitutes his punishment.

Some cups have handles, others are without. In both, the following forms occur: Cups shaped like standing figures (Fig. 203) and kneeling figures (Fig. 204), the latter done in the Bushongo royal statue style. Cups shaped like human heads—some render only the head, using the neck as a base (Fig. 10). Some attached to one leg (Fig. 205). Some have two legs (Fig. 73). Some are double-headed on a common neck base (Fig. 202). Their expression is often of great beauty with a mysterious air of detachment, radiating an intense inner feeling (Fig. 209).

Another large group (also with and without handles) are of geometric design, done with great skill. If we remember that the African carver never traces a design, but cuts directly into the wood, we wonder how he was able to cover a certain round surface with flawless balance, another tribute to his great artistry. These so-called "geometrical pattern" cups are of the following types: many carry no other ornament than the design (Fig. 208); in some the handle is like a head (Fig. 207) or like a hand (Fig. 206).

FIG. 202. *6" high.*

Ceremonial cups. Bakuba, Belgian Congo.

FIG. 203. *9" high.*

FIG. 204. *11" high.*

FIG. 205. *10" high.*

FIG. 206. *9" high.*

FIG. 207. *6" high.*

FIG. 208. *7" high.*

FIG. 209. *Ceremonial cup. Bakuba, Belgian Congo. 6" high.*

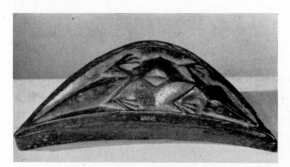

FIG. 210. *Ointment box. Bakuba, Belgian Congo. 9" high.*

FIG. 211. *Ointment box. Bakuba, Belgian Congo. 4" high.*

FIG. 212. *Pipe, Bayaka or Batshioko, Belgian Congo. 5½" high.*

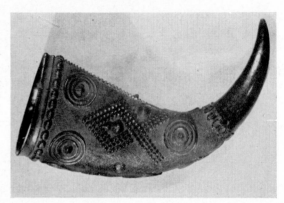

FIG. 213. *Drinking horn. Bakuba, Belgian Congo. 10" high.*

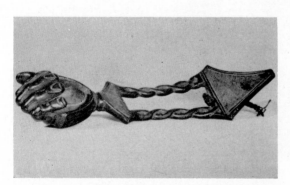

FIG. 214. *Utensil in form of a hand. Bakuba, Belgian Congo. 14" high.*

FIG. 215. *Raffia cloth. Bakuba, Belgian Congo. 26" high.*

FIG. 216. *Statue. Bakuba, Belgian Congo. 16" high.*

FIG. 217. *Mask (Bombo). Bakuba, Belgian Congo. 13" high.*

Each design has its own name and specific meaning, based upon certain objects or symbolic ideas (moon, sun, animal forms, horns, cowrie shells, animal claws, etc.). Often they represent a royal insignia. The same is true of the designs on the raffia cloth.

The human-hand motif (also used on decorated drums) is often isolated. Sometimes the hand is half-closed, possibly commemorating an old custom of a warrior presenting the left hand of a slain enemy for admission into the Yolo secret society (Fig. 214).

In the same style tradition are the *vases* and ointment containers (some in crescent form) richly carved with geometrical patterns, and used to hold the red "tukula" cosmetic powder (Figs. 211, 210).

Similar goblets, cups and boxes are produced by the Bashilele, Bahongo, Bapende, Bambala, Basongo-Meno and Baluba people.

Statues. Contrasted to the highly sophisticated royal portrait statues we have the roughly carved Bakuba figures, stronger in expression and vitality (Fig. 216). There are also wrought-iron figures, poorly executed, with oversize, flat hands, thought to date back to the sixteenth century. Divining instruments (Itombwa) in the form of a stylized animal, with a long body flattened on the back, on which coinlike disks were rubbed during the divination (Fig. 1). Similar divination figures were made by the Bashilele, Bakongo, Basongo-Meno and Bankutu tribes.

Other objects include *stools* and *headrests* supported by figures, *pipes* (Fig. 212) and *spoons* with carved heads, carved buffalo *drinking horns* (Fig. 213).

A tufted *cloth* is woven of Minyoa raffia, in geometric designs (Fig. 215). Such designs, appearing on goblets and boxes, with abstract moon, sun, snake, and animal motifs are believed to have had special meanings and special names handed down through generations.

Masks. Most commonly known in a very diversified output is the Bombo mask used in initiation ceremonies, a huge helmetlike human head, with bulging forehead, small eyes, large nose, and chin extended by a beard (Fig. 217). A triangular-shaped ornament rests on the bridge of the nose; broad bands, encrusted with pearls, are set over eyes and nose; the closed mouth is often covered with a cop-

FIG. 219. *Mask. Bakuba (Bapindi), Belgian Congo. 20" high.*

FIG. 218. *Mask. Bakuba, Belgian Congo. 16" high.*

FIG. 221. *Mask. Bakuba, Belgian Congo. 14" high.*

FIG. 220. *Mask. Bakuba, Belgian Congo. 22" high.*

FIG. 222. *Mask. Bakuba, Belgian Congo. 27" high.*

FIG. 223. *Mask with cowrie shells (Mashamboy). Bakuba, Belgian Congo. 16" high.*

per plate. Between eye and ear, cones are carved in relief. Other copper pieces, pearls and cowrie shells may also stud the masks. They are thought to represent the aborigines now regarded as genii.

The rich variety of Bakuba initiation masks may be seen in Figs. 219, 220, 222, 218, 3.

Another mask, often attributed to the Balubas and Bena Luluas, has a triangular pattern over the whole face, shells and beards often marking the hairline, and raffia cloth in geometrical designs, covering the wearer's head (Fig. 221).

The so-called Mashamboy masks (Fig. 223) have a flat face made of antelope skin or metal plates. Wooden nose and ears and raffia beards are affixed to a webbed cloth base. Eyes, eyebrows, the framing of the face, and often the headdress, are done in rows of beads and cowrie shells.* Tail-like ornaments on top are fre-

quent. The Mashamboy masks are supposed to be worn by chiefs and other dignitaries to commemorate an ancient clan hero. According to Torday, Bo Kena, seventy-third king (*Nyimi*) of the Bushongo invented this mask in 1350.

Maes quotes Torday, and indicates that these masks were also called Mukenga and Mukengo. On his last trip to the Congo, in 1912–14, they were worn by professional dancers. At these dances, women participated.

* Because of the wide use of cowrie shells by tribes in the Congo, the French Sudan, Cameroon, etc., in carvings and on ornamental girdles, it may be of interest to trace its development. The earliest known use of the cowrie shell in Africa was as a fertility symbol, probably because of its resemblance to the female sex organ. They were placed on girdles worn by maidens and marriage-

able women. In other lands, the cowrie was identified with the Greek *porculus* (little pig), token animal of the fertility goddess Aphrodite, and later with the concept of the Great Mother and the womb. Cowrie shells were used as money. Ibn Batuta and Cadamosto who visited the Kingdom of Melle in 1353 and 1455, respectively, reported a cowrie shell currency. These shells, as we have seen, are not indigenous to Africa, but imported from the Maldive Islands in the East Indies, apparently, and spread by Egyptian traders to West Africa. The Egyptian six-cowrie basic unit of money survived in Nigeria until recently. The cowrie is still used in food markets for purchases under a British penny. Two hundred cowries are worth approximately three cents. Its use as money also made the cowrie a symbol of power; consequently, the more cowries on a mask the greater its power.

FIG. 224. *Statue. Baluba, Belgian Congo. 13" high.*

FIG. 225. *Statue. Baluba, Belgian Congo. 11" high.*

Thus the sacred character of these masks was completely lost, and their usage transferred to public amusement.

The Kifwebe masks, with parallel lines, are often attributed to the Bakuba and Basonge tribes, but we list them under Baluba.

Extremely rare are the Bakuba ivory masks (about 5 inches in length). They are of great beauty with reddish-brown or yellow-brown patina (Fig. 24).

BAKWESE

Most *statues* roughly carved with angular shape, large eyes and flat face.

BALUBA (*Also* LOUBA, WALUBA, BULUBA)
on old charts URUWA *from name given them by Arabs*

Inhabitants of southeast Belgian Congo; some are also found in northern Rhodesia. The Balubas were formerly an independent state allied with the Lunda Kingdom, probably around the sixteenth century. The Balubas have a great variety of carving, distinguished by its emotional intensity. Refinement of execution is sometimes sacrificed for the sake of dramatic expression.

Their magical *statues* are in hemispherical forms, the arms set close to the body, the head often round and the eyes deep-set. There are also ancestor figures, characterized by elaborate scarification patterns on the body. Heads have a broad forehead and finely carved features, with an intricate hair pattern (Fig. 224). Some statues have the shoulder squared and the head also square on the neck (Fig. 225), suggesting great power. Composite figures also occur, such as a mother carrying her child, ivory amulets (Fig. 226), the "Katatora" divining instrument (Frontispiece), finely carved stools (Fig. 66) and headrests supported by standing figures (Fig. 227), or by groups of two, three or four figures, or by sitting, crouching or kneeling figures (Fig. 228). All have elaborate scarification patterns. Some authorities explain these supporting figures by the custom of a king sitting on the back of a slave.

Unusual for African art is the kneeling or seated begging figure (Kabila Ka Vilie) representing the protecting spirit of maternity, the hands holding up a Kaliba (wooden bowl) (Fig. 229). These figures were placed before the dwelling of a woman in childbirth, silently

FIG. 226. *Ivory amulet. Baluba, Belgian
Congo. 3" high.*

FIG. 227. *Head rest. Baluba, Belgian Congo.
6½" high.*

FIG. 228. *Head rest. Baluba, Belgian Congo.
7" high.*

FIG. 229. *Figure with bowl (Kabila Ka Vilie).
Baluba, Belgian Congo. 7½" high.*

FIG. 230. *Figure with bowl. Baluba (Buli),*
Belgian Congo. 18″ high.

FIG. 231. *Mask (Kifwebe). Baluba, Belgian*
Congo. 25″ high.

inviting alms from the passer-by. Recent studies show that they were also used for divination. White powder (mpembe) was put into
the bowl and then rubbed on the person seeking advice; or objects representing ancestor
spirits were put into the bowl and shaken,
and from the positions they then took a fortune was read. By the latter method the name
of the child was determined. Also bowl held
by two figures (Fig. 29).

The extremely rare, bowl-holding figures
of the region of Buli (Fig. 230), with elongated faces carved with great expressive force,
belong among the masterpieces of African art.
Only eight examples are known. This type of
carving, however, also appears in the Buli
stools (Fig. 8).

Ceremonial *staffs* and *scepters* are of very
great variety and beauty (Figs. 235, 9). Similar care goes into *adze* and *axe handles* with
the blade inset like a tongue (Fig. 232), *arrow
quivers* (Fig. 234), etc.

The Kifwebe *masks* (formerly attributed to

the Basonge tribe), used by the secret society
of the same name, originated in this territory,
according to recent researches of the Belgian
Congo Museum. However, Maes indicates
that the name Kifwebe was the name of the
mask and was used in a dance called, Makaye
a Kifwebe, which means "dance of the mask."
He further indicates that this mask was used
when the chief of the village died, or when a
chief (Kalala) was appointed, or when an important visitor arrived at the village. There is
also a suggestion that the same mask might
have been used on a large statue, man-size,
made of clay, wood, and fiber.

The Kifwebe masks are of impressive volume, some with extremely large, square-
shaped mouth (Fig. 231), large nose and eyes,
and linear pattern over the whole face (Fig.
233). Some are in the Janus style. Other large
masks have abstract planes and color schemes.
There is a huge mask with curved horns (Fig.
21), of which probably only two are in existence.

FIG. 232. *Head of an ax. Baluba, Belgian Congo. 15″ high.*

FIG. 233. *Mask (Kifwebe). Baluba, Belgian Congo. 13″ high.*

FIG. 234. *Arrow quiver. Baluba, Belgian Congo. 20″ high.*

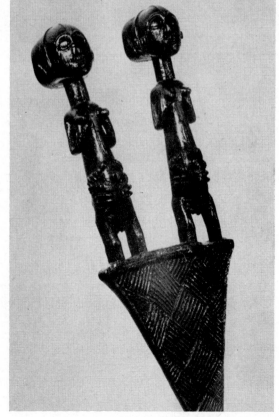

FIG. 235. *Staff's head. Baluba, Belgian Congo. 41″ high.*

FIG. 236. Statue.
Balunda, Belgian
Congo. 12" high.

FIG. 237. Statue. Bambala,
Belgian Congo. 5" high.

FIG. 239. Statue. Bangala
(North Congo), Belgian
Congo. 22" high

FIG. 238. Initiation ceremony
statue (Libwe Society).
Bambola, Belgian Congo.
28" high.

BALUNDA (*Also* ALUNDA, ARUND, MILUA, LUNDA)

Art similar to the neighboring Batshioko.

Their *statues* are unusual in depicting action, pounding a mortar (Fig. 236), smoking, drumming, etc.

Also, the Akish *heads* placed on small earthen mounds, clay figures in animal forms kept in straw huts. Hollow, carved wooden heads with elaborate hairdo.

The *masks* have long hairdress carvings, round eyes, small nose, sharply cut lips, protruding chin similar to the Batshioko masks (Fig. 22).

A large variety of *scepters* with heads carved on the knob, *tobacco mortars, whistles, combs,* etc.

BAMBALA (*Sometimes called Ba-Babala or the "Red People"; connected with the word* babala *meaning "red."*)

Bambala *statues* are characterized by stiff attitudes. Many have the hand on the chin, like the Bayaka figures (Fig. 237). Round head forms, domed foreheads, small oval eyes. Also seated maternity statues, seated drumming figures, and ancestor statues. There are also headrests supported on the arms of single or double figures. The statues are reddened with Tukula powder, also used on the body, from which custom the tribal name was probably derived. Masks resemble those of the neighboring Bayakas.

BAMBOLE

Statues. This northern tribe possessed a distinctive sculpture in the form of a striking type of figure used in the initiation ceremonies of the Libwe secret society (Fig. 238).

BANGALA

Comprising several northern tribes of the region, the Monsembe, Boloki, Ngombe, Ngbaka, Ngbaka-Mabo, Banza, Ngbandi and others.

Statues. Their carving is rudimentary, arms standing apart from the body (Fig. 239), head square or round, legs heavy and usually without feet; the body and forehead with scarifications marks.

FIG. 240. *Initiation ceremony mask. Bapende, Belgian Congo. 22" high.*

Some polychrome *masks*, used also by the Bwaka and Bansa tribes, have been attributed to the Bangala.

BAPENDE *or* BAPINDI

Two separate areas, one adjacent to the Bayakas and the other north of the Batshioko.

Such *statues* as have been accredited to them —some healing figures and some mother-and-child groups—appear to have been imported from other tribes.

Their best-known art products, the Minyaki *masks*, are of great beauty (Fig. 27). They are sensitively carved and have a spiritualized expression, with domed forehead, long stylized eyebrow lines, protruding cheekbones, short broad nose, mouth in the lower angle of the triangular face, half-closed eyes, headdress of black, dyed, palm fiber. The face is painted red or deep brown.

Some masks representing chiefs have a long beard carved from the same block of wood marked by triangular patterns (Fig. 240).

FIG. 241. *Hood mask. Bapende, Belgian Congo. 11" high.*

FIG. 242. *Mask, made of raffia cloth and feathers. Bapende, Belgian Congo. 9" high.*

Some completely cover the wearer's head like a hood (Fig. 243). These masks, used in circumcision ceremonies, were probably also used as a defense against malevolent spirits.

The Bapendes also used a sometimes-horned, helmetlike mask, similar to the Bakuba "Bombo" masks with domed forehead and protruding nose (Fig. 241). There are also polychrome masks: red face, white tubular eyes, black mouth and a white triangular decoration on the cheek (see Bakete).

Completely different from the traditional Bapende masks is a round twig-and-raffia structure covered with woven cloth. The eyes, also of fiber, give an abstract design to the face (Fig. 242).

Delicately carved ivory, wooden, copper and zinc *miniature masks*, about two inches long, with all the typical marks of the large masks (half-closed eye, small nose, etc.), called Dikoko or Buya, worn suspended from the neck. They represented a badge of initiation (Kimpasi) and were also used as protective amulets (Fig. 28). Also larger ivory masks about six inches in size (Fig. 25).

BASHILELE

Closely related to the Bakubas; best known for their *cups*, especially those on a stem.

BASONGE   (*Also called Bayembe, Bassongo, Wasonga,* etc.)

The name *Basonge* probably derives from *Kasongo*, one of the ancient great chiefs of the Balubas. Although the Basonge are relatives of the Balubas, their style differs appreciably.

The Basonge *statues* are carved with great force. Their hands are on paunches filled with magical substance (Fig. 244). There are also busts in the same attitude; also figures without legs or arms (Fig. 72). In the full figures the head is generally rounded in front and outstretched, the long neck often twisted, shoulders generally broad, feet large and flat on the pedestal. The statue may be covered with cloth, with varied objects, animal teeth, bits of wood, etc., hanging from it (Fig. 244). Eyes are indicated either by perforations or cowrie shells. The head is often encrusted

FIG. 243. *Initiation ceremony mask. Bapende, Belgian Congo. 18" high.*

FIG. 245. *Magical statue. Basonge, Belgian Congo. 7" high.*

FIG. 244. *Magical statue. Basonge, Belgian Congo. 35" high.*

FIG. 247. *Hood mask. Basuku, Belgian Congo. 17" high.*

FIG. 246. *Hood mask (Hembe). Basuku, Belgian Congo. 16" high.*

with metal pieces as decoration. These magical statues are used at changes of the moon.

According to Maes, these statues were also used as leopard fetishes, meaning that the medicine man, possessing this statue, was able to acquire command over an actual leopard and could command the animal to kill the person he chose. Many of the statues actually have a number of leopard teeth hanging on a leather band. In smaller figures the magical substance is often placed on the head in the form of an animal horn. Some have pointed, bearded chins.

The Basonge also have an unusual style of sculpture with large head, open mouth pinched together in the center to form a horizontal figure eight design (Fig. 245).

Among the smallest (about two inches) *ivory pieces* of West Africa are the Basonge whistles (Fig. 11). They represent a Bearded male figure with circular patterns on the body. In spite of their small size, and the gemlike feeling of the ivory, they have a remarkably monumental simplicity.

There are also *stools* with carved, supporting statues, similar to the Baluba stools.

The Basonge Kifwebe *masks*, modeled on those of the Balubas, have linear ornament in white color. This becomes more dramatic when the mask is painted black (see Baluba). A variation of these is the miter-shaped Basonge-Batempa masks which have protruding cylinder eyes without mouth.

BASONGO MENO

Basongo means "people," *Meno* "teeth"; thus *Basongo Meno*, "teeth people." The Basongo Menos file their teeth to a triangular shape. They are also called Bankutshu, Bakutu, Batetela, Wafuluka, etc.

The *statues* are half-figures, exquisitely carved, down to the genitals, and set on round pedestals. Heads are small in proportion. Hairdo is sometimes covered with cowrie shells. The trunk is very long, arms ending in large hands, resting on the body, whose rigid attitude imparts an air of grandeur. Navel and abdomen are richly decorated with scarification marks. The head, too, has tattoo marks.

Basongo Meno *cups* are in the form of a

FIG. 248. *Initiation ceremony mask (Badunga Society). Basundi (Bawoyo), Belgian Congo. 17" high.*

human head, similar to the Bakuba goblets, with hornlike hairdo.

BASUKU

The Basukus are sometimes confused with their western neighbors, the Bayakas.

Their two, hoodlike types of *masks* resemble Bayaka work. The type called "Hembe" (Fig. 246) has an angular pattern concentrated on the forehead. The eyes are half-closed. The whole, carved out of a single block of wood, is topped by a seated human figure, an animal figure, or an abstract design. Another type has the face compressed and has flaring ears and a small beard. The expression resembles that of Etruscan statues (Fig. 247).

BASUNDI *or* BAWOYO

The Basundi tribe in the Mayombe region produced a very interesting *mask* (Fig. 248) for their Badunga secret society. This mask is over a foot high and has the features of a Dan mask from the Ivory Coast. Usually painted white (sometimes with colored lines) probably indicating colors used in initiation ceremonies.

FIG. 249. *Statue. Bayaka, Belgian Congo. 10" high.*   FIG. 250. *Double statue. Bateke, Belgian Congo. 11" high.*   FIG. 251. *Statue. Bayaka, Belgian Congo. 19" high.*

BATABWA *or* BAMARUNGU

Statues attributed to this tribe may derive from the neighboring Balubas. Large heads with hemispherical domed forehead, with V-shaped tattooing, and oval eyes. Some heads carry a horn containing magical substance, typical of the Basonge magical statues.

BATEKE

Also called *M'Teke* and *Bakono*. Their name indicates their occupation, *viz.* traders; from *teke* meaning to buy. They live in the Stanley Pool area, in the southern French Middle Congo region.

Statues. Their best-known works are medicine statues, erect figures with large heads, narrow foreheads, short noses, with finely carved vertical scarification ridges on the cheeks and sometimes bearded chin (Fig. 35). Arms are close to the body and usually sharply bent. The feet are roughly carved, with short and slightly bent legs, often in cubistic forms. The beard is short and squared and the hairdo is shaped either like a crown or a crested helmet, in exaggerated, stylized forms, resem-

bling the hairdo of the Bateke, who shave the sides of their heads to give the remaining hair a conic, helmetlike appearance. The small beard resembles the beard worn by the tribal elders. Here again, as so often in African art, natural forms are the basis for abstract forms. The abdomen has a cavity to hold the magical substance (missing in most figures now in collections). The figures had significance to the Africans only when so "loaded" at their consecration by magicians. Some are Janus-type statues, with two faces. Fig. 250 has the magical substance around the body. Sometimes a nail, or in one instance, a shirt button, was used for an eye. The same type was also used by the following tribes: Wabari, Rahumbu, Bamfumungu, Bayanzi, Babwende, Basundi.

No Bateke masks are known.

BATETELA   *see also Basongo-Meno*

Works of the Basonge style, but inferior in artistic quality, especially the *masks*.

Statues. Figures with hand on the accentuated navel or abdomen, filled with magical substance.

FIG. 252. *Initiation ceremony mask. Bayaka, Belgian Congo. 16" high.*

FIG. 253. *Statue (detail). Bayaka, Belgian Congo. 8" high.*

Also *ivory carvings*.

BATSHIOKO

Although a section of this tribe lives in the Bakuba territory and another in southern Belgian Congo, the main body lives in Angola, and their works are discussed in the Angola section (page 227).

BAYAKA or BA-YAKALA

Yaka or *Yakala* means "males, the strong one," *Bayake*, the "strong people."

Statues. The Bayaka style is marked by the prominence and deformation of the nose (Fig. 249) which on some of the masks is bent into an upward hook (Fig. 252). The eyes protrude, the eyelids bulge and are framed by incisions; the ears stand away sometimes in block form; the forehead is often low and flat with vertical lines running from the forehead over the bridge of the nose. In many Bayaka figures both hands hold the pointed chin (Fig. 251). These are generally attributed to the Kwango region. Polychrome effects give an extremely forceful expression. The nose, whether long or short, is turned up. The body

is roughly carved, with unshaped legs, some in strong cubistic form, some without feet. The arms are generally thin and curved, poorly developed and not well integrated into the whole composition.

Of particular interest is Fig. 253, which has all the Bayaka characteristics. When the sculptor wanted both to expose the breasts and put the hand on the bosom, he solved the problem by carving the breasts on both *sides* of the statue, a rendering also to be observed in paintings by Picasso.

The statues are mostly of wood. Some emphasize the genitals; some have crestlike hairdos.

Masks are widely varied in style, but possess one common characteristic; they are all in polychrome. (Through use, however, the paint has disappeared and only hints of the color may be perceived.) Their original, heavy raffia collar, or collarette, has often been removed.

The first main group (masks called Nkisi) are highly stylized. They have a long, upward-hooked nose, open mouth exposing two rows of teeth (Fig. 252). The face is often framed

FIG. 254. *Feather mask. Bayaka, Belgian Congo. 12" high.*

FIG. 255. *Hood mask. Bayaka, Belgian Congo. 11" high.*

by a large painted square or circle according to the sex represented by the mask. A long handle under the chin supported the mask during the dance. They are generally surmounted by a richly ornamented, abstract construction; sometimes resembling a Siamese pagoda; sometimes in animal shapes, made of twigs, covered with fiber cloth, and finally painted.

A variant is the broad-nosed Ndemba mask, with round, protruding eyes and square, block-like ears (Fig. 61). Most are in polychrome. They have the same superstructure as the Nkisi masks.

These two types of masks were used in initiation ceremonies of the Mukanda or Nkanda societies. At the conclusion of the initiation, the masks were held before the faces of dancers.

The characteristics of the second type of mask are puffed cheeks and white painted mouth and eyes. Features are not as exaggerated as in a similar type of Cameroon mask called Bango (Fig. 64).

The third type is made of woven raffia with a large raffia collar and feather headdress. The only marks identifying the human face are

three white rings so placed as to suggest eyes and mouth (Fig. 254). The fourth type is an immense, horned, fiber-cloth, war mask. The fifth type is a hood-mask (Fig. 255), similar in conception to the Basuku type but without the animal on top. The sixth type has a flat surface with extreme abstract design for the eyes (Fig. 257). The seventh type is an animal mask (Fig. 256) similar to the Cameroon Doualla masks.

The Bayakas also carved *wooden panels*

FIG. 256. *Animal mask. Bayaka, Belgian Congo. 26" high.*

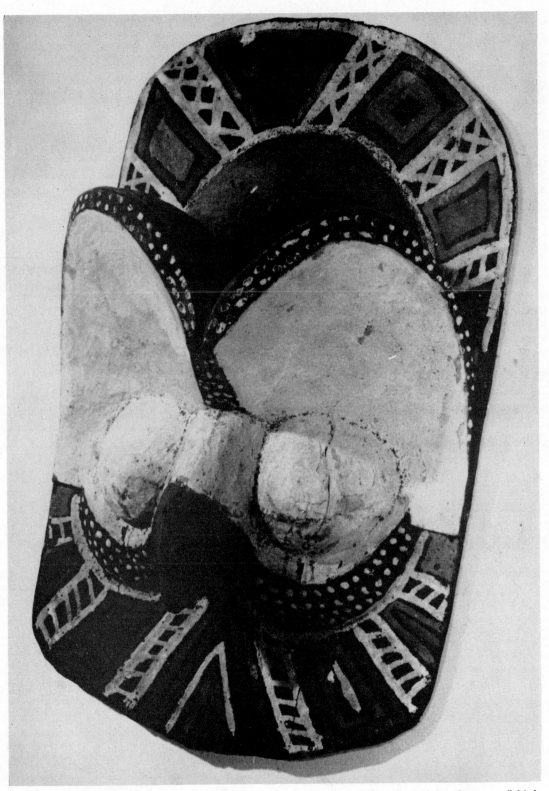

FIG. 257. *Mask. Bayaka, Belgian Congo. 13″ high.*

FIG. 258. *Ceremonial cup. Bayaka, Belgian Congo. 4½" high.*

with human and animal figures, for the Mukenda initiation ceremonies.

The Bayaka ceremonial *cups* are of a graceful octagonal form (Fig. 258), carved with great ease in spite of the difficulties of hollowing out the inside. They are supposed to have been used in marriage ceremonies, the bride drinking from one side and the bridegroom from the other, to seal their union.

BAYANZI *or* BABANGI

Neighbors of the Batekes. Part of the tribe lives in the French Middle Congo.

Statues. Resemble those of the Batekes, but lack the characteristic beard and the helmet-like hairdo (Fig. 261). They are rather roughly carved and the incisions on the face are much heavier than those of the Bateke statues. Nose and mouth form a triangular design. Some, with sex indications, appear to have been used in fecundity rituals. Some are ancestor figures.

BENA BIOMBO

Masks. Polychrome, of monumental structure with large eyes, small nose and small circular mouth (Fig. 262).

BENA KOSH

Hood-mask with bold, richly carved polychrome planes (Fig. 65).

BENA LULUA *or* BENA LULUWA

From the name of the river, on which they live.

FIG. 259. *Mother and child. Bena Lulua, Belgian Congo. 15" high.*

FIG. 260. *Statue. Bena Lulua (Bakwa-Ndolo), Belgian Congo. 15" high.*

FIG. 261. *Statue. Bayanzi,*
Belgian Congo. 6" high.

FIG. 262. *Mask. Bena Biombo, Belgian Congo. 15″ high.*

FIG. 263. *Statue. Bwaka (Ngbaka), Belgian Congo. 20" high.*

FIG. 264. *Mask. Bena Lulua, Belgian Congo. 23" high.*

Their *statues* represent men, women, and mother-and-child groups, all with the same characteristics. Some mother-and-child figures have a prong attached, suggesting that they were attached to other objects (Fig. 259). The figures are slender; with slim, long neck; long chin; long, oval head with large eyes; and crested, pointed, hornlike braided head-dress (Fig. 260). Small male figures have long, intricately braided beards. The hands sometimes hold a scepter, a bowl or a bottle. Rich scarification marks in geometrical design, cover the whole body, with the navel emphasized. It is supposed that the male figures (Lupfingu) represent a chief, and that they were used to bring success in hunting and to cure sickness.

Other figures are in the crouched or squatting burial position (Fig. 7) with the hands on the oversize heads. The feet, also, are oversize. A red color was rubbed into many of them, but in older examples the tint was rubbed off. Probably used as ancestor figures.

Bena Lulua *masks* are elaborate design patterns, and possess intricate hairdos (Fig. 264).

Also: *drums, headrests,* supported by richly tattooed male figures.

BWAKA *or* NGBAKA

Statues. Impressive columnar effects (Fig. 263). Polychrome initiation ceremonial *masks* (Fig. 265).

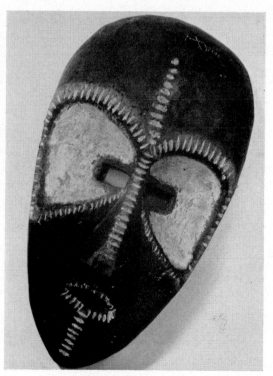

FIG. 265. *Initiation ceremony mask. Bwaka, Belgian Congo. 15" high.*

FIG. 267. *Statue, Mangbetu, Belgian Congo. 19" high.*

FIG. 266. *Funerary figure. Dengese (Ndengese), Belgian Congo. 20" high.*

FIG. 269. *Statue. Nkundo, North Congo. 35" high.*

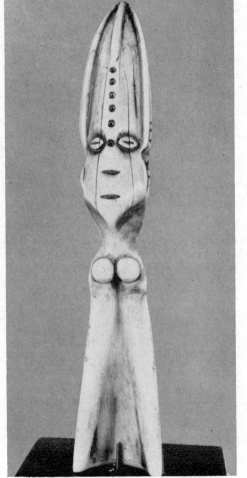

FIG. 268. *Ivory statue. Ngbandi (North Congo), Belgian Congo. 7" high.*

DENGESE *or* DENKESE

A sub-tribe of Basongo Meno whose work is strongly influenced by the Bakuba.

Statues. Interesting funerary figures with large torsos (Fig. 266).

KANIOKA *or* BENA-KANIKA

The name of this tribe means "people of the snake."

Statues. Standing female, seated male; wood and ivory figures; one type a drummer.

Black, red-centered, oval *masks* with white crests, the forehead domed, mouth a cylindrical block.

MANGBETU *or* MONBUTU

This tribe lives near the Anglo-Egyptian Sudan.

The main characteristic of their carvings—*statues* (Fig. 267), *jars, knives, musical instruments, wooden honey containers*—is that the head adorning these works has an elongated cranium, probably due to Egyptian influence spread by the Khartum traders from up the Nile. Their masterpiece is a clay *beer mug,* single- or double-headed (Fig. 18), on which the face is highly stylized and the elongated head shows the tribal hairdo, a work comparable to Egyptian heads.

MANYEMA *or* MANJEMA

(Erroneously classified in other publications as a tribal name. It is a region located between the Lualaba and the Tanganyika.)

MAYOMBE

See Bakongo.

NGBANDI

A northwestern tribe, their artistic works very little known. We know however of an astonishing ivory carving (Fig. 268) with strangely elongated head; breasts and legs rendered in an abstract manner reminiscent in spirit of many modern paintings.

NKUNDO

This tribe also lived in the north.

Statues. Possess strong facial expression (Fig. 269).

FIG. 270. *Statue. Wabembe, Belgian Congo 14" high.*

WABEMBE (*Also* BABEMBE *or* CUABEMBE *meaning "people of the east"*)

One of the rare, eastern tribes living in the mountainous northern Tanganyika Lake region which produced an interesting art style characterized, in common with the general North Congo statuary style, by geometrical, face forms carried out further in cubistic trunks and legs, close to the Warega style.

Statues. Male, with large head, on small necks, broad forehead, large oval eyes, long nose, the small triangular, chinless face ending in a mouth, a zigzag beard design running up both sides of the face, massive hairdo on back of the head. Body is heavy, with arms folded on the breast. Some of these protective statues are used on burial grounds (Fig. 270).

WAREGA (*Also* WAREGGA, OUREGGA, BULEGA)

One of the rare Northeast Congo tribes which produced an interesting art. Their specialty is ivory carving.

Statues. Of great variety are their Bami ivory figurines (about four to five inches

FIG. 271. *Ivory mask. Warega, Belgian Congo.* 7″ *high.*

high) executed with great simplicity in angular forms (Fig. 19). Some have only a head (often with pointed chin) and a round trunk without arms or legs; sometimes the arms are indicated (Fig. 20); or the entire statue is a phallic symbol (Fig. 43). According to one theory the Bami were given by the tribal elders and chiefs as a personal identification or seal to a messenger; another, that they were insignia of rank (Kindi) in the Kwami society called Mwami; another that they were used as a twin fetish.

The Waregas also have wooden figures with raised arms and slender, female ancestor figures, wood dance-scepters with white, diamond-shaped, human-face ornaments.

Masks. Ivory; have a rich patina; 7 to 8 inches high (Fig. 271); some in wood.

Also *headrests* of ivory. Like masks, these are prized by collectors.

WARUWA

This Baluba sub-tribe is also known as Warua, Urua, Uruwa, Uarua, Ouroua, because of the different versions used by Arab writers and carried over into early European maps of the region.

Statues, except that they tend to the spherical, conform to the Baluba types.

WAZIMBA

Southern neighbors of the Warega. Their art also has the strong abstract quality of the northeast tribes, such as Wabembe, Warega, etc.

Statues. Large heads in nearly quadrangular form; the large forehead dominates the small face; small eyes (sometimes inlaid cowrie shells) are imbedded in large sockets; scarification marks cover the bodies. Also medicine figures. Their ivory statues, headrests supported by human figure, resemble those of the Warega.

Kifwebe *masks* (see Basonge) are used with the added characteristic that the forehead is merged with the nose and has a protruding, black ridge for the mouth.

ANGOLA

Northern Angola and Southern Belgian Congo show a certain style unity which can be summed up as follows: There are *Ancestor*, *Demon* and *Totem figures*. These were carved immediately after death to provide an abode for the spirit of the deceased. They were kept in special huts, and before each a wooden or clay plate or bowl was placed for food offerings.

BATSHIOKO

The name of this tribe, which also lives in southern Belgian Congo, has twenty-eight different spellings, among which are: Badjokwe, Badjok, Bajok, Vachioko, Watschiwokwe, Chokwe, Kioko, and Kiokje. The aggressiveness of these people, famous as slave raiders and intrepid fighters, appears in all their sculptures which have cruel expressions and vivid, bold forms.

Statues. Ancestor figures holding in one or both hands a cup or a bowl; head covered with human hair which, mixed with clay, forms stiff braids; hands and feet naturalistic but

FIG. 272. *Statue. Batshioko, Belgian Congo.*
11" high.

FIG. 273. *Chief's chair. Batshioko, Belgian Congo. 15" high.*

FIG. 274. *Chief's stool. Batshioko, Belgian Congo. 8" high.*

exaggerated. The careful carving pays special attention to fingers and nails.

Ancestor figures with violent, snarling, facial expressions; hairdo is most unusual, a structure towering above the head and continuing down the sides, covering the ears, heavily stylized (Fig. 272); one or two small figures may be placed atop the hairdo; feet and hands (four or five fingers, usually holding guns or clubs) are very large and accentuate the cruel, animalistic attitudes. There is often a carved belt from which hangs a knife, a bottle, or other objects; some figures have one arm raised, as if to seize something, the body bent forward, the facial expression predatory.

Also divination figures in human and animal form. Also large wood carvings, covered with clay, kept in huge tobacco containers, the covers surmounted by the statues. Unusual are the chairs with quadrangular seat, a European influence, and chairs with or without backs (Fig. 273). The legs, back and spindles are richly carved with small human and animal figures often representing scenes from tribal life (two men carrying a man in a hammock,

FIG. 275. *Mask. Batshioko, Belgian Congo. 10" high.*

FIG. 276. *Mask. Batshioko, Belgian Congo. 15" high.*

circumcision ceremonies, etc.). Some are legendary symbols. Early stools are made in monaxial blocks with human and animal figures (Fig. 274). Scepters with knobs in the form of human heads or seated figures (Fig. 13). Carved combs with human and animal figures.

Masks are of varied types. One has the same monumental effect as the statue heads, with small nose, very large mouth and strong chins. Another type is rather naturalistic, painted in red, with tribal scarification marks on the forehead and cheeks; hairdo in black fiber (Fig. 276), eyes emphasized, forehead in a rhomboid design. Another type called Mukish, made of tree bark on a wooden base, with different ornamental materials, was used in initiation ceremonies. Other masks, called Kalelwe, have savage facial expressions and gigantic hairdo, often of woven cloth or feathers. Still another type is in hood form, resting on the wearer's shoulder; it has large eyes and extremely large mouth stretched the full width of the mask, producing a fierce expression (Fig. 275).

LOVALE

Statues. Red and white clay human and animal figures.

Masks with broad forehead, pointed chin, small eye slits.

KALUENA

Statues. Seated figure on a chair in the Batshioko tradition, but less tense in expression, and utilizing smaller forms.

MINUNGO

Mukish *masks* similar to the Batshioko masks.

VIMBUNDU *or* M'BUNDU

Statues with small head, very long body, and short legless feet.

BIBLIOGRAPHY

The following list contains only those books and publications which have been consulted in the preparation of this text, and does not pretend to be a comprehensive bibliography of African art or its related subjects.

LADISLAS SEGY (SZECSI)

PUBLICATIONS ON AFRICAN ART

Az Urvezeto, Budapest, May 8, 1930. "A Neger Muveszetrol." (About Negro Art.)

Elseviers, "Amsterdam," August, 1932. "Over Negerkunst. (About Negro Art.)

Art & Archaeology, Washington, May-June, 1933. "Primitive Negro Art."

Ethnologischer Anzeiger, Stuttgart, 1933. Band III, Heft 3. "Stilgebiete der Elfenbeinkuste." (Style regions of the Ivory Coast.)

The Studio. London, 1934. "Negro Sculpture in Interior Decoration."

La Terre et la Vie, Paris, Juillet, 1934. "Sur l'Art Negre." (About Negro Art.)

Negro, Nancy Cunard, Ed., London, 1934. (1) "The Term 'Negro Art' is Essentially a Non-African Concept." (2) "The Different Styles of Masks of the Ivory Coast" (in co-operation with Mr. R. Michelet).

Mouseion (Office International des Musées), Paris, 1934. Volumes 25-26. "L'Art Négre et les Musées." (Negro Art and the Museums.)

Gallery Magazine, New York, December, 1950. "African Sculpture and Cubism."

Phylon, Fourth Quarter, Vol. XII, No. 4, 1951. Atlanta University, Atlanta, Georgia. "The Significance of African Art."

Midwest Journal, Lincoln University, Jefferson City, Missouri, May, 1952. "Bakuba Cups."

Midwest Journal, Lincoln University, Jefferson City, Missouri. "The Future of African Art" (to be published).

Zaire, University of Louvain, Belgium, December, 1951. "Warega Ivories."

Zaire, University of Louvain, Belgium, May 1952. "Bakota Funerary Statues."

Complex, The Magazine of Psychoanalysis and Society, New York, No. 9, Summer, 1952. "African Sculptures and Animism."

Buma, "African Sculpture Speaks." A short moving picture based upon research and story by Ladislas Segy; produced, written and directed by Henry R. Cassirer; photographed and edited by Lewis Jacobs; music recorded in Africa by Arthur S. Alberts. Distributed by Encyclopaedia Britannica Films, Inc.

AFRICAN ART (U.S.A.)

Boas, Franz, *Primitive Art.* Oslo, London, Cambridge, 1927.

Griaule, Marcel, *Folk Art of Black Africa.* New York, 1950.

Guillaume, Paul, and Monro, Thomas, *Primitive Negro Sculpture.* London and New York, 1926.

Harley, George W., *Notes on the Poro in Liberia.* Cambridge, Mass., 1941.

Harley, George W., *Masks as Agents of Social Control in Northeast Liberia.* Cambridge, 1950.

Kjersmeier, Carl, *African Negro Sculptures.* New York, 1948.

Kochnitzky, Leon, *African Negro Sculptures.* New York, 1948.

Wingert, Paul S., *The Sculpture of Negro Africa.* New York, 1950.

Zayas, M. de, *African Negro Art.* New York, 1916.

CATALOGUES (U.S.A.)

Boulton, Laura C., *Bronze Artists of West Africa.* New York, 1935.

Culin, Stewart, *Primitive Negro Art.* Brooklyn Museum, 1923.

Locke, Alain, *The Significance of African Art.* Baltimore Museum of Art, 1946.

Primitive Art. University of Minnesota, 1940.

Sweeney, James J., *African Negro Art.* New York, Museum of Modern Art, 1935.

Wingert, Paul S., *African Negro Sculpture.* San Francisco, M. H. de Young Memorial Museum, 1948.

ARTICLES (U.S.A.)

Barnes, Dr. Albert, "Primitive Negro Sculpture and Its Influence on Modern Civilization." *Opportunity*. New York, May, 1928.

Fagg, William, "The Antiquities of Ife."*Magazine of Art*. Washington, April, 1950.

Hooton, E. A., "Benin Antiquities in the Peabody Museum." *Varia Africana I*. Peabody Museum of Harvard University, Cambridge, Mass., 1917.

Linton, Ralph, "Primitive Art." *Kenyon Review*, Fall, 1941.

Locke, Alain, "African Art, Classic Style." *American Magazine of Art*, New York, May, 1935.

Locke, Alain, "Collection of Congo Art." *The Arts*, New York, February, 1927.

Publications of the University Museum, University of Pennsylvania, Philadelphia:

Hall, H. U., "The Sherbro of Sierra Leone." 1938.

Hall, H. U., "Two Masks from French Equatorial Africa." December, 1947.

Hall, H. U., "Examples of African Art." September, 1919.

Hall, H. U., "African Cups Embodying Human Forms." September, 1924.

Hall, H. U., "An Ivory Standing Cup from Benin." December, 1926.

Hall, H. U., "Great Benin Altar." June, 1922.

Hall, H. U., "A Large Drum from Benin." June, 1928.

Torday, E., "The New Congo Collection." March, 1913.

Wingert, Paul S., "Congo Art." *Transaction*, New York, 1947.

AFRICAN ART (ENGLISH)

Adam, L., *Primitive Art*. London, 1940.

Aderem, Oni of Ife, "Notes on the City of Ife." *Nigeria*, Lagos, No. 12, 1937.

Bacon, R. H., "Benin, the City of Blood." London, 1897.

Bascom, William M., "The Legacy of an Unknown Nigerian Donatello." *The London News*, April, 1939.

Bell, Clive, *Since Cézanne*. London, 1922.

Articles from *The Burlington Magazine*, London:

Meyerowitz, Eva L. R., "Some Gold, Bronze and Brass Objects from Ashanti." January, 1947.

Meyerowitz, Eva L. R., "The Stone Figures of Esie in Nigeria." February, 1943.

Meyerowitz, Eva L. R., "Ancient Nigerian Bronzes." September-October, 1941.

Meyerowitz, Eva L. R., "Bronzes and Terra-Cottas from Ile-Ife." October, 1939.

Palmer, Sir Richard, "Ancient Nigerian Bronzes." October, 1942.

Salmon, Andre, "Negro Art." *Burlington Magazine*, London, April, 1920.

Casson, Stanley, "Negro Art." *The Listener*, London, May, 1933.

Clarke, J. D., "The Stone Figures of Esie." *Nigeria*, Lagos, No. 14, 1938.

Cunard, Nancy, "Negro." London, 1934.

Duckworth, E. H., "Recent Archaeological Discoveries in the Ancient City of Ife." *Nigeria*, Lagos, No. 14, 1938.

Egharevba, Jacob V., "Art and Craft Works in the City of Benin." *Nigeria*, Lagos, No. 18, 1939.

Fagg, Bernard, "Pottery Figures from Northern Nigeria," *Africa*. London, January, 1945.

Friend, Donald, "Masks." *Nigeria*, Lagos, No. 18, 1939.

Fry, Roger, *Vision and Design*. (Negro Art). London, 1920.

Gaskell, W., "The Influence of Europe on Early Benin Art." *The Connoisseur*, London, June, 1902.

Gorer, Geoffrey, "Black Art." *The Listener*, London, August 14, 1935.

Hunt-Cooke, A., and Murray, K. C., "Dahomeyan Craft." *Nigeria*, Lagos, No. 10, 1937.

Kjersmeier, Carl, "Bambara Sculptures." Nancy Cunard, Ed., *Negro*, London, 1934.

Lavachery, Henry, "Essay on the Styles in Statuary of the Belgian Congo." Nancy Cunard, Ed., *Negro*, London, 1934.

Meyerowitz, Eva L. R., *The Sacred State of the Akan*. London, 1951.

Meyerowitz, Eva L. R., "Wood-Carving in the Yoruba Country Today." *Africa*, London, April 1945.

Murray, K. C., "Arts and Crafts of Nigeria: Their Past and Future." *Africa*, London, October, 1945.

Murray, K. C., "Nigeria's First Exhibition of Antiques." *Nigeria*, Lagos, No. 26, 1947.

Olbrechts, Frans M., "Contribution to the Study of the Chronology of African Plastic Art." *Africa*, London, October, 1945.

Pitt-Rivers, L. G., *Antique Works of Art from Benin*. London, 1900.

Plass, Margaret, "The Glory of the Gold Coast." *West Africa*, London, June 2, 1915.

Rattray, R. S., *Religion and Art in Ashanti*. Oxford, 1927.

Read, C. H., and Dalton, O. M., *Antiquities from the City of Benin and from Other Parts of West Africa in the British Museum*. London, 1899.

Roth, H. Ling, *Great Benin—Its Customs, Art and Horrors*. Halifax, 1903.

Roth, H. Ling, "Primitive Art from Benin." *Studio*, London, October, 1898.

Royal Anthropological Institute: *Traditional Art of the British Colonies*, London, 1949.

Sadler, Michael E., *Arts of West Africa*. Oxford, 1935.

Stevens, G. A., "The Future of African Art." *Africa*, London, April, 1930.

Sydow, Eckart von, "African Sculpture." *Africa*, London, April, 1928.

Sydow, Eckart von, "The Image of Janus in African Sculpture." *Africa*, London, January, 1932.

Sydow, Eckart von, "Ancient and Modern Art in Benin City." *Africa*, London, January, 1938.

Thornburn, J. W. A., "The City of Benin." *Nigeria*, Lagos, No. 10, 1937.

Traditional Sculptures from the Colonies. Colonial Office, London, 1951.

Underwood, Leon, *Masks of West Africa.* London, 1948.

Underwood, Leon, *Figures in Wood of West Africa.* London, 1948.

Underwood, Leon, *Bronzes of West Africa.* London, 1949.

Webster, D. W., *Auction Catalogues Nos. 2, 23, 24, 25, 26, 30, 31.* Bicester, England. (From 1899–1901).

AFRICAN ART (FRENCH AND DUTCH)

Afrikaanse Kunst in Nederland. Leiden, 1947. Catalogue.

Apollinaire, G., "Avertissement." *Sculpture Negre*, Paris, 1917.

Ars Exotica. Gand (Belgium), 1950. Catalogue.

L'Art Negre du Congo Belge. Gand, 1950.

Basler, Adolph, *L'Art chez les peuples primitifs.* Paris, 1929.

Baumann, Dr. Herman, "Benin." *Cahiers d'Art*, Paris, Nos. 3-5, 1930.

Bossche, Adr. Vanden, "La sculpture des masques Bapende. *Brousse* No. 1. Leopoldville, Belg. Congo, 1950.

Bossche, Jean Vanden, "L'Art plastique chez les Bapende." *Brousse* No. 2. Leopoldville, Belg. Congo, 1950.

Chauvet, Stephen, *Les Arts indigenes des colonies Francaises.* Paris, 1924.

Clouzot, H. et Level, A., *L'Art Negre et l'art Oceanien.* Paris, 1919.

Delafosse, Maurice, "Au sujet des statuettes en pierre du Kissi" (Guinée Française). *Revue d'Ethnographie et de Sociologie*, Paris, March-April, 1914.

Einstein, Carl, "A propos de l'exposition de la Galerie Pigalle." *Document* No. 2. Paris, 1930.

Fagg, William, "L'art nigerien avant Jesus-Christ." *L'Art Negre*, Paris, 1951.

Fagg, William, "De l'art des Yoruba." *L'Art Negre*, Paris, 1951.

Gaffe, Rene, *La sculpture au Congo Belge.* Bruxelles, 1945.

Grebert, F., "Arts en voie de disparition au Gabon." *Africa*, London, January, 1934.

Griaule, Marcel, "Les symboles des arts africaines." *L'Art Negre*, Paris, 1951.

Griaule, Marcel, *Masques Dogon.* Paris, 1938.

Hardy, Georges, *L'Art Negre, L'Art animiste des Noirs d'Afrique.* Paris, 1927.

Himmelheber, H., "Art et artistes Bakuba." *Brousse* No. 1. Leopoldville, Belg. Congo, 1940.

Kjersmeier, Carl, *Centres de Style de la Sculpture Negre Africaine*, 4 volumes. Paris, 1935–1938.

Lavachery, Henry, "Apparente evolution des masques dans la region de Man" (A. O. F. Cote d'Ivoire); *Bulletin des Musées Royaux d'Art et d'Histoire.* Bruxelles, November-December, 1939.

Lavachery, Henry, "L'art des Noirs d'Afrique et son destin." *L'Art Negre*, Paris, 1951.

Lem, F. H., *Sculptures Soudanaises.* Paris, 1948.

Lem, F. H., "Variété et unité des traditions plastique de l'Afrique noire." *L'Art Negre*, Paris, 1951.

Luquet, G. H., *L'Art Primitif.* Paris, 1930.

Maes, Dr. J., "La Psychologie de l'art Negre." *IPEK*, Leipzig, 1926.

Maes, Dr. J., "Des sources de l'art Negre." *Cahiers d'Art*, Paris, No. 6, 1930.

Maes, Dr. J., *Aniota-Kifwebe.* Antwerp, 1924.

Maes, Dr. J. et Lavachery, H., *L'Art Negre.* Bruxelles, 1930.

Maes, Dr. J., "Les Figurines sculptées de Bas Congo." *Africa*, London, July, 1930.

Maes, Dr. J., *Fetischen of Toverbeelden uit Kongo.* Bruxelles, 1935.

Le Musée Vivant, Numéro Special. Paris, November, 1948.

Olbrechts, Prof. Dr. Frans M., *Plastiek Van Kongo*, Bruxelles, 1946.

Perier, G. D., *Les Arts Populaires du Congo Belge.* Bruxelles, 1948.

Portier, A., et Poncetton, F., *Les Arts Sauvages d'Afrique.* Paris, 1929.

Ratton, Charles, "L'or fetiche." *L'Art Negre*, Paris, 1951.

Salmon, Andre, *L'Art Negre.* Paris, 1922.

Sonolet, Louis, "L'Art dans l'Afrique Occidentale Francaise." *Gazette des Beaux Arts*, Paris, July-December, 1923.

Sydow, Eckart von, "Masques Janus de Cross River." *Documents*, Paris, No. 6, 1930.

Vandenhoute, P. J. L., *Classification Stylistique du Masque Dan et Guere de la Cote d'Ivoire Occidentale.* Leiden, 1948.

Vatican Exhibition, *The Arts in the Belgian Congo and Ruanda-Urundi.* Bruxelles, 1950.

Weyns, J., "Quelques Remarques au Sujet de nos Sculptures Africaines." *Les Arts Plastiques*, Editions de la Connaissance, S. A., Bruxelles, 1949.

AFRICAN ART (GERMAN)

Afrikanische Plastik, Kunst Werk Schriften, Band XVII. Baden-Baden, 1951.

Eberl-Elber, Ralph, "Die Masken der Maennerbuende in Sierra Leone." *Ethnos*, No. 2, Stockholm, 1937.

Eckstein, Hans, "Afrikanische Negerkunst." *Kunst und Kuenstler*, Berlin.

Einstein, Carl, *Afrikanische Plastik*. Berlin, 1921.

Einstein, Carl, *Negerplastik*. Muenchen, 1920.

Esswein, H., "Masken." *Frankfurter Zeitung*. 3 May, 1933.

Freyberg, Hermann, "Urwaldkunst in Angola." *Weltkunst*, Berlin.

Frobenius, Leo, *Kulturgeschichte Afrikas*. Frankfurt am Main, 1933.

Frobenius, Leo, *Das Unbekannte Afrika*. Muenchen, 1923.

Frobenius, Leo, *Die Masken und Geheimbunde Afrikas*. Halle, 1899.

Fuhrmann, E., *Afrika*. Muenchen, 1922.

Hagen, Dr. Karl, *Altertuemer von Benin im Museum fuer Voelkerkunde zu Hamburg*. Hamburg, 1898.

Hansenstein, W., *Barbaren und Klassiker*. Muenchen, 1922.

Hefel, Annemarie, *Afrikanische Bronzen*. Wien, 1948.

Himmelheber, Hans, *Negerkuenstler*. Stuttgart, 1935.

Karutz, R., *Die Afrikanische Hoernermasken*. George Gesell, Luebeck, 1901.

Kuhn, Herbert, *Die Kunst der Primitiven*. Muenchen, 1923.

Luschan, Felix von, *Die Altertuemer von Benin*. Berlin, 1919, 3 volumes.

Luschan, Felix von, *Die Karl Knorrsche Sammlung von Benin*. Stuttgart, 1901.

Marquart, Joseph, *Die Benin-Sammlung des Reichsmuseums fuer Voelkerkunde in Leiden*. Leiden, 1913.

Nuoffer, Oscar, *Afrikanische Plastik und die Gestaltung von Mutter und Kind*. Dresden, 1934.

Schmeltz, J. V. E., "Neue Litteratur ueber Benin." *Internazionale Archive fuer Ethnologie, T. 16.* 1903.

Schneider-Lengyel, Ilse, *Die Welt der Maske*. Muenchen, 1934.

Stephan, E., *Suedseekunst*. Berlin, 1907.

Struck, Bernard, "Die Chronologie der Benin Altertumer." *Zeitschrift fur Ethnologie*, Vol. 1. LV. 1923.

Sydow, Eckart von, *Ahnenkult und Ahnenbild der Naturvoelker*. Berlin, 1924.

Sydow, Eckart von, *Die Kunst der Naturvoelker und der Vorzeit*. Berlin, 1923.

Sydow, Eckart von, *Handbuch der Afrikanischen Plastik*. Berlin, 1930.

Sydow, Eckart von, *Exotische Kunst, Afrika und Oceanien*. Leipzig, 1921.

Utzinger, Rudolf, *Masken*. Berlin, 1922.

Vatter, Ernst, *Religioese Plastik der Naturvoelker*. Frankfurt am Main, 1926.

ANTHROPOLOGY, ETHNOLOGY, HISTORY, TRAVEL

Armattoe, Dr. E. E. G., *The Golden Age of West African Civilization*. Londonderry, 1946.

Baumann, H. et Westerman, D., *Les Peuples et les civilizations de l'Afrique*. Paris, 1948.

Beaucorps, R. de, *Les Basongo de la Luniungu et de la Gobari*. Bruxelles, 1941.

Benedict, Ruth, *Patterns of Culture*. New York, 1934.

Bittremieux, Leo, *La Société Secrete des Bakhimba au Mayombe*. Bruxelles, 1936.

British Museum, *Handbook to the Ethnographical Collections*. London, 1925.

Bryk, Felix, *Dark Rapture, The Sex Life of the African Negro*. New York, 1939.

Burnier, Thomas, *Ames Primitives*. Paris, 1922.

Carnochan, F. G., and Adamson, H. C., *Out of Africa*. New York, 1936.

Cureau, Dr. Ad, *Les Sociétés Primitives de l'Afrique Equatoriale*. Paris, 1912.

Delafosse, Maurice, *Les Negres*. Paris, 1927.

Delafosse, Maurice, *Civilizations Negro-Africaines*. Paris, 1925.

Dennett, R. E., *At the Back of the Black Man's Mind*. London, 1906.

Forde, Daryll and Jones, G. I., *The Ibo and Ibibio-Speaking Peoples of South-Eastern Nigeria*. London, 1950.

Forde, Daryll, *The Yoruba-Speaking Peoples of South-Western Nigeria*. London, 1951.

Goldenweiser, Alexander A., *Anthropology, an Introduction to Primitive Cultures*. New York, 1937.

Gorer, G., *Africa Dances*. London, 1935.

Grebert, F., *Au Gabun*. Paris, 1948.

Haardt, Georges-Marie, and Andouin-Dubreuil, Louis, *La Croisière Noire*. Paris, 1927.

Hardy, Georges, *Vue Generale de l'Histoire d'Afrique*. Paris, 1948.

Herskovits, Melville J., *Dahomey, an Ancient West African Kingdom*. New York, 1938.

Jeffreys, M. D. W., "The Cowry Shell: A Study of Its History and Use in Nigeria." *Nigeria*, Lagos, September, 1938.

Labouret, M. Henri, "Notes Contributives à l'Etude du Peuple Baoule." *Revue d'Ethnographie et de Sociologie*. Paris, March-April, 1914.

Labouret, M. Henri, *Histoire des Noirs d'Afrique*. Paris, 1950.

Latouche, John, *Congo*. New York, 1945.

Lietard, Capt. L., "Les Waregas." *Bulletin de la Société Royale Belge de Geographie*, Bruxelles, 1923.

Lowie, Robert H., *An Introduction to Cultural Anthropology*. New York, 1934.

Maes, Dr. J., *Notes sur les populations des Bassins du Kasai, de la Lukanie, et du Lac Leopold II*. Bruxelles, 1924.

Maes, J. et Boone, O., *Les Peuplades du Congo Belge*. Bruxelles, 1935.

Malinowski, Bronislaw, *The Dynamics of Culture Change*. New Haven, 1946.

Manoukian, Madeline, *Akan and Ga-Adangme Peoples of the Gold Coast*. London, 1950.

McCulogh, M., *Peoples of Sierra Leone Protectorate*. London, 1950.

McCulogh, Merran, *The Southern Lunda and Related Peoples*. London, 1951.

Meyerowitz, Eva L. R., "Concepts of the Soul among the Akan of the Gold Coast." *Africa*, London, January, 1951.

Michelet, Raymond, "African Empires and Civilizations." Nancy Cunard, Ed., *Negro*, London, 1934.

Murdock, G. P., *Our Primitive Contemporaries*. New York, 1934.

Peschuel-Loesche, E., *Voelkerkunde von Loango*. Stuttgart, 1907.

Pitt-Rivers Museum, *General Handbook*. Farnham, England, 1929.

Radcliffe-Brown, A. R., and Forde, Daryll, *African Systems of Kinship and Marriage*. London, 1950.

Richard-Molard, J., *L'Afrique Occidentale Francaise*. Paris, 1949.

Schwab, George, *Tribes of the Liberian Hinterland*. Peabody Museum, Cambridge, Mass., 1947.

Seligman, C. G., *Les Races de l'Afrique*. Paris, 1935.

Shaw, Thurston, *The Study of Africa's Past*. London, 1946.

Talbot, P. A., *The Peoples of Southern Nigeria*. 3 volumes. Oxford, 1926.

Tempels, R. P. Placide, *La Philosophie Bantoue*. Paris, 1949.

Tiarko Fourche, J. A., and Morlinghem, H., *Les Communications des indigénes du Kasai avec les ames des morts*. Bruxelles, 1939.

Torday, E., "The Influence of the Kingdom of Kongo in Central Africa." *Africa*, April, 1928, London.

Torday, E., and Joyce, T. A., *Notes ethnographiques sur les peuples communement appelés Bakuba ainsi que sur les peuples apparentes les Bushongo*. Bruxelles, 1910.

Warner, Esther, *New Song in a Strange Land*. Boston. 1948.

Weeks, John H., *Among the Primitive Bakongo*. Philadelphia, 1914.

Wieschoff, H. A., *Africa*. Philadelphia, 1945.

Woodson, Carter G., *African Heroes and Heroines*. Washington, 1944.

MYTH, MAGIC, RELIGION

Campbell, Joseph, *The Hero with a Thousand Faces*. New York, 1949.

Cendrars, Blaise, *Anthologie Negre*. Paris, 1927.

Diel, Paul, *La Divinité*. Paris, 1950.

Dieterlen, Germaine, *La Religion Bambara*. Paris, 1951.

Dieterlen, Germaine, *Les ames des Dogon*. Paris, 1941.

Feuilloley, B. F., "Magic and Initiation in the Ubanghi-Shari." Nancy Cunard, Ed., *Negro*, London, 1934.

Frazer, James G., "The Magic Art." *The Golden Bough*, New York, 1926.

Frazer, James G., "Taboo and the Perils of the Soul." *The Golden Bough*, New York, 1926.

Griaule, Marcel, *Dieu d'eau*. Paris, 1948.

Gordon, Pierre, *Initiation sexuelle et evolution religieuse*. Paris, 1946.

Harper, "Notes on the Totemism of the Gold Coast." *Journal of Anthropology*, London, No. 36, 1906.

Harrison, Jane E., *Ancient Art and Ritual*. New York, 1913–1948.

Kaigh, Frederick, *Witchcraft and Magic in Africa*. London, 1947.

Kerharo, J., and A. Bouquet, "Sorciers Feticheurs et Guerisseurs de la Côte d'Ivoire—Haute Volta," Paris, 1950.

Lavigotte, Henri, *L'Evur, croyance des Pahouins du Gabon*. Paris, 1947.

Le Roy, Mgr. A., *La Religion des Primitifs*. Paris, 1911.

Malinowski, Bronislaw, *Magic, Science and Religion*. New York, 1948.

Marett, R. R., *Faith, Hope and Charity in Primitive Religion*. New York, 1932.

Potter, Charles F., *The Story of Religions*. New York, 1937.

Tauxier, L., *Religion, moeurs et coutumes des Agnis de la Côte d'Ivoire*. Paris, 1932.

Woodson, Carter G., *African Myth*. Washington, 1944.

Wundt, W., "Mythus und Religion." *Voelker-Psychologie, Vol. II*, 1906.

PSYCHOLOGY

Ankermann, Bernard, *Totenkult und Seelengaluben bei den Afrikanischen Voelker*. 1918.

Blondel, Ch., *La Mentalite primitive*. Paris, 1926.

Boas, Franz, *The Mind of Primitive Man*. New York, 1927.

Carrel, Alexis, *The Voyage to Lourdes*. New York, 1950.

Cotton, E. P., "The Mind of Primitive Man in West Africa." *Journal of Applied Sociology*, Vol. IX. Los Angeles, 1924.

Frazer, James G., "Totemism and Exogamy." *The Golden Bough*, New York, 1926–1930.

Freud, Sigmund, *Totem and Taboo*. New York, 1938.

Freud, Sigmund, *Moses and Monotheism*. New York, 1947.

Hartmann, George W., *Gestalt Psychology.* New York, 1935.

Hess, Jean, *L'Ame Negre.* Paris, 1899.

Lévy-Bruhl, L., *La Mentalite prelogique.* Paris, 1922.

Mueller-Freienfels, *Psychologie der Kunst.*

Parringer, G., *West African Psychology.* London, 1951.

Preuss, K. Th., *Die Geistige Kultur der Naturvoelker.* 1914.

Rank, Otto, *Art and Artist.* New York, 1932.

Rhine, J. B., *New Frontiers of Mind.* New York-Toronto, 1937.

Sydow, Eckart von, *Primitive Kunst und Psychoanalyse.* Leipzig-Wien-Zurich, 1927.

Thorburn, John M., *Art and the Unconscious.* London, 1925.

Verworn, Max, *Zur Psychologie der Primitiven Kunst.* Jena, 1917.

ART APPRECIATION, PHILOSOPHY OF ART

Bergson, Henri, "La Perception du Changement." *Oeuvres Completes,* Geneva, 1921.

Buermeyer, Laurence, *The Aesthetic Experience.* Merion, Pennsylvania, 1924.

Cezanne, Paul, *Correspondence.* Paris, 1937.

Cladel, Judith, *Aristide Maillol, sa vie, son oeuvre, ses idées.* Paris, 1937.

Collingwood, R. G., *The Principles of Art.* Oxford, 1938.

Croce, Benedetto, *The Essence of the Aesthetic.* London, 1921.

Ducasse, Curt J., *Art, the Critics, and You.* New York, 1944.

Faure, Elie, *The Spirit of the Forms.* New York, 1937.

Riegl, Alois, *Stilfragen, Grundlegungen zu einer Geschichte der Ornamentik.* Berlin, 1893.

Scheltema, A. Van, *Die Altnordische Kunst; Grundprobleme Vorhistorischer Kunstentwicklung.* Berlin, 1923.

Schopenhauer, A., *Die Welt als Wille und Vorstellung.* Leipzig, 1859.

Spearing, H. G., *The Childhood of Art, or the Ascent of Man.* New York, 1913.

Taine, A., *Philosophie de l'art.* Paris, 1901.

Worringer, Wilhelm, *Abstraktion und Einfuehlung; ein Beitrag zur Stilpsychologie.* Muenchen, 1908.

COMPARATIVE MATERIAL
(MODERN ART)

Buraud, Georges, *Les Masques.* Paris, 1948.

Clawson, H. Phelps, *By Their Works.* Buffalo, New York, 1941.

Fechheimer, Hedwig, *Die Plastik der Aegypter.* Berlin, 1923.

Goldwater, Robert J., *Primitivism in Modern Painting.* New York, 1938.

Grober, Max von, *Kinderspielzeug aus alter Zeit.*

Gunther, Erna, "Material Culture." *College Art Journal.* The Museum of Primitive Art, Spring, 1950.

Huggins, Willis N. and Jackson, J. G., *An Introduction to African Civilization,* New York, 1937.

Kahnweiler, D. H., "Negro Art and Cubism." *Horizon,* London, December, 1948.

Kutscher, Gerd, "West-Afrika und die Moderne Kunst." *Bildende Kunst,* Berlin, November, December, 1947.

Muenz, Ludwig, und Loewenfeld, Viktor, *Plastische Arbeiten Blinder.* Bruenn, 1934.

Prinzhorn, Dr. Hans, *Bildnerei der Geisteskranken.* Berlin, 1922.

Rothschild, Lincoln, *Sculpture Through the Ages.* New York, 1942.

Shadbolt, Doris, "Our Relation to Primitive Art." *Canadian Art,* Ottawa, Vol. V, No. 1, 1947.

Thoby, Dr. P., "Christ." *Aesculape,* Paris, 1933.

LIST OF ILLUSTRATIONS

Photographs have been supplied by the
collections listed unless otherwise credited